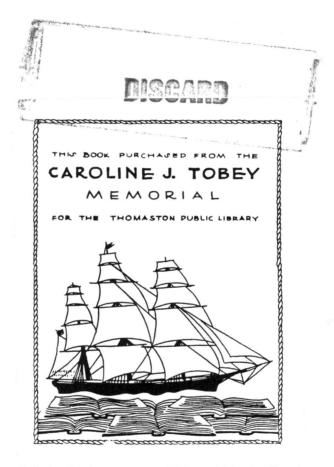

THIS BOOK PURCHASED FROM THE

CAROLINE J. TOBEY

MEMORIAL

FOR THE THOMASTON PUBLIC LIBRARY

THE
SEEKER

**Center Point
Large Print**

Also by Ann H. Gabhart and available from Center Point Large Print:

The Outsider
The Believer

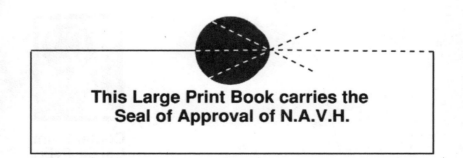

**This Large Print Book carries the
Seal of Approval of N.A.V.H.**

THE
SEEKER

ANN H. GABHART

CENTER POINT LARGE PRINT
THORNDIKE, MAINE

LP
GAB

Published in 2010 by arrangement with
Revell, a division of Baker Publishing Group.

The text of this Large Print edition is unabridged.
In other aspects, this book may vary
from the original edition.
Printed in the United States of America.
Set in 16-point Times New Roman type.

ISBN: 978-1-60285-808-4

Library of Congress Cataloging-in-Publication Data

Gabhart, Ann H., 1947–
  The seeker/ Ann H. Gabhart.
    p. cm.
  ISBN 978-1-60285-808-4 (library binding : alk. paper)
  1. Shakers—Fiction. 2. Kentucky—History—1792–1865—Fiction.
    3. Large type books. I. Title.
  PS3607.A23S44 2010b
  813′.6—dc22

                                          2010012789

To my family
for their unfailing love and support
through the years

A NOTE ABOUT THE SHAKERS

American Shakerism originated in England in the eighteenth century. Its leader, a charismatic woman named Ann Lee, was believed by her followers to be the second coming of Christ in female form. After being persecuted for those beliefs in England, she and a small band of followers came to America in 1774 to settle in Watervliet, New York, and there established the first community of the United Society of Believers in Christ's Second Appearing, more commonly known as Shakers.

When religious fervor swept the Western frontier at the turn of the nineteenth century, the Shakers, whose communities in New England were flourishing, found the spiritual atmosphere in Kentucky perfect for expanding their religion to the west. By the middle of the nineteenth century the Shakers had nineteen communities spread through the New England states and Kentucky, Ohio, and Indiana.

The Shaker doctrines of celibacy, communal living, and the belief that perfection could be attained in this life were all based on revelations that Mother Ann claimed to have divinely received. The name *Shakers* came from the way they worshiped. At times when a member received the "spirit," he or she would begin shaking all over. These sorts of "gifts of the spirit," along with other spiritual manifestations such as visions, were considered by the Shakers to be confirmation of the same direct communication with God they believed their Mother Ann had experienced.

Since the Shakers believed that work was part of worship and that God dwelt in the details of that work, they devoted themselves to doing everything—whether farming or making furniture and brooms or developing better seeds—to honor the Eternal Father and Mother Ann. Shaker communities thrived until the Civil War, which proved to be a very difficult time for the Shaker communities, partly because they never refused to feed those who came hungry into their communities and partly because their normal trade routes to the South were disrupted by the war. On one day after the Battle of Perryville in Kentucky, the Shakers at Pleasant Hill saw ten thousand troops march through their village and they served fourteen thousand meals.

After the war, much change came to the nation. Factories began producing brooms, furniture, preserves, and other products the Shakers had made, and these were sold at prices that pushed the Shakers out of the market. Jobs were easier to find, fewer and fewer young people were willing to accept the strict, celibate life of the Shakers, and the sect gradually died out. The few remaining Shakers reside at the last active Shaker village, Sabbathday Lake in Maine.

In Kentucky, the Shaker villages of Pleasant Hill and South Union have been restored and attract many visitors curious about the Shaker lifestyle. These historical sites provide a unique look at the austere beauty of the Shakers' craftsmanship. The sect's songs and strange worship echo in the impressive architecture of their buildings. Visitors also learn about the Shakers' innovative ideas in agriculture and industry that improved life not only in their own communities but also in the "world" they were so determined to shut away.

1

Mercer County, Kentucky
April 1861

"The Shakers! Have you taken leave of your senses, Edwin? You can't seriously be considering joining the Shakers?" The words came out harsher than Charlotte Vance intended, and Edwin Gilbey stepped back from her until the budding branches of the lilac bush behind him had to be poking holes in his dinner jacket.

"Please, Charlotte. Calm yourself. You know I can't abide a scene." He sounded alarmed as he shifted his eyes away from her face to look longingly over her shoulder toward the veranda door.

Charlotte's irritation grew as she stared at Edwin in the light of the nearly full moon. He didn't even like social gatherings. Behind her the door opened, and laughter mixed with the music of the string ensemble she'd hired from Lexington flowed out into the garden. The party seemed to be proceeding well in spite of the charged emotions in the air.

When her father first sent word from Frankfort that he wanted her to arrange a grand gala for his return home to Grayson Farm after completing his business in the capital city, she'd doubted his sanity. Surely as a senator in the state legislature he was more than aware the country was teetering on the brink of destruction after Mr. Lincoln had taken the oath of office and moved into the White House last month. Half a dozen Southern states had already followed South Carolina out of the Union. That's all anybody was talking about. Whether they could do that. Whether the government should allow them to do that. Whether there would be armed conflict to preserve the Union.

How in the world did her father expect them to have a civil party with half the guests waving the Union flag and the other half shouting states' rights and favoring secession? She'd sent a message back to him saying they might as well lay the dueling pistols on the table in the front hall and let the men take turns out on Grayson's front lawn. But he had made light of her worries and on return post had insisted he had news to announce that required the finest party she'd ever arranged. Astounding news.

Charlotte had surmised he was bringing word back to Grayson that the Constitutional Union Party had pegged him as their next candidate for governor. Certainly reason enough to dare entertaining in spite of the political climate. But no, that hadn't been his news. Instead he had handed a woman dressed to the nines in silk and jewels down out of the carriage and introduced her as his wife.

Not wife-to-be. Wife. A woman from the North. Selena Harley Black. A widow with a young son somewhere still in the North, or so Betty Jamison had whispered in Charlotte's ear while her father escorted his bride from group to group to introduce her. Of course, after the death of Charlotte's mother, Betty had entertained the improbable notion that she might eventually catch Charlotte's father's eye.

When the veranda door closed again and muffled the sound of the party, Charlotte was relieved. She couldn't think about her father and that woman right now. Not with Edwin talking this ridiculous Shaker talk. One problem at a time. She turned her attention back to the man pinned against her mother's favorite lilac bush. He shifted uneasily on his feet and glanced over his shoulder as though considering an escape under the lilac's branches, even if it meant spoiling the knees of his trousers.

"But Edwin," she said as sweetly as she could under the circumstances. "Unless I am greatly mistaken, the Shakers have a ban on matrimony."

Edwin straightened his shoulders and almost looked at her face again before he let his eyes slide down to the ground at their feet. "You are not mistaken. It is one of their strongest tenets. The avoidance of such unions allows them to live in peace and harmony. Hence the name of their village, Harmony Hill."

"I am well aware of the name of their village." The irritation in her voice sounded a bit strident even to Charlotte's ears. Not the way to win arguments. She attempted to pull in a deep, steadying breath, but with the tight lacings of her corset constricting her breathing, she simply ended up light-headed. She fought the feeling. She refused to have the vapors. She could control this. She could control Edwin.

Hadn't she done so ever since they were toddlers playing together in the nursery?

He threw up his hand to ward off her anger as he hurried out his words. "Yes, yes, of course you are. At any rate, I have become well acquainted with an Elder Logan in their village. He has found great peace among the Believers there. A peace I envy." Edwin peeked up at her and went on in a tremulous voice. "You know yourself how unsettled I've felt ever since my dear grandmother departed this world last spring."

"I do understand how difficult the loss has been for you. For all of us. She was a fine lady." It took effort, but she managed to sound sympathetic as she spoke the oft-repeated words. What she actually wanted to tell Edwin was that Faustine Hastings had been well along in years and that no one could live forever. Or grieve forever. Charlotte had resigned herself to a year of mourning before their marriage, even though that would make her nearly twenty when they spoke their vows in May. A mere month from now.

Edwin knew they were to marry in May. He had agreed to the date. Charlotte's dressmaker was putting the finishing touches on her wedding dress. The last time she had tried it on, it had taken Mellie almost a half hour just to fasten its many pearl buttons down the back and from the elbows on the sleeves. Of course part of the reason for that was Mellie had something unfavorable to say about Edwin with every button she fastened.

Charlotte's familiar words of sympathy seemed to allay Edwin's apprehension, and he eased a bit away from the bush closer to her as he said, "Elder Logan thinks Grandmother would have understood and approved of my search for peace in my life."

"Does he? And how can he know that? Did he get a vision as he was doing his worship dances?"

Edwin frowned at her mocking tone. "You needn't try to disparage Elder Logan. He's a fine man and their worship dances are often very sedate and orderly. At least the ones I have witnessed."

"But isn't it so that they spin and at times fall prostrate on the floor in odd fits? That hardly sounds sedate to me." Charlotte's head was spinning every bit as wildly as she'd heard the Shakers did in their worship dances. How could both of the men in her life lose their senses at the same time? First her father and now Edwin.

She tried to block from her mind the vision of her father's beaming face as he presented that woman as the new mistress of Grayson. He hadn't even glanced toward Charlotte, who had been running Grayson with Aunt Tish's help even before her mother's untimely death four years ago. He had without a doubt lost his mind. Proof was surely in how he had sounded almost proud when he said he'd met the woman only six weeks earlier. Charlotte would be surprised if he had even checked into her family lineage. Or given the first thought to why a woman her age would consider marrying a man his. She had to be twenty years younger than him. Perhaps thirty to his fifty.

Charlotte reached up to smooth out the furrows of a frown forming between her eyes. A lady could not chance developing grimace lines to mar her appearance. It was bad enough that she had a too-generous sprinkling of freckles across her nose which no amount of cream could fade. Her mother had laid the fault of that on Charlotte's red hair and her Grandmother Vance back in Virginia, who neither she nor her mother had ever laid eyes on. But her father said his mother's hair was the color of new bricks, and while Charlotte's was lighter than that, more like ginger spice, nobody in the Grayson family line had ever been born with such a flamboyant hair color.

"You have to be among them to truly understand," Edwin was saying. "When the spirit comes down on the Believers, it takes control of their bodies and demonstrates its ecstasy in myriad ways. Not always by shaking as is commonly believed by those of the world."

"Those of the world," Charlotte echoed softly. This was more serious than she had thought. He already sounded like one of them.

Of course Charlotte knew Edwin had been visiting the Shaker village. Aunt Tish had heard as much through the servant grapevine that delivered news between their adjoining plantations faster than a crow could fly between the two great houses. But who would have ever thought Edwin would seriously consider joining with them?

Even Mellie, who held Edwin in considerable disdain, had never suggested that. Just last week while she'd been pinning up Charlotte's hair, Mellie had told her, "That Mr. Edwin, you best stop countin' on him comin' courtin' you any time soon, Miss Lottie."

"He doesn't have to court me, Mellie. We've known we were marrying ever since we were six," Charlotte told her.

"You might be knowin' it, Miss Lottie, but that Mr. Edwin ain't a knowin' it. If ever I did see a man afraid of lovin', it's him." Mellie had twisted Charlotte's hair in a tight roll and jabbed a pin in it as she added, "And you ain't no way lovin' him neither."

"What do you know about loving?" Charlotte spoke shortly as she stared at Mellie's face in the mirror.

"Enough to know it's something a slave like me had best avoid like the plague. 'Fore I find myself on the auction block like my mammy and pappy with me goin' one way and whoever I was fool enough to fall in love with goin' the other."

Charlotte turned on the dressing stool to touch Mellie's arm. "You know I'd never let Father put you on the block. Never. You and Aunt Tish are family."

"I know you wouldn't want to. And I know we as close to sisters as a black slave girl and a rich white girl can be, seein' as how we took turns suckling at my mammy's breast, but things change. That's somethin' we can count on, and if we ain't ready for it, we're gonna get knocked down and trampled into the dirt. Mammy warns me about that all the time, and she knows about them kind of changes."

Mellie mashed her lips together and shook her head a little as she placed her long slender hand over Charlotte's and went on. "And I guess as how you know about them too, what with your mama dyin' how she did. Just steppin' out in her garden and fallin' down there by her red rose-bush. I can still see her layin' there with that rose

18

in her hand like as how she'd pricked her finger and fell asleep like some princess in one of them fairy tales."

Charlotte slowly shut her eyes and pulled in a breath. She would never forget the sound of her mother's gasp as she collapsed on the garden path and how she had run to kneel by her mother's side, but it was already too late. Her mother was gone. Charlotte blinked her eyes to keep back her tears as she said, "Except she wasn't asleep."

"Except that," Mellie agreed sadly as she squeezed Charlotte's hand, then pulled it away to start pinning up Charlotte's hair again. "Things changed then and things is sure to change again."

Charlotte had turned back to the mirror and said, "Some things won't." She hadn't looked at Mellie's reflection in the mirror but instead had stared into her own eyes as if making the promise to herself. She would see that no changes upset their lives at Grayson.

Now she studied Edwin's face as he went on and on about what this man, Elder Logan, had told him. How a person needed to pick up the cross of purity and bear it no matter how heavy it might be in order to find that peace he needed. How at the Shaker village, men and women lived as sisters and brothers without the thorn of marital relationships to disturb their peace. How they owned everything in common, and how, when he joined with them, he would turn his land, Hastings Farm, over to the Ministry there at Harmony Hill. With each word his voice got stronger and bolder until he didn't even sound like the Edwin she knew. The Edwin who had always done whatever she said.

"But, Edwin," she interrupted him. "We are to wed next month."

He did have the grace to look uncomfortable, but he didn't back away from her. "That was more your decision than mine, Charlotte. While I regret disappointing you, Elder Logan assures me a man should not allow himself to be pulled into an unwanted and sinful union simply to avoid a bit of embarrassment. Not when his eternal salvation is at stake."

"Marriage is not sinful," Charlotte said. "I fear you have been listening to bad advice from those who simply want to gather your land in with theirs."

Edwin stiffened at her words, and in the moonlight, the lines of his face looked chiseled out of stone as he stared down at her. The man in front of her little resembled the Edwin she had grown up with. That Edwin had hidden behind his grandmother's skirts until he was well out of knickers. That Edwin had been afraid of his shadow when she pulled him out into the garden to play hide-and-seek. That Edwin listened without argument to her plans for their lives.

When he finally spoke, his voice was harsh.

"And why have you always said we must wed, Charlotte? Isn't it to join our properties? Hasn't that always been your primary purpose? To do your father's bidding and make his holdings the largest in Mercer County."

"Not his holdings, Edwin. Ours. Grayson and Hastings farms together." She pushed the words at him. "We've talked of nothing else for years."

"*You've* talked of nothing else. Perhaps it is time you listened for a change," he said shortly.

Then without waiting for her to say more, he stepped off the path to go around her as if even the touch of the ruffles on her hooped skirt must be avoided. She stared after him, astounded by his rudeness. And by the determined set of his shoulders. That old Shaker elder with his insidious words of peace was the cause of this, but she wouldn't let it be the end. Edwin would marry her. Of course he would. He'd come to his senses and crawl back to her, begging to carry out the plans they had made. She'd find a way to see that he did.

When he opened the veranda door, the noise of the party drifted out. He stepped inside and snapped the door closed behind him, clipping off the sound, but through the glass door and window she could see the guests milling about. Her guests. She was neglecting her hostess duties. Edwin could wait. She touched the pile of hair elaborately styled on top of her head to be sure no strand had escaped its pins and started back toward the house.

A man's deep voice stopped her before she had gone a dozen steps. "He must be an extremely foolish man to turn his back and run from such beauty."

2

Charlotte whirled to face the man who stepped up on the path behind her. He must have been sitting out of her view on the stone bench in the shadow of the dogwood that reached its limbs toward the veranda.

"Forgive me," he said. "It wasn't my intention to startle you."

In the moonlight it wasn't hard to see the amused smile playing across his lips under his mustache that gave lie to his words. That had been exactly what he'd intended, Charlotte thought as she stared up at him with no pretense of demurely lowering her eyes. He was tall, even taller than Edwin, but while Edwin slouched to try to keep from towering above his companions, this man stood straight, completely at ease with his height. He was quite handsome with thick dark hair brushed back from his forehead and a strong profile. She had no idea who he was.

"I don't think we've met," she said in her most reserved, yet still civil voice. He could be a new political friend of her father's who had arrived at the party late and unannounced.

Best to be polite until his importance was determined. He wore a dinner jacket, so surely he was a guest and not just a passerby attracted by the lights and music.

His smile was full now. "My introduction got a bit overlooked after the presentation of the new Mrs. Vance. It's very like her to do a little grandstanding, but your father could have extended the courtesy of letting you in on their little surprise prior to the carriage's arrival. That way you could have been prepared with your smile."

"I smiled."

"That you did," the man said with a half nod of agreement. "Bravely. Staunchly. In spite of the way the color drained from your face and you looked faint."

"I have never felt faint," Charlotte said tersely. She didn't know why she was continuing to talk to this man who was assuming entirely too much about her without the first bit of knowledge, but something about his eyes held her there. Even in the soft light of the moon, they looked sharp and piercing, able to see past shadows, past pretense. Suddenly she wanted to hurry out of sight of those eyes before they stripped away her every defense and laid bare her soul. She was poised to flee up the veranda steps when his next words stopped her.

"Then you are an unusual young woman. Our Selena certainly has never hesitated to feign a swoon if such an action fit the occasion and achieved her end."

Our Selena. Instead of a political acquaintance, he must be a friend or even relation of this woman who had captured Charlotte's unwary father, perhaps by feigning a great deal more than a swoon. Charlotte studied the man a moment before she said, "So are you related to my father's new wife?"

She managed to get out the word "wife" without it choking her. She would get used to it. What other choice did she have?

"Oh no. I fear I am just a hired artisan." The man laughed out loud and bowed at the waist toward Charlotte. "Adam Wade at your service, Miss Vance."

"And for what purpose have you been hired, if I may be so bold to ask? A cupola here in my mother's garden?"

"Perhaps artisan is not the proper word. Artist. Although my grandfather's practical side shudders every time I claim the title. But that is what I am. An artist. A curse I fear I was born with. And I have been commissioned—or a better word might be coerced—to paint a wedding portrait of the lovely Mrs. Vance."

"Coerced? By whom? Our Selena?" She carefully emphasized the last two words.

"Oh no." He laughed again. Easily, without inhibition. "I barely know the woman."

"Neither does my father."

"You have a point, but not one, I am relieved to say, that can poke me. My sister, Phoebe, knew our Selena back home in Boston, and she is the one whose coercion I cannot ignore. Not and maintain any sort of familial peace. I've oft explained to her how I detest doing portraits, but my sister thinks one can slap a few dobs of paint on a canvas, make the subject look beautiful whether they carry beauty or not, collect the commission, and everybody's happy. To Phoebe, one picture is like any other and a brother's duty is to do as she says. Or else." With a rueful smile, he chopped his hand down through the air in front of him before he looked at her with something akin to sympathy as he continued speaking. "I fear you will find the new Mrs. Vance has some of the same characteristics. I will be much relieved to have the portrait finished and hanging over your mantel."

"Where Mother's hangs now."

He raised his dark eyebrows at her. "You can hardly expect her portrait to remain there. Lovely though it is."

"No, I suppose not." Charlotte sighed, surprised at how she was stepping into acceptance of the change coming to Grayson. Change she was beginning to see she could not hold at bay. Her father was married. That would change everything. Perhaps even more than Mr. Lincoln's inauguration. She mentally shook her head at her foolish thought. A house changed couldn't compare to a country torn asunder.

"I'm sorry," Adam said with honest sincerity in his voice.

She shivered slightly, feeling the chill of the night air for the first time since she'd followed Edwin out without grabbing a wrap, but now her anger had drained away, leaving her vulnerable to the cold and a kind word. She pulled herself together and smiled at the man in front of her, determined to be the proper hostess again and not even let her mind consider how much of her conversation with Edwin he might have overheard. It was of no concern to him. But he was a guest to be treated as such.

"Then if you don't generally do portraits except under coercion, what sort of art do you do?" she asked, as if they had just met inside in the double parlor and weren't standing in the shadowy chill of her mother's garden while the party played on with no notice of their absence.

"I daresay you've read *Harper's Weekly* and perhaps leafed through some of the other northern newspapers and magazines your father must bring home on occasion." He didn't wait for her to answer. "If so, you may have seen my work. The illustrations."

"Adam Wade. Of course. I have seen your work in *Harper's*." She stared at the man with fresh eyes. "I should have recognized your name."

"Don't pretend," Adam said. "I liked you better when you were too upset to trot out your manners."

"A lady always remembers her manners."

"Tell your young man that."

Charlotte ignored his words, refusing to let him bait her. He was the guest. She was the hostess. "No, really. A few months back, in a January issue I think, there was a man on horseback somewhere in the Western regions. He was hunched down in the saddle trying to escape the snow and wind. Just thinking about it now makes me cold." Charlotte wrapped her arms around her middle and shivered.

"Quite a compliment to have you shiver just at the thought of the illustration. Believe me, it was every bit as cold as I was able to make it look. But I think your chill now may have more to do with the night air." He slipped off his jacket and stepped closer to drape it around her.

He let his hands linger on her shoulders. She told herself to step back from him, but she didn't move as she soaked up the warmth of his jacket and breathed in his scent. An outdoors odor mixed with a light trace of manly sweat and linseed oil. She wished she could just stay wrapped in his jacket there in the garden until all the guests had gone home. Then she could sneak in the back door and creep up the servants' stairway to Aunt Tish's room. Aunt Tish would help her see what to do. There had to be a way to keep her world from crumbling.

"I'd like to paint how you look right now here in the moonlight. So winsome. So pure." He moved his right hand off her shoulder and rubbed his thumb down her nose and across her cheek, measuring her face for his painting. The pad of his thumb was rough against her skin, but still she didn't pull away. "So beautiful."

"No one has ever told me I was beautiful. No one but Aunt Tish." Her voice was barely above a whisper.

"Not even the young man who was with you in the garden?"

"Especially not Edwin. I frighten him."

"Then he's not much of a man."

"I'm going to marry him." Charlotte didn't know where the words were coming from or why she was saying them. She felt mesmerized by his eyes on her, measuring her, seeing past her façade, doing what she had most feared he could do. Seeing into her soul.

"I think not. That would surely be a waste." His fingertips walked across her face gently probing the shape of her cheekbones.

"That's what Mellie says."

"A true friend if she tells you the truth."

"Do you tell the truth?" Charlotte peered up at him. She thought she would be able to see on his face if he lied.

"Always. If I know it."

"That's the trouble, isn't it? Knowing it. Recognizing the lies."

"And has your Edwin lied to you?" His voice was soft, insistent.

"No. It might be better if he did."

"And why would that be better?" His eyes didn't waver on hers.

"He could tell me he loved me." She couldn't believe she spoke the words out loud. What kind of spell was she letting this man's eyes put on her?

"Sometimes that is spoken in actions better than words." He brought his finger over to trace around her lips. "Has he kissed you? Surely he's kissed you."

She just looked at him without saying anything. She couldn't answer that.

His eyes pierced straight through her as he waited for her to speak. At last he said, "Then have you ever been kissed, my beautiful Miss Vance? Really kissed."

Without giving her a chance to respond, to consider his words, to recognize the alarm rising in her as she thought of her position there in the shadows with a man she didn't even know, he stepped closer and dropped his mouth down to cover hers. And she let him kiss her. Not only did she let his lips touch hers without protest, but her lips reached for his. Sought the touch.

It was as if somebody else had taken over her body. As if she had given up control and now was drifting without thought, without sense, toward disaster. The yearning swelled up inside her to step into his embrace, to slip her arms around his back, to touch his dark hair, to surrender completely to the feelings his lips were pulling up from deep inside her. Even her toes in her dancing slippers felt warm.

His hand moved from her shoulder to slide down her back to pull her closer, to swallow her completely in his strength. She'd be powerless to do anything but lay her head on his shoulder and surrender to his will. There would be no more arranging, no more shaping events, no more making sure things happened as they should. As she planned. As they must. She'd turn into one of those fine ladies who sat in sunny windows, pulling bright-colored threads through flat squares of cloth as they let life drift past them without ever raising a finger to change their circumstances. She would be her mother waiting, always waiting.

The thought was like a dash of cold water and she jerked back to free herself from his embrace. She put her fingers over her lips as her face burned with the ignominy of allowing a stranger such an intimate kiss. A man she'd just met.

The man looked amused at her embarrassment. "Go ahead. Slap me if it will make you feel better."

"Then I would have to slap myself as well." Charlotte dropped her hands to let them hang limply down under his jacket still around her shoulders. Perhaps he had taken advantage of her unsettled spirit and the moonlight, but that hadn't been reason for her to melt into his embrace as she had. She was as much to blame as he was.

He surprised her by laughing. "I don't think I've ever met a Southern belle with such refreshing candor."

She did not allow a smile back on her face. She would not let him charm her again. "If you are a gentleman as well as an artist, I will expect no mention of this. If not, then my refreshing candor will force me to reveal how you startled me and kept me in the shadows against my will."

"Never fear, milady. I may not be a high-ranking gentleman like the scared rabbit you chased back inside, but I don't kiss and tell."

"Thank you." She slipped his jacket off her shoulders and held it out to him. She ignored the shiver chasing up and down her back that was not entirely due to the chill of the night air as she said, "It was kind of you to loan me your jacket. Now I must see to my guests."

"I have no complaints about your fine hospitality." He took the jacket with another infuriating smile.

She turned and lifted her skirts to hurry away from him toward the veranda steps. Behind her, she heard him chuckle, and she hoped he would remain in the garden the rest of the evening. Even better, that he might stop worrying about what his sister said for him to do and instead ride to the West to paint some cacti or sagebrush and take her reason for shame with him.

How could she have surrendered to his kiss so willingly? The evening's events had surely unbalanced her thinking. Something she could not allow to happen again. She was Charlotte Mayda Vance, the daughter of Senator Charles Vance and the granddaughter of Richard Grayson, strong men who knew what they wanted and made it happen. That was the blood flowing through her. And she knew what she wanted. It was more than a casual kiss in the shadows of her mother's garden. Much more.

She paused on the veranda to look out over the land stretching away from the house. She couldn't see past the copse of trees at the edge of the grounds, but she knew how it rolled gently across the horizon. All good fertile land. Grayson land. Her land. Her father speaking a few vows with that woman couldn't change that. Nor could a kiss. Or the lack of one.

3

Adam Wade couldn't keep from laughing softly as the pretty red-haired girl lifted her hooped skirts to race up the veranda steps with no outward show of concern about revealing her well-turned ankles. Her guests would think she'd come across a snake in the garden. His laughter faded. Perhaps she had. One who had entranced her as surely as the serpent in that first garden had Eve.

When she paused on the veranda, he expected her to glance back at him, perhaps with another blushing appeal to not sully her reputation and give her young man more reason to weasel out of his promises to her. But she didn't turn toward him. Instead she became still as a statue as she looked out over the grounds. For what he didn't know or even care, but his fingers itched for his pencils and sketchpad.

Since he didn't have so much as a scrap of paper in his pocket, he traced her figure there on the edge of the veranda in his mind. The ginger-colored hair elaborately curled and piled on top her head, the graceful neck flowing into soft, creamy shoulders bare above the satiny dress the color of emeralds.

Just a shade deeper than the green of her eyes. He couldn't see those eyes now as she stared into the distance, but the lift of her head, the set of her shoulders made him believe it was more than trees and fields she saw. Although she gazed outward, it was something within that she sought, and that's what pulled at the artist in him. The image of yearning.

Then she turned, smoothed the skirts billowing out from her slender waist made even more slender by one of those tortuous corsets women seemed compelled to wear. Even his sister Phoebe wore one, though she had long since passed the possibility of slender no matter how tightly the lacings of her corset were pulled. She claimed such an undergarment was a necessity for the current fashions. So it was little wonder the young ladies who peeked at him from behind their elaborate fans at social gatherings were always so breathless.

Charlotte Vance hadn't seemed at a loss for breath or to fear facing the truth. Even after her father's unwelcome surprise. He had obviously given his daughter's reaction to his new wife no thought at all. He was a man wrapped up in himself. Adam had seen that from the first hand-shake a week ago in Frankfort. A politician through and through with his eye constantly on how to broaden his base of support in the state.

It was hard to understand how the man leaned in the current civil strife. He claimed to support the Union, but a slaveholder and a Unionist didn't seem to go together to Adam, who had spent most of his years in Massachusetts where abolition seemed the only policy for a man of morals. But here abolitionists were looked upon with suspicion and distrust by all, Union or Secessionist. So much so that most of them worked under the cover of darkness or hastened to the friendlier climes of the North to do their campaigning for the end of slavery. That wasn't a problem for Adam. His art trumped his political leanings every time, and he had no trouble observing and recording without revealing his inner thoughts.

At least he knew what those thoughts were even if he didn't bother trying to bring others around to his way of thinking. A man should not be able to own another man. States did not have the right to withdraw from the Union. The federal government in Washington, D.C., had to make that absolutely clear. The Union must be preserved by whatever means necessary.

But the politicians and perhaps the whole populace in Kentucky seemed in a state of denial as they entertained the idea that if war came—and few doubted Lincoln could avoid some sort of armed conflict—then their state, their people could remain neutral without declaring support for the North or South. They were dreamers who were trying to erect a fence of words around their borders. Senator Vance had explained it to

Adam at great length in the carriage ride from the train station to the party in spite of the obvious boredom of his new wife at his political talk.

"Kentucky is a Union state. We believe in the Union first and foremost. That goes back to Henry Clay, our greatest son. The Great Compromiser." His face puffed up with pride. "I knew him well."

"What about President Lincoln? Wasn't he born in Kentucky?" Adam had asked, already knowing the answer, but sometimes he couldn't keep from trying to stir a bit of fire into a conversation.

"While I can't deny Mr. Lincoln was born inside the borders of our great state, I regret to say he shows little evidence of being a Kentucky son now. Illinois seems to have stamped her mark upon him," Senator Vance answered with feeling. "They report he only got one vote in the whole of Lexington even though his wife was born and raised there. That surely tells you something about the man."

"Or Kentucky," Adam said.

The senator glowered at him as if thinking of stopping the carriage to put such a nettlesome Northerner out. But his bride wanted her portrait finished, and she was well practiced in the art of changing the atmosphere around her when change was desired.

She put a gloved hand on her new husband's cheek and spoke to him with the hint of a pout. "Now, Charles, you know how your political blathering wears me down and I do so want to look fresh and lovely for your guests. Can we not find a more amusing topic than the state of the political world?" She flashed her eyes toward Adam with a bright smile that was meant to charm him into submission. "I'm sure our famous young artist didn't mean to raise your dander or bore me into an unladylike frown. Now did you, Mr. Wade?"

"Of course not, Mrs. Vance," Adam agreed with an answering smile that was as empty as her own as he settled back in the corner of the carriage seat with his sketchbook.

The lady lifted her chin and turned her profile to its most flattering side, sure he was practicing his strokes for her portrait. He let her think what she wished even as he began sketching his memory of the village they'd just passed through where a blacksmith had been ringing his hammer down on an anvil while a barefoot black boy had stared at their carriage, his eyes wide and hungry. Adam had come to Kentucky to capture its citizens' confusion of thought in pictures. The senator's wife's portrait was simply a bothersome side venture to placate his sister.

Now he had unwisely complicated the life of the senator's daughter. He had told her the truth when he said he didn't kiss and tell, but he also never kissed and lingered. Often not even long enough for a second kiss no matter how delightful the first had been. And Charlotte Vance's lips had been soft and yielding. While he would not look with disfavor on a second or third such encounter, he had no intention of settling down to one hearth and home. Something the senator's daughter seemed quite anxious to establish in her own life even to the point of browbeating a most unwilling and, to Adam's eyes, unlikely candidate into meeting her at the altar of matrimony.

That was not a trap Adam was about to fall into no matter how delightful the lady's lips. He needed to be free of ties. Even though he'd already been all the way to California and back looking for the father who had disappeared in search of gold when Adam was a child, there was much of the country out there yet to see. He didn't know what scenes awaited him, but he did know he planned to capture the spirit of the country with his artist pencils and brushes so that those who never left the stuffy confines of their sitting rooms could feel the majesty of the country's wide-open spaces. He considered himself more than an artist. He was a reporter.

Still, it might be interesting to get to know the senator's daughter better. She seemed to be as much a contradiction of feelings as her state of Kentucky. Speaking of marrying one man while quite willingly surrendering her lips to another. The strong lift of her chin contrasting to the soft line of her cheek. Her determination in the face of the impossibility of her dream of marriage if the young man fleeing her was serious about joining with the Shakers.

Adam rubbed his fingertips and thumb together in anticipation at the thought of the Shakers. Their village just a few miles from where he stood in the senator's garden—another reason he was not sorry to be in Mercer County. Sam Johnson, the editor at *Harper's Weekly*, was eager to see sketches of their buildings and the graceful winding staircases that so amazed all visitors.

While Adam was ready to supply whatever illustrations the editor requested, he was more curious about the peculiar people who would choose such a life. Men and women who had turned against all that was natural between a man and woman as if they believed the Lord had changed his mind about his initial command to Adam and Eve to be fruitful and multiply.

With a reputation as peaceful, honest, and industrious, the Shakers nevertheless were generally depicted as being dour and exceedingly plain in appearance. Especially the sisters whose uniform white caps and shapeless dresses obscured any hint of feminine charm.

Adam had once visited a Shaker village in the East, but had not been free to wander among the Believers, as they called themselves. Here in Kentucky, he'd heard the public road went straight through the village so a man could surely see much of the Shakers' way of life without being invited into their midst. He wanted to see them when they weren't presenting a face to the world they took such pains to shut away. He wanted to watch the children and see if they looked glad to be in the village or if they were uneasy captives. He wanted to sketch their likenesses when they weren't aware of his pencil strokes, perhaps even sketch them whirling in their worship dances. He liked the challenge of capturing the illusion of movement in a drawing.

Perhaps this Edwin Gilbey who had fled from the beautiful Charlotte could be his ticket into the village. Adam left the quiet of the garden behind with a bit of regret. Parties could be tiresome with too many young ladies concocting ploys to get his attention. Then as he climbed up the veranda steps, he thought of the senator's daughter and how even now he could taste her sweet innocence on his lips. He knew which young lady his eyes would be seeking as the music continued to play into the night.

His time in Kentucky stretched before him with much promise. In spite of the threat of a civil confrontation. Or perhaps because of it. What better place to be than in the middle of a divided state where it would be easy to sketch the faces of both sides.

On the veranda, he paused where Charlotte had stood so motionless, but all he could see was the graceful lift of tree limbs not yet bedecked with leaves as they cast moonlit shadows over the long lane up to the house. His gaze lingered on the road as he wondered if her yearning had been to follow that road away from the life she knew. If so, she shared kinship with him. He'd never seen a road he wasn't eager to travel.

4

It was past midnight when the last guests finally called for their carriages and the door shut behind them. Charlotte was left alone in the entryway with her father and his new wife.

The silence that fell over them beat against Charlotte's eardrums, but she didn't trot out any polite words to ease the tension as she faced this woman who was going to climb the stairs and lie down in her mother's bed. The woman returned her look with the hint of a smile that held little warmth. She wasn't worried about winning Charlotte's approval. She had the approval of the Vance who mattered.

Beside her, Charlotte's father yawned, obviously with no awareness at all of the strained air between the two women, or perhaps simply not caring. "A good gathering, Charley." He clapped a hand down on her shoulder and gave it a squeeze.

The praise and his use of her pet name almost softened her anger at him, but then he went on. "Send Mellie up to help Selena do whatever it is you ladies have to do to retire for the evening." His sleepiness fell away and his eyes brightened as he turned to Selena. "You were especially lovely tonight, my dear Selena. I was, without a doubt, the envy of every man here."

"Thank you, my love." Selena smiled up at him with practiced charm. She turned from him to lay her hand lightly on Charlotte's arm. It was all Charlotte could do to stay still and not jerk away from the woman's touch. "Your father and I do appreciate all you did to make my welcome here at Grayson so fine. I'm sure you have been invaluable to Charles in seeing to so many details of the household, and I'm even surer you will be greatly relieved to have that burden lifted from your young shoulders so that you can pursue the more light-hearted activities suited to a young lady." She raised her perfectly shaped eyebrows at Charlotte. "I hear you plan to wed next month. We shall have to host a dozen parties for you before the big event."

Charlotte stared at the woman in front of her and was unable to push even the corners of her mouth up to fake a smile. The woman might as well have put both hands against Charlotte's back to shove her out the front door behind the last guest. "Yes, well, Edwin is not extremely fond of social gatherings, and it's not the best time for entertaining with the country so precariously divided." Charlotte shifted her feet just enough to move out from under the woman's hand.

Selena pretended not to notice as she actually laughed. A sound as practiced as her smile. Lilting and feminine. Everything about her was lovely, from her rich brown hair swept up in the latest style to her soft white hands with perfectly shaped nails that showed no evidence of ever being used for anything other than fluttering a fan in front of her beautiful china doll face. Charlotte hid her own hands in the folds of her skirt. The woman in front of her would probably shrink back in horror if she knew how only that morning Charlotte had buried her hands wrist deep in dough to help Aunt Tish get the many tarts prepared for the party.

"Oh, but my dear child, that is the very best time for light entertainments to help take our minds off such unpleasantness," Selena was saying. A look of sympathy pulled down her lips. "And I do understand your Edwin's reluctance, but sometimes a man only needs to be convinced of what he truly wants." She glanced up through dark eyelashes at Charlotte's father. "Isn't that so, my love?"

He laughed down at her. "I took little convincing." His eyes drank her in and his voice was husky as he went on, "It's late. Time to retire.

You and Charlotte can discuss the need for such feminine wiles on the morrow." He took Selena's arm and ushered her toward the stairs. He didn't even glance back at Charlotte as he said, "Tell Mellie to be quick, Charlotte."

Rooted to her spot, she stared after them and wanted to yell that Mellie was not his new wife's to order about. Charlotte wanted Mellie to come to her room to help her pull the pins from her hair and undo her stays while they talked about the party. That's how it had always been. Mellie helping her get ready for bed. But there was nothing for it but to do as her father said.

"Don't you be worrying, Miss Lottie. I'll have that woman tucked under the covers 'fore she blinks twice," Mellie promised when Charlotte delivered her father's message. "I can see to the both of you. Come tomorrow maybe he'll be bringin' somebody else up to the house for her."

"He'll dance to whatever tune she decides to play." Charlotte didn't try to keep the disgust out of her voice.

"Ain't no need gettin' your dander up, Miss Lottie." Mellie patted her shoulder. "That's how he was with your mama too. You remember that. Whatever Miss Mayda wanted, that's what we done. He'd a give his fortune to keep her happy."

"It was her fortune," Charlotte muttered, but she knew Mellie was right. Her father had doted on her mother even after she withdrew from life with a multitude of health complaints. Charlotte had always thought the complaints were more in her head than her body, but then she'd been struck down in her garden. Charlotte sighed. "It's all right, Mellie. You see to the new Mrs. Vance and keep everybody happy. I can take down my own hair."

"I ain't hearin' none of that. You best wait on me. You'll get it all in a tangle for sure. And ruin that fine dress tryin' to unbutton it."

In her room at last, Charlotte managed to reach a few of the tiny buttons up the back of the skintight bodice, but Mellie was right. To undo them all, she'd have to be a contortionist or rip them loose. She sat on the dressing stool and stared at her face in the mirror in the flickering lamplight. It was surely the most ridiculous thing in the world to wear a dress—no matter how lovely—that one could not put on or take off without aid.

Of course Mellie had been helping her dress since they were both children, and Aunt Tish before that. Her mother said it was the only way for a lady to live. Cosseted and pampered. Waited on while engaging in refined activities such as poetry reading and that detested needlework. A lady couldn't even lean down and pluck a stray weed out of her own flower garden.

She had people for that. People for cooking and cleaning.

People to open the door to guests and usher them into the parlor. People to empty the chamber pots and fill the lamps. People to drop the dresses over a lady's head and fasten the buttons. People to work the fields and bring in the crops that made life in the big house so fine for the ladies and gentlemen who lived there. Her mother claimed it was how things were meant to be and that it was their Christian duty to take care of their people.

The word *slave* never crossed her mother's lips. Those who did her bidding and kept Grayson running were their *people*. But Charlotte knew the word from her father and from Aunt Tish and from Willis, the gentle black man who brought her pony out to her and taught her how to ride. Still, she was going on ten before she understood, really understood, what being a slave meant.

At a festival in the town, she had gotten separated from her mother, and after wandering down the wrong street, came upon a crowd of mostly men, some dressed rough like her father's overseer, Perkins, and others in gentlemen's coats. A white man stood at a podium like a preacher, and to his side black men wore chains on their wrists and ankles that clanked when they moved.

Charlotte stopped in her tracks and knew instinctively the scene before her was something her father would think unfit for her eyes. One part of her wanted to run from the sight, but another part of her couldn't stop staring as a couple of men prodded a boy in chains up on the block. A black boy surely only a year or two older than Charlotte.

He stared over the heads of the men eyeing him straight at Charlotte. She had expected to see fear on his face or perhaps dismay, but instead there was smoldering anger. Somehow she knew without a word passing between them that he hated her. Not because of anything she'd done, but because she had no chains to keep her from going where she willed. She looked straight at him, hoping he would see how sorry she felt, but he jerked against his chains as his look grew fiercer. Later she decided it must have been the same as hot coals dropping on his heart to think about her walking away in freedom he would never know.

"Keep your eyes down, boy," the man behind him had shouted as he hit the boy so hard he fell to his knees under the blow.

Charlotte whirled and ran back up the street the way she had come until she found her mother shopping for parasols while Willis sat in the carriage and waited.

She didn't tell her mother what she'd seen. She didn't tell anyone, not even Mellie. Especially not Mellie. The raw hatred in the boy's eyes haunted her sleep for weeks until Aunt Tish took her aside.

"What's the matter with you, chile? My Mellie says you ain't sleepin' hardly none at all. That you toss and turn till the sheets is all a-tumble on your bed. You best be comin' clean to your Aunt Tish with whatever is tormentin' you."

And so she let the words come out to say what she'd seen.

Aunt Tish got too quiet as she sat beside her at the kitchen table. Charlotte couldn't remember her ever sitting so quietly for so long.

Finally Charlotte said, "I did see it. I'm not lying."

"I knows you did, chile. You don't have to do no explainin' what it looked like to me. I been there. Me and my Mellie both, though she was just a babe with no sense of nothin' but her mammy's arms. The Massah bought me off the block so's I could wet-nurse you."

Charlotte looked at Aunt Tish. She'd always been part of her life, warm and kind. Full of wisdom and sometimes laughter. There was no laughter now. "Did you hate him?" Charlotte whispered. "The way that boy hated me."

"I didn't think it would help anythin' for me to let hatred build up in my innards. But I had to fight against it when he stopped shoutin' out bids on Jonah. We'd done jumped the broom before Mellie was born. I thought then right at first maybe he didn't have the money and as how I ought to be glad enough me and Mellie weren't goin' downriver. Little babies die goin' down the river. That's what Jonah told me. Not to worry none about him. He could take whatever they threw at him on those cotton plantations."

Charlotte had no words to say as Aunt Tish looked away at the wall as if she could see beyond it to the south where her Jonah might still be picking cotton. "But then when we got here and I saw the Massah had a mess of slaves, I had to fight powerful against the bitter gall that wanted to poison me. It still rises up to smote me at times."

Tears pooled in Charlotte's eyes and dripped down her cheeks. And she felt the boy she'd seen was right to hate her. She choked out the words. "Do you hate me too, Aunt Tish?"

"Now, now, chile. You's like my own." Aunt Tish laid her calloused black hands on Charlotte's cheeks. "You knows my heart could never hate you. And that poor boy you saw wasn't hatin' you either. He was hatin' how life is. And fact is, I can see it in your eyes. You'd a turned him free as you be right now if you coulda done it. That's what you got to 'member, chile. You'd a set him free if'n you coulda."

Charlotte stared at the black woman's loving face. "But Aunt Tish, I can't even set you free, can I?"

"No, chile, you can't. Not now, but maybe someday. And then I knows you'll do the right thing by me and Mellie."

Charlotte hadn't thought about the slave boy

for a long time. She had blocked him from her mind, blocked it all from her mind. Things were the way they had to be. The way her mother and father had always told her they were meant to be. Why the memory came sneaking back to unsettle her thoughts on this night, she had no idea.

Perhaps because everything was different, thrown up in the air to land who knew where. Certainly not as she'd ordered or planned. Edwin standing up to her. That artist, a man she didn't even know, kissing her. Her own wantonness to allow such a happening. Her father lying down beside that woman in her mother's bed. A woman young enough to perhaps bear him the son he'd always wanted. Mellie not there to unfasten her buttons. Grayson slipping out of her hands and with it the power to do that right thing by Aunt Tish and Mellie the way she had promised in her heart as she sat beside Aunt Tish at the table that day so many years ago.

Now there were those who said the country was going to war because Lincoln seemed poised to do what she had not had courage or strength to ask her father to do already.

5

Charlotte was still staring in the mirror when Mellie slipped into the room to help her out of her dress. "You done had to try, didn't you, Miss Lottie?" she fussed as she pulled the rest of the buttons loose with quick fingers.

"I don't like being captive to a dress."

Charlotte stood up to let Mellie untie the top of her hoops. They fell to the floor with a soft clatter as the silky skirt collapsed against her legs. She pulled her arms out of the sleeves and stepped out of the piles of emerald fabric. Mellie gathered up the dress quickly and spread it out on the bed before it could get too rumpled.

"How about squeezed half in two with a corset?" Mellie said as she pulled loose the ties on Charlotte's stays. "It ain't no easy thing bein' a lady. Same with that Miss Selena. She had her stays pulled so tight it took me five minutes to work the lacings loose enough to get her out of the contraption. It's a wonder she wasn't faintin'."

"I've heard she does at times." Charlotte rubbed her sides and pulled in a deep breath that felt wonderful as she sat back down at the dressing table in her camisole and pantalettes.

"I ain't surprised," Mellie said as she began pulling the pins out of Charlotte's hair and brushing it out. "You want me to massage your feet, Miss Lottie?"

Charlotte took the brush from Mellie and began pulling it through her hair herself as she said, "You're every bit as tired as I am, Mellie. You need to go on to bed and massage your own feet."

"I didn't have to dance with ever' man in the state," Mellie said, but she didn't try to take the brush away from Charlotte. Instead she sat down on the bench at the end of Charlotte's bed, slipped off her shoes, and held her feet out in front of her to wiggle her toes inside her black stockings. "I was watchin'. How many times did that old Mr. Robertson step on your toes?"

"Too many." Charlotte groaned at the memory. "But he's always generous whenever Father needs funds for his campaigns."

"Then let that new woman your daddy brung home get her toes stepped on."

"I don't want to talk about her tonight, Mellie. Please." Charlotte put down the brush and began plaiting her red hair in a thick rope.

"Fine with me." Mellie stood up and pushed Charlotte's hands aside to finish the job quickly and efficiently. "Then how about we talk about that Mr. Wade what come with them? Now, he is one fine-lookin' gentleman. And did I hear somebody say he was paintin' that woman's portrait?"

"You did, and I don't know about gentleman." Charlotte's cheeks warmed at the memory of her lack of control. How could she have been so wanton?

Mellie leaned back and eyed Charlotte in the mirror. "Sounds like you must have run up on him in your mama's garden. I did note you looked a mite breathless when you come in from outside."

"Nobody can breathe with those stays squeezing your ribs in a vice." Charlotte pointed toward the corset she'd shed moments before.

"Then it didn't have naught to do with Mr. Edwin chasin' in like some storm had hit out there and then you runnin' in all aflush some minutes later followed by that painter feller with a grin like as how he'd just eat the last of Mammy's dried apple tarts."

"You see entirely too much," Charlotte said.

"What else I got to do but look, and you know you like hearin' about what I see. Like that Janie Preston. You'd think that girl would figure out yellow makes her look like yesterday's leftover gravy, but it didn't seem to bother Mr. Matthew. I think he's about to get caught." Mellie was always a fountain of information after any party on who was making eyes at who or which men were plotting political alliances. " 'Course tonight most all the young ladies were findin' ways to sashay up to that new man. The 'no gentleman' from the garden."

"He's famous," Charlotte stared down at her

hands. "Has illustrations in *Harper's Weekly* all the time."

"You don't say? On top of bein' so fine lookin'." Mellie tied off Charlotte's braid and sat back down on the bench. She folded her white apron in pleats for a minute before she said, "Fact of the matter is, you might not be the only one the likes of him is gonna cause trouble for."

"What do you mean, trouble?" Charlotte turned on the dressing table stool to study Mellie.

"I kept my eyes down, Miss Lottie. I swear I did. I didn't even take a peek up at him, but he talked to me." Mellie glanced up at her and then down at the pleats she was folding and unfolding with nervous fingers. "I mean like I was a person. Not a slave. Like you talk to me. Like I matter."

"What did he say?"

"He asked me if I liked it here. Like I was one of the party ladies instead of a servant there holdin' a tray of tarts." Mellie reached up and yanked off the cap she'd been wearing for the party and ran her hand through her black curls. "I didn't know what to say—he just stood there till I had to say somethin'."

"And did you tell him you liked it here?" Charlotte kept her eyes on Mellie's face, but she was seeing the boy on the block again. She held her breath as she waited for Mellie's answer.

Mellie didn't look at Charlotte. Instead she

stared at the flickering light of the gas lamp beside the door for a moment before she said, "You know I wouldn't want to be nowhere 'cept with you and Mammy. But . . ." She let her voice trail off as she looked back down at her apron and began folding it in pleats again.

"But what?" Charlotte reached over and touched Mellie's arm. "You know you don't have to worry about what you say to me. I want you to talk to me."

Mellie finally looked straight at Charlotte. Her dark brown eyes looked sad. "I do know that, Miss Lottie. Mammy says that's part of my problem. How you've been more sister than mistress. Mammy says it's give me ideas I might be better off forgettin' about. That slave girls ain't supposed to know how to read like you taught me. And I taught Mammy. She says I'd best never be lettin' on about none of that. Or lettin' myself fall in love with no long-legged field hand. She understands how I might want to, bein' all of twenty now, but she says that would set my feet on a sure path to sorrow."

Charlotte searched for something to say to make Mellie feel better, but nothing came to mind. There was truth in what Mellie said. They sat there in silence a minute before Mellie went on.

"But not ever knowin' about lovin', that's reason for sorrow too, ain't it, Miss Lottie?"

Finally Charlotte said, "I don't know, Mellie."

Mellie shook her head as her mouth hardened into a thin line. "You speakin' the truth there, Miss Lottie. That's sorrow you gonna know too if you settle on Mr. Edwin. There ain't never gonna be no lovin' between the two of you. It ain't in the man." She stood up and carefully gathered up the dress. "You sure did look pretty tonight," she said as she hung the dress on a padded hanger in the wardrobe. She laid out Charlotte's nightgown before she started toward the door. "If you don't need nothin' else then."

"Wait, Mellie." Charlotte stopped her before she could turn the knob.

Mellie looked back at her, ready to do whatever she asked. Her training from childhood on. Take care of Miss Lottie. Charlotte was relieved to see no hint of the hate she remembered in the slave boy's eyes, but she could still see the sorrow there like the glint off water down a deep well. "Did you ever think maybe love is glorified too much?"

"I don't know, Miss Lottie. Could be won't neither one of us ever find out for sure unless'n we try it for ourselves. But the Good Book that Mammy is always after me to read speaks highly of it."

"But that's love for God. Or for your neighbor. Not love between a man and a woman."

"He made Eve for Adam and told them to have babies. He put the want to for that kind of love in a body's heart too. And you know if you'll think on it, there ain't all that much difference between folks no matter what color their faces is when it comes to thinkin' on love. That's how come Mammy still looks to the south and wonders about my daddy even all these years after they carried him off."

Charlotte shifted uneasily on the dressing table stool. Of course she'd thought about being in love the way Mellie meant. Her imagination had tingled as she read great love stories, but real life didn't often mirror the fantasy of stories. In real life a person had to be practical. A person had to do what was expected. She looked at Mellie and sighed a little before she said, "I guess I've always thought there were more important things than love. The kind of love you're talking about."

Mellie's face softened. "That might be a good thing if you stay fixed on Mr. Edwin. I heard him talkin' last night. About goin' to them Shakers what don't think the Lord intended no Adam and Eve lovin' the way I'm thinkin' on it."

"I know. Everything's turned upside down tonight. Everything."

"You'll figure it out, Miss Lottie. You just need to get some sleep so's your head can think up the ways. Come mornin' you'll find a way to turn things back right."

Come morning. Charlotte echoed Mellie's words in her head as she pulled on her nightgown and crawled under the covers Mellie had turned back for her. And she did always find a way. This wouldn't be any different. She could turn things back right. Come morning.

But the morning sun didn't ease Charlotte's worries. For the first time in her memory, she felt out of place in her own house as she got out of bed and dressed for the day. Mellie had slipped in while she slept and filled her pitcher and washing bowl and laid out her clothes, but she'd probably been ordered to the new Mrs. Vance's aid.

Charlotte ran her hands along the cherry banister as if absorbing the familiar feel of it as she went down the stairs. She loved Grayson. She knew every corner, every floorboard squeak, every angle of sunlight through the windows. It was her house, warm and loving and home. But now a stranger was going to be climbing Grayson's stairs and inspecting all the rooms and wardrobes not as a guest but with permanence in her step.

Plus the other stranger, the artist, was some-where under the roof. She might turn a corner, open a door, and encounter him face-to-face at any moment with the truth of her shamelessly allowing him to kiss her vibrating in the air between them. So it was a relief when she went into the kitchen and Aunt Tish told her the man had been up at first light and gone from the house as the sun was rising.

"But he'd best be back here by half past noon or it'll be his head," Aunt Tish added with raised eyebrows as she looked up from taking three of the leftover dried apple tarts out of the warming oven and arranging them on a plate for Charlotte. "Miss V done been askin' where he be when I carried a tray of coffee up to her and the Massah. She done told your papa in my hearin' that he'd best be tellin' that man he weren't to go off paintin' some lowdown field hand's face instead of her own. Like as how such might spoil the man's brush."

"Unless I miss my guess, Mr. Wade will be painting whatever he likes," Charlotte said as she sat down at the table. She always ate breakfast in Aunt Tish's kitchen when her father wasn't at Grayson, and this morning he'd hardly note her absence with Selena filling his eyes. She liked it in the kitchen with the bacon sizzling in the skillet and the pots boiling on the stove. To Charlotte, it felt like the center of Grayson, where she could see the whole of whatever might be happening.

"Here you are, Miss Lottie. I saved you the ones with the most apples." Aunt Tish set the plate of sweet tarts in front of Charlotte and poured them both a cup of tea. She wiped her face with her apron, but Charlotte saw the smile that sneaked up from her lips to her eyes.

"Sit down and tell me what's so funny."

Aunt Tish lowered herself into the chair opposite Charlotte with a little groan. She'd put on a few extra pounds around her middle over the last years and had trouble with rheumatism in her back. "That Mr. Wade, he ain't doing nothin' with a brush."

"How do you know that?" Charlotte peered at her over the rim of her cup.

"He done been in here drawin' the likes of me. Can you believe that? Had this great big pad of paper and some pencil sticks. Had me sit right here while he sat there wheres you are. Stared holes plum' through me, and when I looked down 'fore I got in a mess a trouble for starin' bold at his white face, told me to keep lookin' at him. You shoulda seen how he moved his hand fast as anythin' over that paper." A look of wonder came over Aunt Tish's face as she drew quick lines on the tabletop with her fingertip. "Then he turned over the page and did it all ag'in."

"Did he show you what he drew?" Charlotte was wishing more and more that the kiss in the garden had never happened. Adam Wade sounded like someone she might enjoy getting to know better, but she could hardly stay in his company now without him thinking she was chasing shamelessly after him.

"He done better than that. He give me one of 'em." Aunt Tish reached under her apron to pull a folded sheet of paper out of a hidden pocket.

"I hated to fold it up, but I couldn't leave it layin' out where anybody might see it." She smoothed it out on the table between them.

Aunt Tish stared up at Charlotte from the paper as if Adam Wade had lifted the likeness of her face out of a mirror. And while the sketch was bare bones, just a few lines, there was more to it than just the image of Aunt Tish. In those few strokes he had captured a look in her eyes. One Charlotte had seen often enough herself when Aunt Tish stood out on the back steps and looked beyond at the horizon.

"And he did this in just a few minutes?"

"Ten, fifteen at the most." Aunt Tish lightly rubbed her flat palm over the paper. "He caught me, didn't he now?"

"He did." She thought of him measuring her face with his thumb and fingers the night before, and she wondered what the sketch would have shown about her if he'd drawn the lines. Maybe she was just as glad he hadn't had a pencil in his hand. "I think there are some old frames up in the attic if you want to get Mellie to climb up there and look for one."

"I might just do that," Aunt Tish said as she folded up the paper to slide back in her pocket with great care.

"Where is he now? Do you know?" Charlotte asked before she bit into one of the tarts.

"That weren't none of my bus'ness." Aunt

Tish stood up to fork the bacon out of the pan.

Charlotte eyed her broad back. "But you know."

Aunt Tish didn't say anything for a long moment as she stirred a pot of grits and lifted the lid on the coffeepot. Charlotte didn't ask her again. She just waited, and finally as if Aunt Tish could feel Charlotte's eyes on her, she sighed and turned around. "I don't know if'n that's where he really went or why he would want to." She hesitated again.

Charlotte lifted her shoulders in a show of unconcern. "It doesn't really matter to me where he went. I was simply curious about what he might be sketching next."

"Uh-huh," Aunt Tish said with one peaked eyebrow that showed she was seeing right through what Charlotte was saying. "Looks to me like as how he done caught your eye. Guess that's why it's so odd him askin' the way to Mr. Edwin's place."

"Edwin's?" Charlotte didn't even attempt to hide her surprise. She shifted uneasily in her chair. He'd promised not to kiss and tell.

"I couldn't figure him wantin' to be drawin' Mr. Edwin's long skinny face, but then I couldn't figure him wantin' to draw my round black one neither. I overheard him talkin' to Willis as he was leavin'. He was wantin' a horse. Course when Willis come in later for his breakfast, he was tellin' how the man was full of questions on how to get to the Shakers' town too. Askin' all manner of questions about what Willis knew about them and the way they lived and such."

"What'd Willis tell him?"

"Well, you know Willis. He ain't much for talkin' to white folks. Says the less said, the better. He just tol' him all he knew was they had some mighty fine workhorses."

Charlotte played with one of the tarts on her plate, breaking edges off it but not putting them in her mouth.

Aunt Tish sat back down and reached across the table to touch her arm. "Somethin' botherin' you, Miss Lottie?"

"Edwin says he wants to go to the Shakers."

"I knowed it. Mattie tol' me so some weeks ago. Says that Shaker man is in and out of the house over there like as how it was his."

Mattie was Edwin's longtime housekeeper. "What's she think about it?"

Aunt Tish pulled her hand back and wrapped it around her cup. "She ain't upset." She stared straight at Charlotte. "No way she could be. Folks join the Shakers, they has to set their people free. Them Shakers don't abide with slave-holdin'."

"Or marrying either."

"You speakin' the truth there."

The bell in the dining room tinkled and Aunt Tish pushed herself up out of her chair. "Sounds

63

like the Massah's wantin' his bacon. You goin' out there with 'em?"

"Not today, Aunt Tish. If Papa asks, you can tell him I've already eaten."

"There's little truth in that," Aunt Tish said as she eyed the tarts still on Charlotte's plate. "You gonna waste away to nothin', chile."

6

Edwin Gilbey wasn't home. Off to the Shaker village, according to the servant who met Adam in the driveway to hold his horse. The man had the biggest smile on his face as any Negro Adam had seen since he got to Kentucky. When Adam asked if he could sketch his picture holding the horse's head, the man's smile got even wider. He was missing a couple of teeth.

"Ain't nobody ever wanted to use up no pencil markings on the likes of me." The man ran a hand through the fuzz of gray hair on his head as the horse snuffled his shoulder. "You any good at it?"

"No Michelangelo, but I do a fair likeness." Adam opened his pad to the sketch of the senator's cook and turned it around where the man could see it.

"Well, I'll be if Latisha Sparrow ain't a-starin' up at me off 'n that paper plain as day. I reckon if she let you draw her, won't be no harm in you drawin' my old face too." He tilted his chin up a bit the way he'd surely seen white men's portraits posed.

Adam turned over to a blank page and made some quick marks. "What's your name?"

"Redmon."

"Last name or first?" Adam asked.

"Last name, first name. All the name I needs."

"Well, tell me, Redmon. Are you always this happy?"

"Ain't no good lookin' like you got hold of a sour persimmon. No sir. Best to keep on grinnin' cause that's what ever'body wants to see."

"Your smile's looking pretty genuine this morning, Redmon. Is it because Mr. Gilbey's gone?"

"You done tryin' to get me in trouble, Mr. Sir. But no sir, I've known Massah Edwin since he was in knickers. Taught him to ride a horse. Now that was a task, let me tell you." Redmon chuckled a little. "Young Massah Edwin was some timid as a boy. But he done seems to be growin' out of it. What with wantin' to learn them Shaker twirls and spins."

"I met him last night, and to tell the truth he didn't look like the dancing type." Adam looked up at the black man and then quickly back down as he sketched his hand on the horse's bridle. The man's fingers were bony but strong.

65

"You got that right. But them Shaker dances is different. We's all hopin' he might take to them."

"Oh, why's that?" Adam had the sketch done, but he added a little shading here and there just to keep the man talking.

"Them Shakers set a ton of store by their folks keepin' their rules. Not marryin' fer one, but they got another one that matters more to us'n around here. No ownin' nobody. We's thinkin' on breathing some free air."

"What would you do, Redmon?" Adam glanced up at him. "Join up with the Shakers too?"

"I ain't thinkin' on that. No sense tradin' one massah for another no matter how kindly they might be. And I wouldn't be wantin' to give up my Mattie. We jumped the broom long time back." He looked off to the north. "No sir. Me and Mattie, we'd go north. They say a man like me can get a job up there holdin' horses and such."

"You could get a job here too, couldn't you? As a free man."

Redmon looked down at the ground. "It ain't all that easy. They has this law about freed slaves leaving the state or so I been told. Besides, around here, some scalawag might grab my free papers away from me and make him some money sellin' me south. That kind a thing wouldn't be worth noticin' here, but they tell me it's different in the North." The man peered up at Adam and his smile faded away. "You sound

Northern. Is it true we're gonna go to war? The North agin the South?"

"It looks that way."

The black man shook his head. "We best pray the good Lord has mercy on us all."

"Guess I'll have to depend on your prayers, Redmon. I've never been much of a praying man," Adam admitted with a smile.

"Ever' man is a prayin' man if times is bad enough, and could be times is gonna be bad enough for a bunch of folks soon if shots start firin'."

"You could be right." Adam turned the pad around for Redmon to see, and the man's smile came back.

"I do declare, Mr. Sir, you done grabbed old Redmon's face and put it down on that paper. And the horse ain't bad neither. My Mattie ain't gonna be believin' it."

Adam turned the pad back around and scribbled Phoebe's address on the bottom of the drawing. She owed him after pushing him into the unwelcome task of painting Selena Vance's portrait. He tore off the drawing and held it out to the black man. "Here. You take this and show Mattie. Then she'll believe you."

"Oh no sir, Mr. Sir. I couldn't take that from you." Redmon held up his free hand with his palm toward Adam and stepped back a couple of paces. The horse danced backward with him.

"Sure you can, Redmon. I'm giving it to you. Just fold it up and put it in your pocket." He pointed to the address he'd scribbled on the bottom of it. "And if you get your free papers and go north as far as Boston, you go to that address there and show them this picture. They'll hire you on to handle horses just like you do here. That's a promise."

Adam folded the drawing a couple of times and handed it to Redmon, who took it from him as though he thought the paper might ignite in his hand. The man stared at the folded paper a few seconds before he slipped it out of sight in his pants pocket.

"That's mighty generous of you, Mr. Sir." He flipped his eyes up to Adam's face and then back at his feet. "You makin' a promise to old Redmon, I'll be makin' one back. Seein' as how you ain't on familiar terms with the good Lord, I'll do some prayin' for you. Just in case things start goin' bad."

"Thank you, Redmon. A man would be foolish to turn down a believing man's prayers." Adam smiled and took the reins to his horse. "And you say Mr. Gilbey's over at the Shaker village. Can you point the way?"

The sunshine was warm on Adam's shoulders as he rode along the road past cattle grazing on the spring grass in the rolling pastures. In the plowed fields, black men with hoes walked in an up-and-down wave across the smooth dirt, planting seeds. In the distance the redbud blooms brightened up the tree line of woods. All in all, a day to make a man glad to be out riding a horse down a sunny Kentucky road.

A dozen times, Adam wanted to stop and get out his sketchpad. But the morning was speeding past and he'd told Selena Vance he'd be back to work on her portrait that afternoon. For the hundredth time he wished he hadn't let Phoebe talk him into such a tiresome task. The woman was not a pleasure to paint. Full of vanities and not the least interested in a portrait that revealed her nature. She wanted something pretty. Her comfortable image of herself. He could do it, but it was tedious, uninteresting brushstrokes to paint flattering poses that he had no pleasure signing his name to. He liked stripping away a person's pretenses and drawing the stark lines of truth. But there was nothing for it but to make her as beautiful as artistically possible and move on to more interesting subjects. Like Redmon or the senator's cook. Or perhaps the senator's lovely redheaded daughter.

He'd like to try to capture the spark in those green eyes. He'd never known a girl quite like her, although he did have to admit a quick kiss in the garden was hardly enough to claim knowing her. But sometimes he could watch a person and guess much about them. His artist eye, his grandmother told him. She'd had an artistic bent. As a young lady she had tried her hand at painting delicate wildflowers, which she told Adam was one of the few acceptable subjects a young lady might try to capture with brushstrokes.

Later she taught art to inept young ladies to supplement the income of Adam's grandfather, headmaster of a school that touted itself as preparing the best young gentlemen for Harvard and Yale. A respectable profession and one that supplied their needs, but few extras. Especially after Adam's father left to seek their fortune in California and was never heard from again. Adam's mother had no choice but to take her three sons and daughter and move back in with her parents.

While she had been greatly relieved to be back in the urbane society of Boston instead of stuck in the uncivilized area of Louisville where Adam's father had run a store, there was always a shortage of funds to keep up proper appearances. Satisfying her need for the luxuries of life was probably the primary reason his father had been lured away from his family by the siren of gold panned from creeks. If she could have been satisfied with a storekeeper's clerk as a husband, then all of their lives might have been different. But she had been raised on the cusp of society in the East and wanted her children to climb up to a higher rung on the social ladder.

Phoebe, Adam's elder by three years, had grabbed the higher rung with great enthusiasm and married well some years back before producing an appropriate number of offspring for her contented husband. Adam, on the other hand, cared nothing for social standing. That had been knocked out of him in his grandfather's private school where all the true gentlemen's sons had peered down their noses at the lowly headmaster's grandson. It didn't matter to them that his mind had been quicker than many of theirs, or perhaps that was the reason for their disdain. A disdain that he learned to return in spades.

His grandfather had often caned him for posting irreverent sketches of this or that student. Or perhaps not for the irreverence but just for the sketching. His grandfather wanted to beat the artistic dreamer out of him, but some things can't be altered in a man's spirit. Art was one of those things for Adam. That and his streak of independence that made him say no when his grandfather tried to force him into Yale to spend four more years being the charity case of the school. He didn't need Yale. He only needed his pens and his brushes.

When he had told his grandfather he would not enroll in college, that instead he would concentrate on improving his art, his grandfather had almost spit out the word. "Art." His voice was

71

full of contempt, and his hands curled as if he were wishing for the headmaster's cane to attempt one more time to bring Adam into line. "You're as much a fool as your father before you. Chasing off after some dream that will never come to fruition."

Adam braced his shoulders as though expecting a blow from the old man, but he didn't back down. "I am an artist." Those were words he'd practiced for just that moment, and he spoke them with conviction.

His grandfather had once been tall, like Adam, but years of studying and bending over students to instruct them had rounded his shoulders until he had to peer up at Adam through gray eyebrows that grew in wayward paths. But his light blue eyes were as sharp and as accusing as ever. "Artists starve in garrets."

Adam had lived in the man's house since he was twelve years old, but little affection had grown between them. He had realized early on that his grandfather saw Adam's father whenever he looked at him and that he could never be good enough, smart enough, or pliable enough to override the anger his grandfather still carried for the man who had ruined his daughter's life. So Adam never tried. He didn't try that day either as he answered his grandfather's near curse. "Then I will starve."

He had not exchanged a word with his grandfather since. His grandmother had written him encouraging letters that caught up with him occasionally as he traveled to the West searching for his father. He still carried regret that he had not returned to Boston when his grandmother fell ill. He hadn't thought she would die so quickly.

By the time he received word of her death, she'd been underground for days. He saw little need to rush to Boston then. His mother had Phoebe and the boys, his two younger brothers, to hold her hand and pull her through. As for his grandfather, the man needed nothing from Adam. He would simply shut himself away in his library and hardly notice the good woman's passing.

The truth was, Adam didn't have the money for the trip to Boston and to New York both. And it was to New York he had finally been summoned. To interview with *Harper's Weekly*. He didn't believe in angels, but sometimes he wondered if his grandmother had whispered his name in Sam Johnson's ear as she passed through the air on her way to heaven. He had not looked back since except to send his mother money to help pay the younger boys' tuition.

Jake was in his first year at Harvard. A hothead who didn't have art to turn to. Instead he had fought his way through their grandfather's school with his fists and had earned a measure of respect from the gentlemen's sons that allowed him a more accepted place in their society. That had carried through for Harry, who at sixteen was almost ready to matriculate at the college of his choice. He had a love of books and the feeling that teaching was a calling. His calling. Phoebe wrote that Grandfather Tyler was a changed man when he was around Harry.

Perhaps the old man was changed with Harry, but there was no change that could bridge the rift between him and Adam. Adam had proved him wrong, and that was something he could never accept.

Adam shook away the thoughts of his grandfather as the landscape alongside the road changed. Stones stacked on stones with no masonry to hold them in place kept the cows in the lush green fields. Even the cattle seemed different, fatter with little sign of having just come through a hard winter. The sturdily built barns had wide doors that slid back on long iron rods attached to the barn instead of swinging open. But perhaps the most telling difference was that, among the many workers in the fields, he spotted only two black faces under the straw Shaker hats.

Adam didn't stop. Up ahead, the buildings of the Shaker village rose up into the sky. The main houses were every bit as large as the manor houses he'd just come from but built without the first curling bit of ornamental trim work that adorned the local gentry's mansions. Yet somehow the straight, simple lines of the Shaker structures lent them a kind of natural elegance Adam's artist eye admired.

As he rode into the village, a bell sounded, and men and women in uniform dress began filing out of the various buildings to make their way to the large stone building in the center of the village. None of the people seemed to be engaged in conversation as they walked, and few even cast a curious glance toward him riding past them. He was part of the world and so of little interest.

Adam glanced up at the sun straight over his head. The bell had evidently summoned them to their midday meal. He slid off his horse and held the reins while he pulled out his sketchpad. He didn't see Edwin Gilbey. Or any person who stood out. They were all as alike as ants trailing into an anthill as they filed past him. The women wore white caps and large white collars lapping over their bosoms to tuck down in their aprons, covering their plain dresses. The men wore straw hats with wide brims and suspenders to hold up their butternut brown or gray pants.

As he began to sketch them flowing into the white stone building in front of him, one young girl peeked over at him curiously before an older sister shot her a stern look. The girl quickly lowered her eyes to the path once more.

"I mean no harm," he said with a winning smile as the older sister looked at him with suspicion.

She made no response except to narrow her eyes on him with evident distrust before she shooed the young women with her past him like a farm woman trying to pen up a gaggle of geese.

Before his eye could forget the two women's faces, he turned a page and drew the young Shaker girl with the bloom of youth in her cheeks and the older woman drained of cheer. He was still filling in the details on the three sketches when the Shakers began coming back out of the building to return to their duties.

With a look up at the sun, Adam reluctantly put away his sketchpad and mounted his horse.

It was two hours past noon before he got back to Grayson. Selena Vance was not pleased.

7

In the days that followed, Charlotte felt as if she had been tossed into a spinning vortex with no way to break free. She had no control in her own house. Her father's new wife wasted little time in assuming her role as mistress of Grayson. All sweetness and light disappeared with Selena's party dress on that first day as she settled at

Charlotte's mother's writing desk in the morning room and began handing out orders.

The house would be scrubbed from top to bottom. Wardrobes were to be emptied out to make room for her things that would be arriving in trunks in the coming days. The Grayson china with its delicate rose pattern would be packed away and replaced with a pattern of her choice as soon as she had the opportunity to travel to Boston to purchase it. Work on redoing rooms for her son, Landon, who would be arriving with his governess at the end of the month, would begin in earnest at once.

Charlotte felt as if she should run up the stairs and bar the door to her room to at least keep the woman's changes from it. Her father may have felt the same, because each day as soon as breakfast was over, he retreated to his library. The library with its great cherry desk was his sanctuary and the place where he plotted his political campaigns and curried favors from influential visitors and backers. His political strategy room.

He cared little for the books filling the shelves from floor to ceiling on one side of the room. That had been her Grandfather Grayson's passion when the library had been his retreat before her father. Grandfather Grayson claimed to have read every book on the shelves, some over and over until those books fell open to his favorite passages when Charlotte pulled them from the shelves to read. As she curled in the chair in front of the library's fireplace, Charlotte often imagined the old gentleman reading over her shoulder.

After her mother died, Charlotte had free access to the books as there was no one to tell her which books were proper fare for a young lady and which were not. Her father certainly didn't know. He had little time for literature or even history. He claimed to be too busy making history to worry about dwelling on the mistakes of the past.

Charlotte had no argument with that. She also shared her father's passion for politics, and some of her best times with her father were spent in the library listening to the political news from Frankfort. She saw no need to give up these talks just because he had brought a wife home. If Selena's strained look was any indication whenever Charlotte's father began talking of the necessity of preserving the Union at all costs, the woman had little interest in politics.

But Charlotte was eager to know her father's thoughts on whether the Southern states could be wooed back into the Union. President Lincoln hadn't been able to do so in his first month in office, but diplomacy took time. Or so her father always told her. Coaxing an opponent back to your side could be more difficult than doing so by force, but the extra effort was well spent.

However, from what Charlotte read in the

newspapers, the South didn't seem to look with favor on any sort of compromise. Even before President Lincoln took office, the Secessionist states had already established their own government—the Confederate States of America. Charlotte had read about their meeting in Alabama, but surely saner heads would prevail as they had in crises of the past. Those in positions of power would want to find a way to heal the breach without picking up arms.

Charlotte was anxious to hear her father say as much. Plus she was eager to know his plans for the next campaign. That was more than a year away, but a man who wanted to be reelected couldn't wait too long to get his name on the right people's lips. While it was unseemly for a candidate to go out begging for votes for himself, it was vital to have a great many supporters who would. Even more, she wanted to laugh with him about the ridiculous bills some of his fellow senators at times tried to push through the Kentucky legislature.

She wanted to feel his hand patting her head and hear him saying, "Charley, you should have been a boy. You could have been the next governor. Right after me. We could have kept it in the family for years." Even though he always said it as if he'd made a big joke, she knew that thinking about running for the governor's office wasn't a joke to him.

But Selena managed to steal those times with her father from Charlotte too, for now when she carried coffee to him after breakfast, he wanted to talk of nothing but Selena. Selena this. Selena that.

It didn't seem to matter what the woman did. On the very first day, she ordered Gibson, their butler, to carry Charlotte's mother's portrait to the attic, and her father didn't protest. On the second day, she demanded access to the account books not just for the household but for the whole farm, and he handed them over with a smile. Charlotte began to fear that if Selena asked him to burn down the house and build it back to her specifications, he might strike the match on his boot. As long as she kept calling him "my love" and flashing her ingratiating smile at him.

It was almost beyond bearing. But Charlotte had never spent much time pretending. Not since she was twelve and her mother had handed over the keys to the pantry and linen cabinet. She had never pretended her mother would rise up off her couch and take control of the household again. She had never pretended that her father would notice and appreciate the way she, Charlotte, kept the household running. She had never pretended that she loved Edwin or that he loved her. Love had nothing to do with the agreement between them.

And now she didn't pretend that she could stop

Selena's onslaught on Grayson. Not without her father's help, and he was so enamored with the woman it was obvious he thought she could do no wrong. Charlotte saw little choice but to bide her time and carry on as if her life wasn't getting turned upside down. She wasn't exactly pretending that things hadn't changed or that her carefully arranged future wasn't slipping out of reach, but with time, she was sure she could step out of the vortex. She could take control of her future again. Just as soon as her head stopped spinning.

Meanwhile, it didn't help that she often caught Adam Wade's much-too-perceptive eyes on her as she put forth a polite front at the dinner table each evening. It didn't help that the only news she received from Hastings Farm was of Edwin visiting the Shaker village. It didn't help that her father began talking of six-year-old Landon, whom he hadn't even met, as if he was the son he had always wanted. It didn't help that Selena began to speak of the dowry Charlotte would take with her when she married in May, when it was becoming more and more apparent that there might not *be* a wedding in May.

It especially didn't help that Charlotte's father told her Selena thought she spent an inappropriate amount of time in the kitchen with Aunt Tish and had suggested Charlotte should go visit his Virginian relations for a few months to broaden her horizons beyond Grayson. When Charlotte asked which relatives, since the redheaded grand-mother had passed on years since, her father said there was a cousin but he would have to find out her name. Even so, he was sure Charlotte would be quite welcome as a houseguest.

Charlotte felt as if she had been bowled over by a runaway horse, and every time she tried to stand up and get her bearings, the same thing happened all over again. Selena was outflanking her at every turn. And all with a too-sweet smile and the claim that she only had Charlotte's best interests at heart.

On the third day, she summoned Charlotte to her while she was sitting for the portrait. If it hadn't been her father delivering the message, Charlotte would have ignored Selena's summons. Not forever. Just until after the sitting because of how assiduously she had been avoiding the artist except at the evening meal when she could hardly be absent from her place without a good excuse. Cowardice would not be an acceptable reason or one she would like to explain to her father. Nor could she come up with a reasonable excuse to delay talking to Selena when her father found her in the garden.

"Charley, I've been looking for you." He sat down on the stone bench beside her and shifted his weight from side to side with a little groan. "These things need some padding." He was a man who liked his comfort.

"But the sunshine is nice." Charlotte smiled as she dropped her book to her lap, keeping her finger on the page to mark her place. The extra weight her father had put on in the last few years had aged him. He was barely past fifty, but he winded easily and preferred his easy chair to any sort of sporting activity. At least before Selena.

Charlotte hadn't seen him for several months, since he had been staying in Frankfort. With the country in such a state of turmoil, she had not thought his extended absence from Grayson odd. He had to keep abreast of legislative issues and work for his constituents. But it seemed this year there had been time for more pleasurable pursuits as well.

He glanced up at the cloudless sky as if he hadn't noticed whether the sun was even shining until she mentioned it. "So it is," he said.

The bright light in the garden made it easy to see how thin his hair was getting on the top, even though Ruben, his longtime valet, had carefully combed his remaining hair over the balding spot. Gray was creeping back from his temples and taking over his eyebrows. His moustache was almost completely gray. A light sheen of perspiration moistened his forehead even though the air was cool enough that Charlotte had considered going back inside for her shawl.

"Are you feeling all right, Father?" Charlotte asked with a worried frown.

"Now don't you be worrying about me." He patted her arm. "I've never been better."

"You look tired."

"Well, things were busy in Frankfort what with the current unrest in our country, and of course once I met Selena, things started hopping. Not much time for relaxation. Not that I'm complaining," he said with a little laugh. "Most certainly not. Selena's the best thing to happen to me in a long while. And to Grayson too, or I miss my guess."

Charlotte had no words to answer that, but her father didn't need her words as he went on. "You can't know how very glad I am that you and Selena are getting along so well. She thinks of you as a favored younger sister, you know."

"Does she?" Charlotte stared down at her book as she carefully marked her place with a ribbon before she closed it. "Not a daughter, then."

Her father laughed. "You can hardly expect that, since she's only a few years older than you."

"That's good anyway. I had a loving mother." Charlotte looked up at him as if the next question just came out of thin air. "How old is Selena anyway?"

He raised eyebrows that Ruben must have forgotten to comb that morning before he said, "I haven't been a politician these many years not to know there are some questions a man dares not ask, and a woman's age is one of those."

"What do you know about her?" Charlotte looked directly at her father. When the color rose in his cheeks, she wasn't sure if it was due to anger or embarrassment.

He frowned a little. "I know enough and I should think you know enough not to be disrespectful to your father."

"I'm sorry. I didn't mean to sound disrespectful, Father." She stared down at her book a moment. *The Scarlet Letter* by Nathaniel Hawthorne. A story of impropriety. "I was merely curious about her. And her son, Landon. Have you met him?"

"No, no, but I am anxious to have him here at Grayson. Selena planned to send him to Georgia to spend some time with relations there, but I've talked her out of that. He needs to be here with his mother. And me. He's only six, but Selena says he's smart as a tack." Her father's good humor returned as he looked up and off across the garden. "It will be good to have a boy running about the house."

"Georgia? I understood Selena was from Boston."

"That's where she was living when her late husband made his tragic departure from life. Some sort of wasting sickness, she says. All very sad. But her extended family owns a plantation in Georgia. Very well-to-do, I surmise. That's why she's so capable of looking at Grayson and seeing where we might have been neglectful over the last few years in managing our people. A soft heart is fine in church but can get you in trouble on the farm."

Charlotte sat frozen on the bench, almost afraid to breathe, but she had to ask the question pushing at her lips. "What does she suggest? For our people?"

"We have to cull them out the same as we would our horses. She's already talked to Perkins about it and he's giving her names."

"You're going to sell them?" Charlotte's voice sounded wrong in her ears. "To the South?"

"That's where the best market is. Selena says the plantations down there are always anxious to get Kentucky-bred Negroes. And with Mr. Lincoln's abolitionist leanings, who knows what might happen. A person has to protect his investments."

"President Lincoln hasn't put forth a plan to free the slaves, has he?"

"Not as yet, but there are many who think it could be in the offing if a compromise isn't reached with the Secessionist states. I don't know what those governors and representatives down there can be thinking." He rubbed his hands up and down his thighs as his voice got a little louder. "Just because the President spoke against allowing slavery in new territories in the West doesn't mean he planned to ban it in states where it already existed. He won't do that. Not if he wants to keep Kentucky in the Union."

"Would you vote for secession?"

"No, no. I can't imagine any situation where Kentucky wouldn't stay with the Union." He pulled his eyebrows together in a frown just thinking about it. "But at the same time I can't see surrendering my property to the federal government without proper recompense. It's better to leave things status quo. And not keep stirring things up like those copperheads up north with their abolition talk."

"I wish we could just set all our people free."

"My dear girl, you don't know what you're saying." Her words obviously shocked her father. "No, no, my dear, that would be the ruin of us all. Perhaps them even more than us. What would become of them without us to feed and clothe them?" He shook his head at her as his look turned from indignant to indulgent. "Being so young, you can hardly be expected to understand all the ramifications of freeing the slaves, and it is something you shouldn't concern your pretty head about. What you need to remember is that our people are well cared for."

Charlotte wanted to argue with him, but she knew it would be useless. Better to pick her fight. "Is Mellie mine? Mother always told me so. That Aunt Tish was hers and Mellie was mine."

"She did say that."

Charlotte opened the book in her lap and tore out the blank page at the back of the book.

"Would you write that down for me? That Mellie belongs to me. And Aunt Tish too. It can be an early wedding present."

"Not Aunt Tish," he said. "We have to have a cook here at Grayson."

"Then Mellie," Charlotte insisted.

He looked at the paper she handed him. "I don't have pen and ink."

Charlotte reached under the bench where she'd laid her writing tools when she started reading. "I was making a list earlier. Of things I need to do before the wedding." It wasn't exactly true, but close enough. It was actually a note to Edwin to try to ensure there was a wedding. She dipped the pen nib in the ink and handed it to her father.

He held the pen in the air above the paper as he hesitated. "I don't know about this, Charlotte."

"You were going to let Mellie go with me when I married, weren't you?"

"Well, yes, I suppose so, but that was before Selena. I really should speak to her about this. Besides, isn't there some doubt of the wedding going on as planned in May?"

"Even if I don't wed in May, I will wed eventually. And Mellie was promised to me by Mother." Charlotte spoke the words with quiet firmness.

"Yes, your mother was always sentimental about the servants. Something Selena says we can't be. She says it could be we should have found a new place for Mellie years ago when it was apparent you were getting too attached to her." He frowned as he stared down at the paper while the ink dried on the pen's nib.

Charlotte's heart went cold inside her. How could her father even listen to such a suggestion? That woman had spun a spell over him. Charlotte moistened her lips and managed to keep her voice soft and insistent without letting the panic she was beginning to feel leak through. She had to protect Mellie. She had given Aunt Tish her word. "Mother didn't think I was too attached. She said it was good to have servants we could depend on. You do remember that she promised Mellie to me, don't you? A promise she had no doubt you'd keep."

He stared across the walkway at the dogwood tree whose buds were already showing white. "I did so love your mother. I planted that tree for her with my own hands on our first anniversary to prove how much. She sat on this very bench and laughed when I showed her the dirt under my fingernails. She had just felt the stirrings of the first child she tried to carry for me." He smiled at the memory, but then the smile slipped off his face. "She lost that baby two weeks later. You and our poor little baby boy were the only two she carried past the first five months. And then the baby boy never drew breath."

"I remember," Charlotte said.

"Yes, I suppose you do. What were you four, five?"

"Almost six," Charlotte said. "He was born in May before my birthday in June."

"So many years ago and yet even now I can close my eyes and see that round little face, so perfectly formed. So silent and still. Mayda held him to her breast and whispered the name she'd planned for him as if at the sound of her voice he might yet gasp and begin to breathe. Charles Grayson after me and her father. I didn't want to use the names. I wanted to save them for the baby son we might yet have, but she would not hear of naming him anything else." Her father let out a breath heavy with the sadness of his memories. "I had to peel her hands from his tiny body to let Aunt Tish prepare him for burial. Mayda was never the same after that."

"But she kept loving us." Charlotte needed to hear him affirm that.

"Yes. As much as she was capable. She put too much on you when you were little more than a child, and I suppose I did as well. We should have let you go away to school."

"I never wanted to leave Grayson. Grandfather taught me to read and write before he died," Charlotte said. "And I went to Miss Lucinda's school in town. I'm not uneducated."

"Not in history and letters, but there is an art

to being a lady and rules that must be observed by young women in your position."

"I have observed the rules." Charlotte pushed her words at him. "Haven't I always managed to show Grayson in the best light whenever you wanted to entertain here? You have never had reason to be ashamed of me."

His eyes came away from the tree back to Charlotte. "Oh, my dear girl, I didn't mean to make you think that. You've always been a very dutiful daughter."

Dutiful. Is that how he thought of her? As only dutiful. She let her eyes fall shut a moment as she composed herself. She didn't want to lose her focus. Not until he wrote the paper giving her Mellie. She opened her eyes and smiled at him. "And you a loving, caring father. That's why I know you will honor Mother's promise to me."

"Promise?" He had gone so far back in memory that he seemed to have forgotten what promise she meant as he looked down at the pen in his hand with a little frown.

"Mellie. Mother's promise to me." Charlotte held the little pot of ink out toward him. "My wedding present." She wanted to ask for Aunt Tish again, but feared pushing him too far.

"Oh, Mellie. Well, I suppose you're right. I should honor your mother's promise." He dipped the pen into the ink and wrote the words on the paper. He handed it to her.

She read his writing. "This is legally binding?"

"It is. You are now a slaveholder."

"Yes," Charlotte agreed as she stared at the paper. "Thank you, Father." She reached over to kiss his cheek before she carefully folded the paper and slipped it down into her pocket.

After that, she could hardly refuse to obey his request to heed Selena's summons to the parlor. She had Mellie's promised freedom in her pocket.

8

Adam Wade mixed the paint on his palette as quickly as possible. Time was wasting while he stood in the senator's parlor painting the senator's wife as scores of better subjects were going undrawn. He would have even preferred sketching the lines of the senator's florid face. Sam would probably welcome that, along with a few of the senator's words stating his seemingly sincere belief that his state could remain a neutral buffer zone if the confrontation between the states escalated. And the senator would be happy to have the notoriety of being in *Harper's Weekly*. The man had ambitions. Beyond senator in the Kentucky Senate.

Governor, the new Mrs. Vance claimed, which

perhaps explained why she was the new Mrs. Vance. Adam doubted love had much to do with it, even if she did liberally sprinkle her conversations with the senator with words of devotion. Plus the senator was old money or at least had inherited such from his first wife. The wife whose portrait had been removed, leaving behind a darker square of forest green striped wallpaper over the mantelpiece behind Adam. Across the parlor the new wife sat by the window in a shaft of afternoon light.

Adam hadn't warmed to her. Something he generally did when he was painting someone. Perhaps his reluctance to do the portrait was the cause, or perhaps it had more to do with the way the woman ordered him about like one of her husband's servants as he stood behind the easel and wielded his brush. Twice he'd had to wipe away his brushstrokes depicting her eyes because of the hard glint he kept letting the paint on the canvas reveal. He wished he was back at the Shaker village painting the old sister whose suspicious glower had wiped away every trace of feminine beauty from her face. At least there he could be honest with his brush.

Selena Vance hadn't seen her painted eyes. He knew better than to let a subject see a portrait in progress. Especially someone like the woman in front of him. She seemed—if that could be possible—even wearier of the whole process than he was. She came to each sitting wearing a cream-colored dress with an edging of delicate lace around the plunging neckline. Her skin was very white, almost too white, but it contrasted nicely with the pink of her cheeks, which she kept pinching to give them color whenever she thought he wasn't watching.

He could have told her he could paint in the color without her resorting to the painful pinches, but he didn't. Her dark hair was piled high on her head in an elaborate style that had to take an hour to pin and arrange. So he supposed it was no wonder the woman was tired of sitting still even before she came to the parlor to perch on the Victorian chair and, with a bare word of greeting, demanded he begin.

Paint her pretty and get it over with, he told himself every ten minutes. It didn't matter that the more he looked at her, the less attractive she seemed to him in spite of her perfectly aligned features. He had an imagination. While he had never used that imagination to intentionally change the looks of one of his subjects, that didn't mean he couldn't this time. For his mental sanity he needed to think of Selena Vance as beautiful and portray that on the canvas. He needed to be free to get back to drawing subjects that mattered. The nation was boiling and he was stuck inside a parlor painting lace on the bodice of a dress.

The finer points of the lace might be missing in the portrait, for he planned to be gone from the senator's house by the end of the week. If the senator wasn't pleased with the finished portrait, he had plenty of resources to contract another artist who might be as captivated by the new Mrs. Vance's beauty as the senator was.

Of course Adam would miss Aunt Tish's cooking. Plus he had entertained a few hopes of coming across the senator's daughter alone in the garden again. While a repeat of their earlier encounter wouldn't be unwelcome, it was not likely the way she had avoided him since. The only time he'd seen her was at the dinner table, where she seemed a pale shadow of the girl in the garden who had met his eyes so brazenly in the moonlight and spoken so honestly. She let no honest words brighten the dinner conversation as she kept her eyes on her plate and only perked up if the senator began talking politics.

From memory, he had sketched the senator's daughter gazing off her veranda into the darkness. He thought Sam might print it with a caption saying something like, "With war on the horizon, a Southern belle ponders her future." Sam was a genius with captions.

Adam wasn't worried about the senator's daughter not wanting her picture in the newspaper. Truth be known, she might not even recognize herself, since the illustration would lack color to show her red hair. But he hoped to find a time to show her the drawing before he left Grayson so she'd know in case the newspaper eventually found its way into her hands. It was like a gift he could give her to perhaps make up for taking advantage of her at a vulnerable moment. Although he was hardly averse to catching her in another such moment or too much of a gentleman to seize the advantage if it did happen again.

So he was surprised when the daughter appeared at the parlor door in the middle of the afternoon's sitting. By command, it turned out. Selena had been browbeating the butler, an old black gentleman named Gibson who seemed totally overwhelmed by the new Mrs. Vance's stream of orders. There was little doubt he was going to forget most of them before he got out of the room.

Adam had tried to help by telling Selena how important it was that she sit quietly for him to capture the best image on the canvas.

She glared Adam's way for a brief moment. "I sat quietly yesterday. Today you will have to find a way to work around my words. This is all taking much too long. I've had my portrait done before without the need for so many sittings."

If only she had called on that artist again, Adam thought as he had to stay his brush from turning the jeweled combs in her elaborate hairstyle into horns. He sent Gibson a sympathetic look, but the butler kept his eyes on the floor. Adam's fingers itched to capture his dejection. The old fellow had probably been accustomed to opening the door to guests and ushering them into the receiving parlor, to making sure the stair spindles and furniture were properly dusted, and to seeing that fires blazed in Grayson's hearths if the weather turned cool.

While that might have satisfied the senator's daughter, he had a new mistress in residence now, one who was changing things too rapidly for Gibson to take in. Each new word from the woman in the chair by the window seemed to bend his shoulders a little more, as if she were loading bricks into a sack on his old back while he mumbled, "Yes'm."

When the senator's daughter came in the room, the old man's face brightened. Something his new mistress noted with evident displeasure.

"This is useless." Selena heaved an elaborate sigh of disgust. "You're dismissed, Gibson. Send that other girl in here. The one who does my hair. She at least seems to have a memory."

"Mellie," Charlotte told Gibson as he looked at her. "Tell Mellie Mrs. Vance wants her." Her voice was soft and kind with none of the sharp edges in Selena's commands.

"Yes, miss. Right away, miss." The old fellow started out of the room, but stopped to ask, "Do you want her to bring tea?"

"Just . . . get . . . her." Selena spoke the words one at a time with force.

"Yes'm."

Adam was surprised at how fast the old man got out of the room. He wished he could follow on his heels, and he thought the senator's daughter would have been right behind them if she could have done as she wanted. But then she seemed to find some courage as she looked directly at Selena and said, "Gibson has been with the family for many years."

"Perhaps too many years." Selena didn't bother to hide her annoyance whether with Gibson or the senator's daughter or life in general.

Without thought Adam painted in the frown lines between her eyes and then had to smooth them away with his brush. Paint her pretty and quickly, he reminded himself. Neither woman was paying the least bit of attention to him.

"He's a great favorite of many of Father's political friends," the younger woman said.

Selena mashed her mouth together in a thin line. "Politics can't rule everything."

"Elections are won by a thousand little things."

"More like a few thousand votes. But I didn't call you in here to discuss political maneuvering. I get an overabundance of that from your father, you can be sure."

"Father is committed to serving his state as

best he can. A difficult charge now with all the divisions."

Selena's eyes narrowed on Charlotte. Adam was pleased to see the girl didn't wilt under her glare. "Are you attempting in your clumsy way to take me to task?"

"Oh no. I do beg your pardon if such seemed the case." She sounded sincere as she turned to bring Adam into the conversation. "I certainly wouldn't want Mr. Wade to think there was any kind of ill feeling between us. Forgive me, Mr. Wade, if my words appeared uncharitable."

Adam twisted his mouth a little to the side to keep from smiling. "Don't mind me. I'm just the portrait painter."

"How is it coming? May I look?" Charlotte took a step toward his easel.

"No." Selena stopped her in her tracks. "Our dear Mr. Wade claims he can't allow anyone to see the portrait until it is finished. Not even me."

Adam let the smile leak out to his face as he made a few brushstrokes. "You know how artists can be. Temperamental about their work."

"Of course," Charlotte said and stepped back. "But I've heard you are very good with portrait sketches."

"Sketches of whom?" Selena's eyes were sharp on Adam.

"I've seen his work in *Harper's Weekly*." Charlotte didn't really answer the woman's question as she turned back to her. "I've been going through some of our old newspapers, and every illustration Mr. Wade has done is quite remarkable. I'm surprised Father was able to convince him to take time out from such work to do your portrait."

"Charles had little to do with it. I am a friend of Mr. Wade's sister."

"How fortunate for you," Charlotte said.

She acted as if Adam hadn't already told her the same thing in the garden. Perhaps she had wiped that encounter out of her mind. Perhaps he should do the same. He pretended to turn his full attention back to the canvas in front of him.

Charlotte continued to stand in the middle of the floor instead of settling in one of the chairs which she surely had a right to do even if the senator's wife didn't ask her to sit. After a brief and uncomfortable silence, Charlotte said, "My father said you wished to speak to me."

"Yes, so I did." Selena's voice sounded almost as superior as it had moments ago when she was speaking to the old butler. "The servants have been packing up your mother's things. Something that should have been done years ago."

"I suppose you're right, but there never seemed any urgency." Charlotte's voice held a whisper of sadness. "Until now. Do you want me to go through the things?"

"No need," Selena said with a wave of her hand. "We've already disposed of them."

"Disposed of them?" The color drained from Charlotte's face. "Without consulting me?"

"Really, Charlotte, those dusty old clothes would have done nothing but make you sneeze. I had them sent to a charitable group." Selena swept her eyes up and down Charlotte from her shoulders to her toes. "You certainly could never tighten your stays enough to fit into any of those garments. Your mother must have been stylishly slender."

"Please, Selena, this hardly seems proper conversation in mixed company." Red bloomed in Charlotte's face as she glanced sideways at Adam.

Selena laughed at her innocence. "Never you fear about Mr. Wade. I'm sure he's quite familiar with the workings of corsets."

Adam looked up from his paints and searched for a way to ease Charlotte's humiliation. Humiliation Selena was relishing. It was becoming obvious that she was as ready to pack up the senator's daughter and ship her off as she had been the first Mrs. Vance's dresses. He pushed out a little laugh. "You've got me there, Selena. My first paying job was drawing corsets for a catalogue advertisement." He mixed some colors on his palette and told himself to forget about painting her pretty. Just finish the job. He hadn't promised satisfaction to her. Or to Phoebe. He cleaned his brush. "Perhaps I should leave so you can continue your talk in private."

"That won't be necessary, Adam. Charlotte and I are almost through here." Selena pointed to a small wooden box on the table beside her. "Your father says that was your mother's jewelry, and he insisted you would want it even if there is little of worth in the box. Nothing but a few old tarnished pieces."

"Mother preferred books and flowers to jewelry," Charlotte said as she swooped up the box.

"So Charles has told me. And that's another thing." Selena looked out the window. "The garden needs major renovation. Everything has been sadly neglected here for too long."

"Grayson has its own unique charm," Charlotte said.

"But all charms can be enhanced. Isn't that so, Adam?"

"In a perfect world perhaps," Adam said.

"There are no perfect worlds. Or are there, Charlotte?" Selena turned her sharp eyes back to Charlotte, who halted her backward edging toward the door but stayed silent as she stiffened her posture and waited for the woman to go on. "Your young Mr. Gilbey seems to disagree with me there. The night of the party he was telling me all about this Shaker village nearby where he seems to feel a perfect life might await him. Have you heard any more from him on the status of your planned wedding? Will it be a Shaker wedding?"

Charlotte's face lost all pretense of a smile. "No. The Shakers don't believe in marriage."

"I thought that was the case." From the smug look on Selena's face, it was obvious she had known that all along but had merely been baiting Charlotte. "Then, my dear, don't you think it is time to look in a new direction? Find a new plan for your future? I'm sure your father shared with you the opportunity of going east for a while. That would save you the embarrassment of being the subject of many whispered conversations at all the spring gatherings."

"Grayson is my home," Charlotte said.

"Of course it is. I certainly don't mean to imply any differently." Selena's voice was honey-coated but underneath was steel. "But you do have to realize it is no longer your home only. Your father has a new family now. I'm sure he's told you about his plans for Landon."

"Plans? It was my understanding he'd not yet met the child."

"That's true, but I've naturally enough shared a great deal about Landon, and your father has generously offered to adopt him. He says my son is his son. Just as his daughter is my daughter. And of course we have hopes of having a child of our own." Selena smoothed her hands down over her midsection and raised her eyebrows knowingly at the girl.

Two bright red spots burned in Charlotte's

cheeks as she looked down at the floor and spoke barely above a whisper. "Of course."

Selena let out a short burst of unladylike laughter at Charlotte's evident discomfort. Adam was sorry he hadn't left the room earlier in spite of the woman's orders to the contrary. He could have simply walked out. He wasn't her slave. It was painful watching the calculating woman attempting to dismantle the world of the girl in front of her. A few days ago the girl had been the senator's beloved daughter with all of Grayson at her feet. Now all she could claim as her own was the box of jewelry clutched so tightly against her side the wooden corners had to be digging into her ribs. Ribs that were obviously free of the type of tortuous corset Selena had immodestly mentioned earlier.

Charlotte had no need of the slimming stays. She had no need of any beauty enhancements. In her everyday blue flowered dress flowing about her legs without multiple petticoats and her red hair falling free down on her shoulders, she easily outshined the polished woman he was painting. Even with no hint of a smile on her face.

He suddenly wanted to cross the room and put his arm around her. To protect her from the hard truths of life. He wanted to see her smiling, embracing life. Embracing him. The thought pulled him up short. He couldn't let himself get carried away by a pretty face. He didn't need those sorts of complications in his life. What he needed to do was paint faster and get away from this house. He needed to be back searching out the scenes to capture the truth of the country's current upheaval. He needed no upheaval in his own life. Especially not the kind a girl like Charlotte Vance could bring him.

When the girl mumbled some words of thanks for the box and almost ran out of the room, he told himself that was good. With her out of sight, he could concentrate on finishing the loathsome portrait and be gone from the senator's house. He was no knight in shining armor ready to rescue every damsel in distress he met. Especially not when the dragon in question was only the damsel's stepmother. It wasn't as if her life was in danger. Merely her immediate happiness.

9

Selena was right. Most of the tangled pile of necklaces and brooches were old and tarnished and of little value other than to Charlotte's heart. She remembered playing with some of them when she was a child. She fished out an emerald ring and a strand of pearls that had belonged to her Grandmother Grayson and held each of them for a long moment as if testing their weight and value.

Then she carefully freed a locket on a fine gold chain from the other strands of jewelry in the box. Inside was a wisp of baby hair clipped from her baby brother's head before he was laid in his tiny casket. Her mother had never taken the locket off after that day. Charlotte thought her mother had worn it to her grave, but now here it was tossed aside in a box and forgotten. Charlotte shut the locket and held it tightly in her palm.

Be strong. Miss Mayda would want you to be strong. Aunt Tish's words echoed in Charlotte's mind. And that had been easy for Charlotte to do in spite of her mother's sudden death, because everybody had helped her. Everybody knew Grayson would be hers. In time. Even if she had thought about her father remarrying, she would have never considered Grayson passing to someone who didn't carry Grayson blood. Her whole life centered around that belief.

But now she'd been betrayed. By her own father. They were going to ship her off to Virginia and do what they willed with Grayson and their people. No, not what they willed. What Selena willed.

She couldn't let it happen. But what could she do? She had sent the letter to Edwin demanding to know his intentions. Willis had carried it to Hastings manor house at noon. She had to know. She couldn't just hide in the shadows and hope without knowledge. If Edwin stayed true to their agreement, then she could wait out Selena. The flattery of the woman's attention had obviously blinded her father, but his eyes would clear and he would see through the woman's pretense in time.

Meanwhile. That was the problem. Charlotte had never been one to sit on the side and simply let things happen. Not the way her mother had. Charlotte made things happen. But now nothing was working. She closed her eyes and held the locket against her cheek. Perhaps she should pray about it. Ask the Lord to make things come out right, but that hadn't worked for her baby brother. His life had ended on the day of his birth. It hadn't worked for Aunt Tish. Her husband had been sold down the river.

Charlotte had no doubt Aunt Tish prayed then. Aunt Tish believed in prayer. She had taught Mellie and Charlotte to pray over their food as soon as they could sit at the table. She had prayed over Charlotte's mother. She probably covered Charlotte with prayers every morning now. But that didn't mean things were going to turn out right. Aunt Tish told her once that a person couldn't expect God to hand out favors on a silver tray.

"Then why pray if you don't think the Lord is going to answer?" Charlotte had asked.

"I never said the good Lord don't answer. He always answers. That don't mean his answers is gonna match up with the answers you think you're wantin'. But the one thing a child of his can count on is that, no matter the answer, the Lord is right there with you. Walkin' through them valleys right along 'side you. Liftin' you up when you fall. Helpin' you bear up under the trials." Aunt Tish had put her work-roughened hand on Charlotte's cheek. "And we all, ever' last one of us, has trials and tribulations."

"But is that any reason to collect them like charms and gather them close and moan over them without trying to do something about them?" Charlotte said.

"No, I guess not, child. You ain't much a one for moanin'." Aunt Tish had smiled at her as she patted her cheek. "The good Lord done give you a fightin' spirit and the freedom to use it."

A fighting spirit. That's what she needed now. Charlotte opened her eyes and stood up. There was a time for praying and a time for doing. This was the time for doing. Edwin had her letter. She had her mother's jewelry. And Mellie's path to freedom. She slipped her hand in her pocket and felt the paper. She hadn't given up. It might have seemed that she had lost the battle in the parlor. She was sure Adam Wade thought so. She'd felt him looking at her with pity. But she didn't need pity. Pity or prayers. There'd be a way. She just had to find it.

She'd make her father see that Grayson was

108

meant to be hers. The same as he had realized Mellie was hers. Of course, if he had known her plans to free Mellie, she doubted he'd have given her the paper. He claimed freed slaves did nothing but foment trouble and unrest if not made to leave the state. That was why he'd supported the Kentucky Colonization Society that up until a couple of years before had worked to buy passage back to Africa for emancipated slaves.

Mellie wouldn't want to go to Africa. Her home was here at Grayson the same as Charlotte's. That shouldn't mean she couldn't be free to decide her own fate. Free to fall in love as she wanted. Actually Charlotte was beginning to suspect it wasn't only a dream of falling in love for Mellie. She'd been volunteering to carry the leftover food from their dinner to the slave quarters nearly every night before Selena began to demand so much from her. And hadn't Charlotte caught a worried look in Aunt Tish's eyes more than once when she looked at Mellie?

One thing at a time. She had the paper. She'd figure out the rest eventually. First there was the locket warm in her hand. Charlotte pulled the top off a nearly empty powder tin and dropped the locket down inside. It should have been buried with her mother. She would rectify that first thing in the morning.

She slipped the emerald ring on her finger. She'd never seen her mother wear it. It would have been too large for her mother's dainty fingers. She had favored an opal ring in a ruby setting. Charlotte searched through the jumble of jewelry. That ring wasn't in the box. So perhaps she had worn it to the grave.

Charlotte stuffed the box of jewelry up on the top shelf of her wardrobe. She started to hide Mellie's paper under the box, but changed her mind. It was too important to let out of her sight.

When Mellie came in a few minutes later to help her dress for dinner, Charlotte slipped the paper out of her pocket and down into the top of her camisole when Mellie had her back turned. She couldn't show it to her yet. Not until she had a plan, and before Charlotte could make a plan, she had to know her future with Edwin.

If she didn't get an answer from him by noon tomorrow, she would ride over to Hastings Farm. She'd make him state his intentions. But tonight she would go down to the dining room and listen to Selena's false chatter at the table. She would pretend there wasn't a battle drawn up between them. Just as many in the North and South were pretending the same thing. It was better to keep the illusion of peace as long as possible.

Even as they ate their dinner that night with a pretense of good humor and fine manners, the illusion of peace for the country had already been shot down at Fort Sumter in South Carolina.

A messenger brought the news the next morning. Charlotte didn't see the messenger ride up. After breakfast she had stopped in the kitchen and hid a heavy stirring spoon in the folds of her skirt before going out the back door to the family cemetery. She didn't want help from anyone for the job at hand.

The ground was soft from a late afternoon shower the day before, and she had no trouble cutting out a circle of the greening grass and scooping out a hole at the base of her mother's stone. She pushed the metal powder box down into the hole and tamped the dirt back in around it before carefully replacing the bit of grass sod. When she stood up and looked down, the disturbed ground was barely noticeable.

Charlotte ran her hands over the carved letters in the stone. Mayda Grayson Vance. Beloved wife and mother. Aug 5 1816–May 24 1857. Her baby brother's small tombstone was beside her mother's. In behind were the stones for her grandparents and her mother's sisters, Alice and Emma, taken by cholera in 1833. Another stone that towered higher even than her grandparents' stone bore the name of their one son, Richard Grayson III, in deeply chiseled granite letters. He had gone west to seek adventure and broken his parents' hearts by getting killed in an Indian skirmish. His body wasn't actually under the stone but was instead in an unmarked grave somewhere on the prairie.

Charlotte thought how different her life might have been if her uncle Richard had lived to come home and marry. His family would be living in the Grayson manor house. His son the descendant to carry on the Grayson name and tradition. But there were no Grayson sons. No sons at all. Up until now.

She raised her head to look out between the tall oaks that shaded the graveyard. Grayson land stretched as far as she could see in every direction. Good land. Her land. She could almost feel the roots attaching her feet to the ground as strongly as the roots holding the towering oaks around her. It would take a mighty storm to break her free.

She was so immersed in her thoughts that she didn't notice the artist walking up behind her until he spoke.

"I've been looking for you," he said.

She whirled to face him.

"I must beg your forgiveness once again, my lady," he said with a smile as he stopped a couple of paces away from her. "I really didn't intend to startle you. This time. I should have whistled a tune or something to warn you I was coming."

"Can you whistle a tune?" Charlotte asked to give herself time to recover her poise. She hid her hands in her skirt so he wouldn't see the dirt under her fingernails.

"Of course," he said and began whistling "Yankee Doodle Dandy."

She couldn't keep from laughing even as she wondered if such joviality was proper in a graveyard. "You are a man of many talents, Mr. Wade."

"So I've been told." His eyes settled on her face. "But don't you think we've shared enough familiar moments for you to call me Adam?"

Her cheeks warmed and her lips tingled at the memory of some of those moments with him. She fixed her eyes on the blades of grass at her feet and tried to ignore her heart thumping in her chest as she said, "I daresay some familiar moments are best not remembered."

He stepped closer to her and put his fingers under her chin to tip her face up to look at him. It was a replay of the moments in the garden, except this time the sun was shining brightly and there was no chill in the air to necessitate him offering her his jacket. But he seemed to be offering something more. Understanding, or perhaps compassion. Why, she didn't know. He couldn't read her thoughts.

"Don't say that, Charlotte. I quite enjoyed the moments of which you speak."

She told herself to step away from him. To look away from the blue gray eyes that were probing her soul. But she stayed still as she said, "And how many times have you enjoyed like moments in other gardens?" Her voice was barely above a whisper.

"I won't deny there have been other gardens, but no girl so lovely. Or lips so enticing." He moved his fingers from under her chin to trace her lips.

She pulled herself together and stepped back from his touch. It was colder there but safer. Much safer. "We're not in a garden now, Mr. Wade."

"Adam, please." He kept his hand in the air reaching toward her face for a moment before he dropped it to his side and looked around. "And you're right. I do have to admit I've never enjoyed such a moment in a graveyard." He nodded toward the stone behind her. "The beautiful first Mrs. Vance, I assume."

"She was very pretty," Charlotte said as she glanced back at the stone. "I don't look anything like her."

"Did you want to?"

His unexpected question brought her eyes back to him. "What?"

"Look like her. Be like her." His eyes were probing her again.

"No. I always thought her too fragile." Her words sounded disloyal in her ears, but she didn't stop talking. "At times she seemed almost afraid to leave her couch. As if she feared the day would be too difficult to face."

"Are you afraid of your tomorrows?"

She looked at him, not sure how she should answer, but his eyes demanded honesty. "I don't know," she said at last. "Last week I would have said not, but now if not afraid, then I do admit to being unsure of my future." She stared straight at him with wanton disregard of proper behavior, but a graveyard seemed a place to pitch aside social conventions and reach for the truth. "What about you?" She hesitated before she added, "Adam."

The corners of his lips lifted in a brief smile at the sound of his name. Then he grew solemn again as his eyes shifted color to more gray than blue. "I don't entertain fear. Instead I seek opportune possibilities."

"But there are oftentimes reasons for fear."

"Unfortunately you're speaking truth even not knowing the news that's come to us this morning."

"What news?" Dread woke inside her. The news couldn't be good.

"The Confederates fired on and forced the surrender of Federal forces at Fort Sumter. War is now inevitable."

"War," she echoed. She looked away from him out toward the horizon once more and now she couldn't keep from picturing cannons lining up against cannons. Perhaps even eventually on this very ground.

"The dark war clouds will no longer hang back. The storm is upon us," he said as if he too was imagining what war would bring to them. "But I didn't follow you out here just to deliver that unhappy news. I wanted a private moment with you to say goodbye before I left Grayson."

Her eyes came back to him. "Are you off to fight the South, then?"

"No, I'm not a soldier. I see other possibilities. I will go but only to draw the scenes to break the hearts of those far from the battlefields."

"Surely there are no battlefields as yet."

"Battles rage in many places. People will be choosing sides. In the legislatures. Village streets. Drawing rooms."

His look sharpened on her with the last, but she pretended not to know his meaning. "So Selena's portrait is finished?"

"I plan to add the final strokes to it this afternoon and be on my way come morning."

"Then you could have said goodbye in the morning."

"Perhaps, but you seem to lose a bit of that honesty I find so enchanting when others are in our company." A smile was back in his eyes.

She let his words slide past her. She had no answer for that. Instead she shifted the subject. "I'm sure Father will be leaving too. Back to Frankfort to be in the middle of the decision making for our state."

"He was ordering his servant to begin packing when I left the house."

"I do hope Selena plans to accompany him." Charlotte mashed her mouth together. She shouldn't have spoken that aloud.

Adam's smile reached his lips. "Your father said the same, but in a much different tone of voice." His smile faded as he peered at her with a good deal of sympathy. "Unfortunately for the happiness of you both, she feels she has too much to do here at Grayson to return to Frankfort at this time."

"She has many plans." Charlotte kept her voice as free of expression as she could.

"Many plans," Adam agreed. "Sometimes all a person can do is get out of the way of a woman like Selena."

"I can hardly pick up and leave the way you can." She looked at him with a bit of envy even as she thought of poor dead Richard who had done that and never come home. If there truly was war between the North and the South, how many more gravestones would rise in the family graveyards around them?

"What about your gentleman friend?" Adam's eyes were sharp on her again.

"The one going to the Shakers?" Something about this man kept her from pretending even to herself.

"I suppose that does present some difficulties."

"Certainly few of your opportunities." She wanted to keep her voice strong and sure, but the way his eyes were trying to swallow her was taking her breath away. She stepped back and felt the cold edge of her mother's gravestone against her legs.

"Opportunities can pop up in the most unlikely places, but sometimes you need to know the right opportunity to pursue." He stepped closer to her. "It's good Edwin Gilbey is going to the Shakers. That sets you free."

"Free to do what?" Charlotte's voice fell almost to a whisper again. She tried to back up and put more distance between them, but the gravestone stopped her.

"Live your life." Adam softly traced the curve of her cheek with his finger. "Enjoy the moment. This moment."

A tremble swept through Charlotte at his touch. Not of fear but of desire. She couldn't move. She didn't want to move. His eyes had her mesmerized.

"Seize the opportunity." His voice deepened and sounded husky as he bent his head down toward her, but he stopped before he touched her lips. She could feel his breath against her face as he went on. "Do you have the courage to do that, my beautiful Charlotte?"

It took all her strength to keep from melting against him and raising her lips to meet his. He was going to be gone from Grayson in the morning. She'd likely never lay eyes on him again. What good purpose could there be in yanking her heart out of her chest to throw at his feet, even if that was what she wanted to do? And yet what could one kiss hurt? A kiss she could remember and treasure no matter what happened in the days ahead.

Surrendering to his embrace would take no courage. The courage was in putting her hands flat against his chest and turning her head away from his lips as she pushed him back from her.

"I don't think you have honorable intentions, Mr. Wade," she said as she scooted to the side to put a bit of space between them and immediately wondered if she'd made the biggest mistake of her life. Even with the sun warm on her shoulders, she felt as cold inside as the gravestone behind her.

A look of regret to match her own flashed across his face before he said, "You surely didn't expect a proposal for a harmless farewell kiss."

"I expected nothing. Except the goodbye you claimed to seek me to deliver."

He shut his eyes for a moment before he made a sound that was somewhere between a sigh and a laugh. "Then I suppose your expectations will not be disappointed." He reached out and touched her cheek. He was smiling again now. "Goodbye, my beautiful Charlotte. If only we had met at a different time with no war on the horizon."

She didn't pull away from his touch even as she said, "There would always be those possibilities on the horizon for you."

"I think my eyes might be feasting on a possibility now. One I may regret turning away from." His eyes were swallowing her again. "Perhaps our paths will cross again someday."

"There's always that possibility."

"Tonight?" He raised his eyebrows at her. "In the garden?"

"Goodbye, Mr. Wade." She softened her implied refusal with a smile as she moved away from him. "I will look forward to seeing your illustrations in the news. Stay safe." She didn't wait for him to say any more as she turned and began walking in measured strides toward the house. She'd have to come back later to retrieve Aunt Tish's spoon. But now it was time to remember who she was and not be carried away by a handsome face and smooth words. The only possibility Adam Wade held out to her was the possibility of trouble.

When she got back to the house, Edwin's return letter was waiting for her on the table in the hallway. She carried it to the privacy of her room before she pulled the letter free of its envelope.

Dear Charlotte,
   You are quite within your rights to demand the truth of my intentions and I

am now ready to reveal such to you and to the world. I am going to the Shakers at Harmony Hill for a month's trial. Elder Logan thinks that an excellent way to test my determination and spirit. I myself feel no need of a trial period. I have no doubt that at the end of those thirty days I will feel unchanged and will at that time commit completely to the Society's rules and be ready—nay, not simply ready but eager—to shut away the evils of the world, accept the true salvation they offer, and begin walking the path of the true Believer. I feel such peace in the village as I see the order there and the brotherly love just as the Good Book teaches.

I do realize you had other expectations and I regret disappointing you by denying you those worldly desires. However we can still join together in a meaningful and spiritual way if you want to join with me in the Society of Believers as a sister. That is the sort of love more than anything of romantic nature that we have always known for each other. I have spoken of this possibility with Elder Logan and he gives me his assurance the Shakers would welcome you into their midst even as they welcome me. I know we could both attain a level of happiness there that

*would never be possible in a common
marital union as the world knows it.*

*If you wish to respond to this message,
please forward your answer to me at
Harmony Hill.*

*Ever your loving <u>brother</u> in Christ,
Edwin Gilbey*

Charlotte stared at the underlined word *brother*
written in Edwin's neat script for a long moment
before she looked up and met her eyes in the
mirror. What was it Adam Wade had asked her?
Did she have the courage to face the possibilities
awaiting her?

She stared at her image in the mirror until it
seemed as if she were looking at a girl she'd never
met as she considered the possibility Edwin
offered her. She didn't flinch from the truth.
Selena was taking control of Grayson. She
already had Charlotte's father dancing to whatever tune she wished to hum into his ear. Hadn't
he already spoken of Charlotte being sent away?
Her place here at Grayson and in her father's
heart was being crowded out. At least at the
Shaker Village she would be standing on land
adjacent to her land and not hundreds of miles
away in Virginia.

And she would have thirty days to convince
Edwin he was making a mistake. Something she

would have no way of doing if he was there and she was here or in faraway Virginia at the home of some unknown relative. Perhaps it might even open her father's eyes to the truth of his betrayal of her mother's trust. Of the Grayson trust.

Best of all, she could take Mellie with her. Charlotte reached into her pocket and touched the paper there. Shakers required converts to free their slaves. Did she have the courage to step through the Shaker door long enough to assure Mellie's freedom?

10

"Miss Lottie, you has done gone and lost your mind." Mellie plopped down on the bench at the end of the bed and stared at Charlotte with wide eyes. "You go to those Shakers? That's crazy talk."

"Aunt Tish doesn't think so. She thinks it will work."

"Then my mammy's done lost her senses too. Work is a good word for you to think on, Miss Lottie. The' ain't no ladies over there in that Shakertown. Just women more like me than you that them preachers put to work makin' hats and cookin' jams." Mellie frowned. "What could Mammy be thinkin'?"

"What's best for me the way she always has. And for you."

"Then she's done mixed up on that. How's you goin' to those Shaker people gonna be any kind of good for you or for me? I better go talk sense to her."

Mellie stood up, but Charlotte put a hand out to stop her. "First you have to listen, Mellie."

Mellie sank back down on the bench. "All right, Miss Lottie. You tell me what's got you and Mammy thinkin' on this crazy stuff."

Charlotte rubbed her forehead as she looked at Mellie and wondered where to start. "It's not crazy. Aunt Tish wouldn't tell us to do anything crazy. But this is the best way. I think it may be the only way."

It had been an eventful day from the moment they had assembled in the parlor for the unveiling of the portrait that morning. Her father had made a big deal of pulling off the cover sheet, but Adam Wade had stood to the side as though completely bored with the whole production. Selena was pleased, clapping her hands like an excited little girl as she moved to view her painted face first from one perspective, then another.

Charlotte moved back to get a better look. She had expected it to be better. It was a flattering likeness of Selena's face, but yet the portrait seemed lacking in some way.

"You're frowning." Adam stepped up close behind her and spoke the words in her ear.

"Not a frown of displeasure, you can be assured. I was merely concentrating on your work." Charlotte smiled at him even as she ordered her heart not to start beating faster just because his arm grazed hers. Her heart wasn't obedient. "It's lovely."

"A good word for it. A lovely painting of a lovely face." He lowered his voice even more. "But rather dull and lifeless. A cardboard image."

"Perhaps if you'd had more time." Charlotte kept her voice as low as his, but it hardly mattered. Her father and Selena were busy celebrating the empty loveliness of the portrait.

"Or a better subject." Adam moved even closer to her until she could feel the heat of his body before he said, "I went out to the garden last night."

"It was a pleasant spring evening for a walk." Charlotte kept her eyes on the portrait, but she was no longer seeing Selena's painted face. She was imagining what might have been if she had succumbed to the temptation to go out into the garden the night before.

"But very lonely."

"I'm sure you'll find other gardens more populated."

"That could be." She could hear the smile in his voice even though she didn't look back at him. "But I will always be left to wonder if I might have gone down on one knee to capture that kiss I so wanted to carry away with me."

"I doubt there would have been much chance of that." She bit the inside of her lip to keep an answering smile off her face. She knew he was toying with her, but at the same time she thought she caught the hint of wistful truth in his voice.

"I don't know. Redheads have a way of making a man do unexpected things."

She finally turned a bit to look at his face and let her smile appear. "You live for the unexpected, Mr. Wade."

"So I do." He laughed softly. "I think you may be the first woman I've ever met who understood that." His smile faded. "And what are you going to do, Miss Vance, in the face of the conflict before us?"

She wasn't sure if he was speaking of her personal or their national conflict. It didn't matter. Her answer was the same. "The unexpected."

He looked straight into her eyes. Neither of them was even aware of Charlotte's father and Selena in the room any longer. "Perhaps you will. I left something for you in the garden last night. I was going to give it into your hand, but that was not to be." He lightly grazed her hand with his fingers. "Please seek it out else the little field mice may carry it away to line their burrows."

When they left the parlor, Willis had been waiting in the carriage to take him and Charlotte's father to the train station. Charlotte didn't follow them out. She had no desire to witness her father and Selena's fond farewells. Instead she went out the veranda door into the garden.

The sketch was anchored against a stray wind by a couple of rocks on the bench near where they had shared the first of those familiar moments Adam had referred to in the graveyard. The paper felt a bit soft from being out in the dew as she unfolded it to stare straight into her own eyes. At the bottom, he'd written, "Your face will add beauty to a thousand scenes."

"Now there is a portrait with some sparkle," he spoke behind her. "Even only in pen and ink."

She couldn't keep from jumping. "Do you ever give a girl some warning?"

"No." He smiled.

"I thought you left."

His smile got broader. "I had to come back for my favorite sketching pencils. I thought I remembered leaving them here in the garden." He reached down under the bench, picked up a couple of pencils, and held them up in the air. "And here they are."

She laughed. "You'll miss your train."

He waved his hand in a gesture of unconcern. "They'll delay its leaving a few minutes for the senator. But I forgot something besides my sketching pencils. Something I couldn't leave without." His eyes fastened on her face.

"What's that?" When he reached for the sketch, she surrendered it with regret.

"Never fear. You can have it back, but we wouldn't want it to get crumpled." He dropped it on the bench beside them before he said, "Always expect the unexpected."

Then without another word to warn of his intent, he grabbed her and pulled her close in an embrace. His lips were on hers before she had time to utter a word of protest. And she was glad. She let herself be swallowed up in his embrace and gave the response his lips demanded. As the ground seemed to shift beneath her feet, she didn't worry about what was going to happen next. She simply surrendered to the joy of the moment.

But the moment ended. He raised his lips from hers. When he spoke, he sounded as out of breath as she felt. "And that is what I couldn't leave without."

Then just as suddenly as he had appeared, he was gone. Running away from her to his future. Leaving her behind to find hers.

That future is what she and Aunt Tish had worked out in the kitchen that afternoon after Selena had gone to visit a new acquaintance in the town and what Mellie couldn't believe she was serious about now. She was staring at

Charlotte as though she had sprouted an extra head. "I ain't knowin' how you tryin' to turn into one of them dried-up old Shaker crones can be the best anything."

"Those old crones dance. Or so I've heard," Charlotte said. "They can't be too dried up. Or all old. They have a school there. So there must be children."

"None of their own making. Them people don't hold with the general Bible beliefs on the matter of Adam and Eve."

"Their beliefs do sound strange, but maybe that's just because we haven't tried to understand them." Charlotte hadn't expected Mellie to argue with her. She'd thought she'd agree to do whatever Charlotte said. Whatever Aunt Tish said.

"Ain't no understandin' how they live. Or worship. Rollin' around on the floor in fits."

"They don't always do that. I've been told that sometimes they simply dance in up-and-back marches. Not a lot different from a cotillion except the men and women stay separate."

"Separate for sure." Mellie shook her head a little, resisting Charlotte's every word. "What's got this in your head? That Mr. Edwin goin'? You's done better off without him anyhow, Miss Lottie. You need to latch on to the likes of that artist man."

Charlotte couldn't keep the color from rising in her cheeks. "He's gone, Mellie. I doubt I'll ever see him again. And getting Edwin to change his mind is my only chance to save Grayson."

Mellie frowned at her. "How's that gonna save anythin'? Mr. Edwin don't own Grayson. Massah Charles does."

"Father will come to his senses and see Selena for what she is. But I can't be off in Virginia when that happens. I need to be here close by."

Mellie leaned over to touch Charlotte's hand. "Even if you had to go to Virginia, it would just be for a little while and you might meet some other fellers like that artist gentleman. Somebody better'n poor Mr. Edwin who lacks any kind a starch in his makeup."

Charlotte hesitated. For some reason she'd been reluctant to tell her what Willis had told Aunt Tish. What Charlotte had confirmed in an ugly confrontation with Selena that afternoon. "It's not just Grayson I'm trying to save," she said finally. "It's you."

"Me?" Mellie jerked back from Charlotte. "What? Has Mammy done tol' you I been makin' eyes at Nate?"

When Charlotte just looked at her without saying anything, she went on. "I love him, Miss Lottie. And he loves me. He done ask't me to jump the broom with him. You ain't wantin' to say no to that, are you?"

Charlotte sighed. "It doesn't matter what I want to say, Mellie. Selena's the one that matters now here at Grayson. She's put your name on the list Perkins is making. She aims to sell you."

"She can't do that." Mellie looked shocked and her next words were barely above a whisper. "Not send me down the river."

That's what Charlotte had told Selena just a couple of hours before. "You can't do that."

Selena had pretended a look of concern. "I certainly understand your reluctance to part with a servant you've had for so many years, but our Mellie is very pretty. She'll fetch a high price and help to stabilize Grayson's somewhat precarious financial position in the face of the looming war. Such is sure to disrupt the markets for our crops. Charles has been understandably, but regretfully negligent in his business matters what with the political crises he's had to deal with in Frankfort, but it can't go on. Grayson has more people than the land can support. This is an opportune time to remedy that before Mr. Lincoln finds a way to confiscate and steal our property."

Charlotte stood stiff with her hands clenched at her sides. She could barely speak through her anger. "You can't sell Mellie."

"What are you going to do? Tell your father on me?" Selena arched her eyebrows a bit. "I think we both know who'd win that battle. Besides he agrees with me that you have allowed Mellie to grow much too familiar with you. She is not your sister. She is a servant."

Charlotte kept her voice controlled. "Did you tell Father your plan?"

"He was much too concerned with more important matters to bother with which slaves might be culled from our holdings. He has entrusted me to do what needs to be done."

Charlotte took a deep breath and made herself uncurl her fists in spite of the way she was trembling with anger. "Then I suppose in his hurry to be off to Frankfort he must have neglected to let you know that he gave me Mellie. She belongs to me. Not to him. Or to you."

Selena looked at her for a long moment before she smiled a little and said, "And how do you propose to feed and clothe your slave?"

"She has a place here at Grayson the same as I do. Grayson is not yours."

"Are you so sure? I am your father's wife. And while your father and I will certainly always feel bound by charity to see that your needs are met, we might not extend that charity to your servant. A slave must earn her keep. Having been raised on a plantation, you are surely aware of that." Selena paused a second to let her words sink in before she went on. "But your Mellie is strong. She can probably learn to work fast enough in the fields to stay away from the whip."

"Father would never let you send Mellie to the fields."

"Your father is not here, Charlotte." Selena

spoke each word slowly and distinctly as though Charlotte were a child with limited understanding. "I am here. Perkins has been told to take orders from me. Not you."

Charlotte stared at her a moment before she could push the words out. "Why are you doing this?"

"My dear Charlotte, this is all for your own good. Your father and I are in complete agreement. It is past time that you learn the proper behavior of a lady and stop consorting with the help." As the woman kept talking, the fake look of concern on her face made Charlotte feel ill. "I daresay much of this comes from your father letting you read so many improper books and newspapers. It's well known a young female brain can't stand up under the strain of too much education except, of course, in the finer arts. The sort a proper finishing school will teach you so that we can hope you won't chase away the next young gentleman who calls on you as you did young Mr. Gilbey."

"You cannot sell Mellie. She is mine." Charlotte kept her voice ice cold in spite of the way the hot knot of anger was burning in her chest. "And I am not going to Virginia. You will never take Grayson from me."

Now Selena's laughter dismissing her words rang in Charlotte's ears as she looked at Mellie. "We don't have a choice, Mellie. Either of us.

It's the only way we can keep you safe. And maybe Grayson too."

When Mellie simply kept staring at her as if she knew no words to say, Charlotte went on. "We won't have to stay with the Shakers forever. Just for a while until Father sees through that woman's pretense or we find another way."

"What about Nate?" Mellie sounded ready to cry.

"I don't know, Mellie. But you'll be safe as soon as we enter the village. And free. I promised Aunt Tish that I'd set you free years ago. As soon as I could." Charlotte reached over to squeeze Mellie's hands. "This is the only way I can keep that promise now."

"Once I'm free I can go wherever I take a mind." Mellie pulled her hands free and lifted her chin with a hint of defiance.

"I guess so. You might make your way across the river to Indiana where it's safer to be a free Negro. But what if one of those horrible slave trackers grabs you? They might not listen if you say you're free. They could just tear up your papers and take you wherever they wanted."

"Massah Charles wouldn't let them do that."

"He wouldn't know. He doesn't know what's happening here in his own house." Her voice sounded shrill in her ears. Charlotte sat back and pulled in a slow, deep breath to calm herself. She had to convince Mellie. "You'll be safe with the Shakers. With me. We'll be sisters."

"We's already sisters, Miss Lottie."

"Free sisters." Charlotte stared into Mellie's eyes. "Please. I don't think I can do this without you."

Mellie mashed her mouth together a moment before she blew a burst of air out her nose and gave in. "All right, Miss Lottie. When do we leave?"

"At daylight."

"Sneakin' away like a couple of runaways."

"I don't want to have to see her again." They both knew who Charlotte meant.

"I don't know, Miss Lottie. This done feels like you's givin' up and that ain't like you."

"I'm not giving anything up. I'll be back. We'll both be back."

"I always believed most everythin' you ever tol' me, but this time I don't have no certain feelin'." Mellie sighed as she stood up. A frown creased her face. "What about Mammy?"

"I tried, but Father wouldn't give me her papers. Said Grayson needed a cook. And it does. She wouldn't dare bother Aunt Tish."

"We better pray that's true," Mellie said right before she slipped out Charlotte's door.

Pray. Charlotte shut her eyes, but no prayer words came. Instead her thoughts jumped from here to there and back again. She was feeling Adam Wade's arms around her. She was remembering the words in Edwin's letter. She was hearing Selena's words pushing her out of Grayson. She was wondering exactly how one did join with the Shakers. Edwin said he was going to the Shaker village to find peace. And the Shakers prayed about everything, or so she'd heard. Perhaps if she gained nothing else in the weeks ahead, she'd learn how to pray to find her own kind of peace.

Finally she whispered, "Give me courage to face tomorrow."

She sat there for a long moment with her eyes closed, listening to the steady ticking of her clock as she waited for some kind of answer. Nothing happened except that she became even more aware of the hard knot of fear inside her chest. She opened her eyes and stared at her face in the mirror. She was going to have to come up with her own answers for the morrow. The way she always had.

Maybe that was her answer.

11

Charlotte's heart began thumping in her ears and her hands grew stiff on the reins of the mare as the large stone and brick buildings of Harmony Hill rose up in front of them. Mellie's grip on Charlotte's waist tightened until Charlotte worried the buttons on her riding jacket would pop off. Mellie had been terrified ever since Charlotte made her climb up behind her on the mare. She'd never been on a horse.

Now she whispered in Charlotte's ear, "Where has we come to, Miss Lottie? I done feel like Jonah about to get swallowed by that big fish."

Charlotte knew what she meant. They were entering a different world. One where the buildings had no porches for sitting to catch the evening breezes or even a decorative gable to please the eye. Everything was plain and solemn. Including the people. Men and women walked between the buildings, but Charlotte caught no sound of talk or laughter. It was as if they were on the way to somebody's funeral except nobody was wearing black. The women were dressed in like blue or brown dresses with large white collars that lapped across the front of their bosoms above a white apron. White caps covered their hair.

Of course Charlotte had seen Shaker women before. She'd ridden carriages through Harmony Hill on the way to Lexington on occasion, but then she'd just looked upon them as an oddity. She'd never given the first thought of someday being one of them.

Even now, riding her mare with Mellie behind her, it still seemed an impossible thought. A

137

laughable thought. Her in Shaker dress, meekly walking to some task she'd been ordered to do. She wasn't concerned about the idea of work in spite of how Mellie had looked at her when she first talked of going to the Shakers. Charlotte could work. She wasn't a vapor-prone Southern belle who could barely manage to raise a glass of tea to her lips without a servant's help.

At the same time, she had never had tasks imposed on her. She was the one who ordered her life. That was the reason she was ready to pretend to be a Shaker for a few weeks. To get her life back. She could learn some new ways to make that happen.

The new ways had begun that morning when she had eased open the stable door to keep it from creaking as night began to give way to the first gray light of dawn. She hadn't wanted anyone to see them leaving. Not even Willis. She was afraid Selena might find a way to hold it against him and add his name to her list for Perkins.

When she had held the lead rope out toward Mellie to hold while she got the saddle, Mellie had stepped back. "I can't hold no horse."

"Of course you can. All you have to do is stand still and hold this rope." Charlotte grabbed Mellie's arm and placed the end of the lead in her hand before she turned to get the reins and saddle. She had never saddled the mare without help from Willis, but she knew how. Willis had taught her. He'd said a person shouldn't be riding if that person didn't know how things worked on a horse.

Mellie stared at the mare with evident fear, ready to give up their plans. "This ain't gonna work, Miss Lottie. I can't ride no horse. I'll fall off and break my head for sure."

"I won't let you fall off," Charlotte said as she pulled the cinch tight. She hadn't picked the sidesaddle because she didn't see how Mellie could ride with her on that. Sometimes when her father was in Frankfort and she wanted to ride across Grayson's fields jumping fences, Charlotte got Willis to bring out a regular saddle for her mare. It was far too easy to get unseated making a jump in a sidesaddle. Nevertheless it was highly improper for a lady to ride astride a horse even if her riding habit skirts were sufficiently full to modestly drape all the way to her ankles. Proper or improper didn't seem to matter today.

"I knows you won't aim to, but there's some things even you can't make happen, and me stayin' on this horse might be one of them." When Charlotte just looked at her across the mare's back without saying anything, Mellie went on. "And what about Massah Charles? What's he gonna think when he hears you've run off from Grayson?"

"I don't know," Charlotte answered honestly. She'd left a letter with Gibson to be posted to her father explaining where she was without dwelling on the reasons why. Right now with his total infatuation with Selena, he'd refuse to believe anything bad about the woman anyway. He'd think she was doing this because of Edwin, and she supposed there was some truth in that. Just not the truth her father would assume. Certainly she had no broken heart. Only ruined plans. Not ruined, she corrected herself. Sidetracked. She didn't mention Mellie at all in the letter. There was no need.

Here in the heart of the Shaker village, Charlotte thought about her father opening her letter, and she worried that she might not have chosen the best words. Or made the best plan. Still, she had no choice now but to see it through. For Mellie's sake if nothing else. By the time Gibson gave the letter to Perkins to post and then it made its way to her father in the Capital City, Mellie would be free with nothing Selena could do to change that. Charlotte could bear a week or two of captivity here with these strange people to assure that.

Even so, when she stopped to ask one of the Shaker men how to go about joining with them at Harmony Hill, her voice trembled, and the mare, sensing her unease, danced to the side. The man looked to be quite old, but his movements were quick as he reached out to take hold of the bridle and calm the horse with a soft-spoken command before he answered Charlotte.

"We welcome all who would live the perfect life, my sisters," he said with solemn kindness. "Let me take your horse and I will call one of the sisters to help you."

Charlotte's hands tightened on the reins for the barest moment before she pulled in a deep breath and forced a smile as she surrendered the reins to him. She expected him to step up to help them off the mare, but instead he pulled his hat down low on his forehead and turned his back on them.

"I'll lead you to a block where you can dismount." He kept his face straight forward as he led the mare to a round wooden block in front of a large brick building.

Charlotte slid out of the saddle down onto the block and then helped Mellie dismount. The man kept his eyes averted as he promised to send someone to help them before he led the mare away.

Mellie sank down on the wooden block as though her legs would no longer hold her up. She looked up at Charlotte. "You sure we's doin' the right thing, Miss Lottie?" Her voice carried the same tremble Charlotte's had a moment earlier.

"As sure as I can be." Charlotte tried to sound sure as she sat down beside Mellie and took her hand, but inside she felt anything but confident. She stared down at her fingers clasped around Mellie's dark hand and wished Aunt Tish were there with them. She would tell them they were doing the right thing. The only thing.

The next mornig when Charlotte had given up on sleep, she climbed out of bed in the pre-dawn darkness and pulled on her riding habit. She hadn't allowed herself to think about what she was getting ready to do. She simply eased her bedroom door shut and crept down the stairs to the kitchen where Mellie and Aunt Tish waited. Shadows cast by the lone candle Aunt Tish carried hovered on the wall behind them and then seemed to leap and dance after them when without a word they moved toward the door. A lump formed in Charlotte's throat at the sound of Grayson's back door clicking shut behind her, but she refused to cry. There was no reason for tears. This was all temporary. She'd be back soon enough.

But Mellie had fallen on Aunt Tish's neck and wept as she begged her, "You'll tell Nate where I am, won't you, Mammy? You'll tell him I didn't have no choice. I don't, do I?"

"No choice but freedom, Melana." Still holding the candle, Aunt Tish stepped back and grabbed Mellie's chin with her free hand to raise her face up until she was looking straight into Mellie's eyes. "You keep that in the front of yo' mind and think on it."

"Yes'm." Mellie choked back a sob before she went on. "But what's the good of bein' free without you? Or Nate?" Mellie's voice trailed off as she pulled away from Aunt Tish's hand to look toward the slave quarters.

"I'll be next." Aunt Tish let her eyes slide over to Charlotte. "And then who can know what might be happenin' after that? What with ever'-body saying a war is comin' 'cause of how Mr. Lincoln talks 'bout freedom for the people."

Freedom. That's what Charlotte felt like she was giving up as she and Mellie followed two Shaker sisters up the steps into the brick building and down a broad hallway with polished wood floors. Lines of blue pegs on both walls held candle sconces, cloaks, and hats. The room they were shown into was small and bare except for a lone table. Two chairs were suspended on the blue pegs that lined this wall too, but nobody offered to lift down the chairs for anyone to sit.

Charlotte fought the urge to run back out the door as she waited for someone to speak. Both women looked to be well past their middle years, and as they solemnly studied Charlotte and Mellie, Mellie's old crone description wormed into Charlotte's thoughts. She couldn't imagine either of these women ever dancing or singing. In worship or not.

Sister Altha spoke first. She was tall and thin with angular features. The few strands of hair that peeked out around her white cap were steel gray. She looked at Mellie and then settled her sharp eyes on Charlotte as she said, "You are not our usual novitiate. What has made you consider this choice? Are you concerned for the condition of your soul?"

Charlotte searched for words to say that wouldn't be false without giving the real reason she had come knocking at the Shakers' door. She had the uneasy feeling the woman in front of her would know immediately if she spoke lies. Finally she said, "All right-minded people should surely worry about their souls, especially in these uncertain times with war on the horizon."

Sister Altha moved her hand in a dismissive gesture. "We have no part in wars. Our testimony is for peace now and always. No Christian can use carnal weapons or fight, and so we have separated ourselves from such conflict and live in peace with all."

"Peace seems a good way, but how will you keep the cannons from your land if the armies decide to come?" Charlotte asked, truly curious about how they planned to maintain peace in the midst of war.

"Mother Ann and the Eternal Father will protect us. But you will have time to learn of our ways of peace if you decide to stay among us."

"That's why I'm here. Why we're both here." Charlotte looked over at Mellie, who seemed poised up on her toes as though any second she might break for the door. Charlotte reached over to lay her hand on Mellie's arm.

Sister Altha's frown deepened. "You must be aware that none come among us with slaves. Such must be set free to make their own decision to live among us or not." Her eyes shifted from Charlotte to Mellie, and a bit of regret came into her voice. "Nor can we take in runaway slaves against the laws of the land, no matter how wrong those laws may be."

Mellie spoke up. "I'm not a runaway. I belong to Miss Lottie."

Sister Altha's face softened. "That will no longer be, my sister, if you choose to stay among us here at Harmony Hill. We belong only to the Eternal Father and Mother Ann." Her eyes came back to Charlotte.

"I have her papers." Charlotte reached into her pocket and pulled out the folded paper. "I am ready to do whatever is required to set her free."

"That is good." Sister Altha's eyes narrowed on Charlotte again. "You say the right words, but are you truly prepared to give up your place in the world, your life of ease, to work among us?"

"I am here to find out about the Shaker life. We both are." Charlotte spoke the words as if coming to the Shaker village was something they'd been planning for months instead of a desperate midnight plan. She squeezed Mellie's arm to give her courage before dropping her hand back to her side.

"Once more the proper words, but I hear an unspoken undertone." Sister Altha frowned. "Here in our Society of Believers we do not hide our wrongs, but confess them in order to receive forgiveness. If you have some sin you are running from, my sister, you must reveal it. Have you done some wrong that has compelled you to come among us?"

Both sisters watched Charlotte intently while waiting for her to speak and explain why a young woman of her position would be presenting herself to the Shakers. Beside her, Mellie was as still as the sisters, as if afraid to breathe. Somewhere in the building outside the room, a clock gonged out the time. Charlotte counted. Nine strikes. The clock fell silent and the same sort of silence seemed to seep out of the very walls of the room where they were standing. She had no doubt that the clock could strike its next hourly total before either woman broke the silence if she did not answer Sister Altha's question.

Charlotte swallowed and opened her mouth to tell as much of the truth as she thought wise, but Mellie, spooked by the women's silence, jumped in front of her words. "Miss Lottie's doin' it for me. To save me. That woman Massah Charles married was gonna sell me down the river."

Sister Altha frowned. "How could that be if

Miss Lottie owns you?" She looked at the paper Charlotte had handed her. "As appears to be the case. Melana, isn't it?"

"I don't know." Mellie sounded ready to cry. "But Miss Lottie thought it might happen. And if you knew Miss Selena, you might think so too."

"Who is this Selena?" Sister Altha looked at Charlotte.

"Perhaps I should explain," Charlotte said.

"That would be well," Sister Altha said.

"Selena is my father's new wife. As you may know, my father is a state senator."

Sister Altha inclined her head a bit. "Is your father aware that you have come to Harmony Hill seeking admittance?"

"I wrote him of my intentions," Charlotte answered truthfully. The truth or at least part of the truth seemed the best story to tell. "He is very involved with the political situation of our state right now, and it may be a while before he can respond to my letter. In the meantime, his new wife and I have not seen eye to eye, and I thought it best if Mellie and I left. That it would be a way to keep peace in our family."

She used the word "peace" purposely, since the Shakers claimed such a fondness for peaceful living, but Sister Altha only lifted her eyebrows a bit as if she knew Charlotte was merely attempting to sway her opinion with words and not with honest feelings. After a slight hesitation,

147

Charlotte went on. "I also had planned to marry Edwin Gilbey who has come among you, and he suggested, since he seeks to follow your way and thus will no longer consider marriage, that I might think about joining him here." Sister Altha's eyebrows shot up a little higher and Charlotte rushed on. "As a sister, of course. Plus I wanted Mellie to be safe from those who hoped to do her harm in order to injure me."

While Sister Altha continued to look doubtfully at Charlotte, the other sister, the one named Cora, moved forward with the touch of a smile that gentled the lines of her face. "We do not turn those away who come to us seeking peace. So we welcome you among us as long as you both abide by the rules we set forth. There is no consorting with the opposite sex. All work at the duties assigned by the Ministry, and you must open your minds and attend to the telling of the Believers' way to salvation."

"We are ready to do as you say," Charlotte said.

"Each must answer for herself," Sister Cora said quietly as she looked at Mellie. "Are you ready to bend your will to our way, sister?"

Mellie shot a look at Charlotte, but Charlotte stayed silent. They were right. If Mellie was to be free, she would have to answer for herself.

"Well, sister, do you have an answer?" Sister Altha demanded without the gentleness of the other sister.

"I can do what you want," Mellie finally said as she lowered her eyes to the floor.

"That is a good beginning. Now we will find you a place and proper clothing." Sister Cora reached for Mellie's hand. "Come, Sister Melana."

When Mellie sent another panicked look at her, Charlotte pushed confidence into her smile and her voice. "It's all right, Mellie."

"But who will take care of you, Miss Lottie?"

Sister Altha's frown deepened while Sister Cora was kind in her answer as she ushered Mellie out of the room. "Have no concern for your sister. Sister Altha will summon another sister to introduce her to our way the same as I am doing for you."

"I thought we'd be able to stay together," Charlotte said after the door closed behind Mellie and Sister Cora.

"Nay, you both need to find your way on your own. If that is what you truly want." Sister Altha gave her another suspicious look. "If you have doubts of the path you've chosen, you may stay in a visitor's room for a few days while you dwell on the matter more fully."

"I have no doubts," Charlotte lied.

"That is good." For the first time Sister Altha lifted the corners of her lips up in a small smile. "First you must sign Sister Melana's manumission papers. Then you will begin your journey on the true way. The simple life and salvation await those who come to us with expectant hearts." She motioned Charlotte toward the door. "Come, my sister. For as we learn in Mother Ann's teachings, we must not waste one moment of time, for we have none to spare."

Charlotte wasn't sure who this Mother Ann was, but she had no problem agreeing with that teaching. She had no time to spare. Somehow she would have to find Edwin and convince him that he was wasting time here. They both were.

As she followed Sister Altha down the hallway once more, they stopped between a matching pair of winding stairs that curled along opposite walls up three floors with little visible means of support. She had never seen anything to compare with them in any manor house. No outward decoration adorned the cherry handrails or steps, but even so the stairs rose upward in such a graceful spiral that surely no eye could gaze upon them without admiring their beauty.

"What lovely stairs," Charlotte said before she thought better of breaking the silence between her and the stern sister.

Sister Altha looked at the staircases and then back at Charlotte. "Many of the world say the same, but to us their beauty is in their usefulness. That is where true beauty resides."

Whoever built this stairway had more in

mind than utility, Charlotte wanted to insist, but she bit her lip and remained silent. She wished Adam Wade was there to see it with her. She could almost hear his words echoing her own marvel in her ears.

She shook away the thought. Adam Wade was gone. He was not part of her future. He had never been part of her future in spite of the way her heart leaped up inside her just at the thought of him and the memory of his lips on hers. While she was here among the Shakers, she would practice the discipline and plainness of the woman beside her. She would push his memory completely from her mind.

Yet in spite of her determined thoughts, she slipped her hand in her pocket and felt the corners of the folded sketch. His lines drawing her face. That and her grandmother's ring and pearls were all she had brought from Grayson.

12

Charlotte tried to quell her growing trepidation as she followed Sister Altha outside and along the walkways. She hadn't thought they would separate her and Mellie, for she had spoken the truth when she'd told Mellie she didn't think she could do this alone. And now they were both alone. Both being swallowed up by this strange group of people. At her request.

They stepped from the sunshine on the steps into the deep shadow of the brick building behind them. The morning air felt immediately cooler, and a shiver crawled up Charlotte's back. What was she doing here, trailing after this unsmiling woman in her plain brown dress? Maybe Mellie was right. It could be she had abandoned her senses.

She had told Adam Wade that she was going to do the unexpected. She'd certainly done that in the last couple of days. Allowing a near stranger to kiss her without the slightest hint of resistance. Riding away from Grayson and leaving her home to the clutching designs of that woman. Pretending to want to be one of these unsmiling Shaker women. Imagining that such a crazy plan would bring back the expected life she longed after.

As the shadow enveloped Charlotte, her prayer from the night before echoed in her head. *Give me courage.* A prayer that was not being answered if the tremble inside her was any indication. Perhaps courage wasn't one of the blessings the Lord doled out. The Bible spoke of forbearance and longsuffering, gentleness and meekness, joy and love as gifts of the Spirit one should seek. But what of courage? Surely Daniel had been gifted with courage when he continued to say his prayers in full sight of his enemies even though he knew he might be thrown into a den of hungry lions.

But she wasn't Daniel. She hadn't spent all that much time in prayer or reading the Bible. She had little reason to believe the Lord would shut the mouths of any hungry lions ready to devour her. *Be strong and of a good courage.* The words popped into her mind, and while she knew not where they came from, she was sure they were Bible words.

She pulled in a deep steadying breath and looked ahead. Sunlight splattered the path only a couple of steps in front of her. She had done the unexpected. She had left Grayson. She had freed Mellie and kept at least part of her promise to Aunt Tish. She wasn't giving up on her future. She was fighting for it even if she was walking a very strange path to achieve her aim. Perhaps the Lord did attend to her prayers. Courage didn't mean the absence of fear. Courage meant walking forward through whatever shadows lay across her path toward the future she had to find a way to make happen.

Ahead of them, the sun bounced off the windows and stonework of the large white building in the center of the village and lent it a special glow that made Charlotte hope it might be their destination. But when Sister Altha paused in front of her, she didn't even glance over at the stone building. Instead she pointed to the frame building opposite it. "Our meetinghouse," she said.

Without waiting for any sort of reply, the woman turned and began walking again. Sister Altha kept her capped head bent with her eyes down and her hands tucked under her apron, but now with her newfound courage, Charlotte saw no need to copy her. She wanted to see it all. If she was being swallowed into the belly of the whale as Mellie had suggested, at least she could be familiar with each rib that made up her new home.

The paths between the houses were mostly deserted. When she dared to ask Sister Altha why no one was about, the sister looked back at her with evident irritation before she answered, "The brethren and sisters are attending their duties."

"All of them?" Charlotte asked.

Sister Altha frowned slightly. "You will discover the answers to your questions in due time without the need for idle conversation on the walkways."

So Charlotte bit back her questions as they walked on through the village past smaller buildings with open windows that let out the peck of hammers, the sweep of brooms, and numerous other sounds of industry. Now and again, she spotted a man's head or the white cap of one of the sisters through the windows. In the gardens between the buildings, several sisters dressed in like fashion to Sister Altha were bent over or on their knees raking leaves and debris away from the roots of the herbs and other plants. Only a couple of the women looked up at them when they passed, and even those two quickly lowered their eyes back to their work.

Sister Altha finally stopped in front of a three-story brick house with separate stone steps up to two identical front doors. The sister led the way up to the door on the left of the house.

"You will be given a bed here at the Gathering Family House. Those who come among us live here while being instructed on the true path to salvation. There will be much for you to learn. Such as always using the proper door to go in and out of our houses. Sisters use the west doors and the brethren use the doors on the east."

"The church my father and I attend has two doors, one for the women and one for the men."

"Yea, it is a common custom, but where worldly worshipers fail is in thinking that such is only necessary for their Sabbaths. We pick up the cross of purity of body and soul and carry it every day of the week." Sister Altha paused inside the door and peered over at Charlotte. "It is a cross that is oft too heavy for many who come to us."

"What happens then?" Charlotte looked straight at her face. "If they are unable to follow the Shaker way?"

"They go back to the world. We force no one to stay with us who finds the true way too intolerable. But we mourn their return to the miry pit of worldly sin when they had every opportunity to walk the way of peace and love."

"Do many leave?"

Sister Altha looked grieved as she said, "Yea. Few can walk the narrow road. I will pray to Mother Ann that your feet will not wander from the path to salvation while you learn our ways."

A young sister came down the hall to meet them. Her face looked as opposite of Sister Altha as was surely possible. While she wore the solemn Shaker expression, her brown eyes sparkled with friendliness and the bloom of youth was in her cheeks.

Even Sister Altha's face brightened as she looked at her. "Ah, Sister Cora has sent Sister Gemma to be your guide to the more physical elements of our lives. She will instruct you on proper Shaker dress and explain your work duties, Sister Charlotte." A hint of a frown returned to Sister Altha's face. "I would not wonder if you might need a great deal of instruction in how to perform some such duties, but all who are able-bodied labor with their hands here at Harmony Hill. The Lord intended us to be useful, and you will discover it is a gift to so work for the good of all."

"Yea, laboring with our hands increases the

strength of our spirits," Sister Gemma said. "And gives us good sleep at night. Never fear, Sister Altha. I will take good care of our new sister. Charlotte, did you say?"

"Yea. She can go with you to your work duty after the midday meal," Sister Altha said.

"I am helping to package the seeds for the brethren's selling trips next week."

"An easy task. That will be a good beginning for her."

"What about Mellie?" Charlotte asked as Sister Altha turned toward the door.

Sister Altha looked back, a frown deepening the furrows between her eyes again. It was clear she did not like being questioned. "She is no longer your slave," she said sternly. "She is your sister now."

"She has ever been my sister," Charlotte said quietly. "I was only concerned for her because she was so nervous on the way here and not sure what to expect. She has always depended on me."

"You need not worry. Your sister will blossom like a flower in the sun in the warmth of the freedom you have rightly given her." A fleeting look of approval softened Sister Altha's face for just a second. "Sister Cora will see to her needs. It will be good for you to learn that decisions of the elders and eldresses cannot be questioned. Obedience is necessary for the peace of our society."

Sister Gemma waited until the door shut behind the older sister before she let a smile lift the corners of her lips. "Don't fret. It's not near as hard as Sister Altha makes it sound, Sister Charlotte. Come, we will begin." She moved toward the left staircase. "This is the west stairs, the sisters' stairs. You must always use them and not the ones on the east side of the room. Those are for the brethren." She stopped at the bottom of the stairs. "And always step up on the first stair with your right foot first."

Charlotte did as instructed and followed the woman who appeared to be near Charlotte's own age up the stairs stepping with her right foot first, but she couldn't keep from asking. "Why?"

The question seemed to surprise Gemma, who paused in the middle of the flight of stairs to look around at Charlotte. "Because the Ministry decided it should be so many years ago. Long before I came to be here."

"When was that?"

"I was eight. My father brought me here to go to school."

"And he never came back to get you?" Charlotte thought of her own father and wondered what he would do when he got her letter. Would he come storming through the Shaker gates and demand to talk reason to her?

"Yea, he so intended. I'm sure of that. But he and my mother succumbed in the cholera epidemic of '51. My baby brother too. My uncle took in the other two boys, but it seemed to be the sensible thing for me to stay here where I could keep going to school and learn other useful occupations. The Believers have always been kind to me. And with my folks gone, it felt more like home here than anywhere else I could imagine going." She turned to climb on up the stairs.

"So you like it here." Charlotte made it part question, part statement of fact as she followed the sister. After all, Gemma looked happy, as if she'd found that peace Edwin talked about seeking for himself.

"I am content. There is much love between the sisters and brethren. And when the spirit comes down in meeting, I sometimes feel light as a feather with no concerns or worries. I often simply float away on the joy of the moment." At the top of the stairs, Gemma turned to smile at Charlotte. "Sister Altha says that's a spirit gift. Have you ever felt such a gift of the spirit in your worship times?"

"Nothing that made me think I was floating away. Joyful or not." The only time Charlotte had felt anywhere near that way was in the garden with the artist's lips touching hers, but that was hardly something to reveal to these odd people who considered such joy shared between a man and woman sinful.

"Spirit gifts can be much different. Many feel they receive fruit from heaven to eat and enjoy. Others are gifted with song or a gift of whirling. Some draw spirit pictures."

"You mean a picture of a ghost?"

The girl actually laughed out loud. The sound was so unexpected after Sister Altha's solemn attitude that Charlotte jumped a little. Gemma put her hand on Charlotte's arm.

"Nay. Of a surety, nay. Have you been told ghost tales about us here? I have heard that those of the world tell many wild stories about us Believers, but I don't think I've been told of any such that claim our village is haunted." Suddenly she looked more solemn. "Of course, there are those spirits of our departed brothers and sisters who come back to deliver messages to us from Mother Ann at times."

Charlotte looked behind her at the stairs and wondered if she should go back down them to search out her mare and ride back to Grayson. She'd done what she intended and set Mellie free. But she hadn't accomplished her other aims. She hadn't seen Edwin. She hadn't given her father time to regret letting Selena push her out of Grayson. But people who got messages from spirits and ghosts might be more than she had bargained for.

Gemma tightened her hand on Charlotte's arm. "Don't look so concerned, my sister. It will become clear to you after you learn more of our ways. Trust me, there are no ghosts to fear. The gifts of the spirit bring joy, not fear. And so it is with the spirit drawings as well. A special gift that can bless us all. You will see in the days ahead and gain understanding of our ways."

Gemma led the way into a room that held five narrow beds that looked hard and uncomfortable with little room for even a shift in position while sleeping. Nothing at all like Charlotte's soft featherbed under its ruffled, white lace bedspread at Grayson. A tall narrow chest sat against the outside wall. It had many drawers but absolutely nothing upon it. No flower, no pot of cream or box for hair ribbons or combs. Not even a speck of dust. Three chairs were suspended on the blue pegs that seemed a fixture in every Shaker room.

"How do you comb and arrange your hair with no mirrors?" Charlotte asked.

"We only have the need to adjust our caps, and there is a small mirror in the bathhouses and dressing rooms for that purpose." Gemma touched her cap and then smiled as she reached over to touch Charlotte's curls. "Your hair looks as cheerful as a candle flame on a dreary winter night. It does seem a shame to cover it, but it is our way for the sisters to cover their hair. You will grow accustomed to the cap, and if your hair proves to be a bother Sister Melva is good at clipping it short."

Charlotte's hand went instinctively to her hair in a protective gesture. She had not considered submitting to a shearing.

"Your hair will grow less important to you in time, but until then Sister Melva will not force her scissors upon you." Gemma laughed again.

"That's a relief," Charlotte said as she lowered her hands and studied Gemma a moment. "Are more sisters like you or Sister Altha?"

Gemma looked puzzled. "I'm not sure of your meaning."

"Sister Altha seemed so . . ." Charlotte hesitated as she searched for an acceptable word. "So solemn. I cannot imagine her laughing."

"She has many duties and little time for frivolity," Gemma said. "Plus it is only fitting to maintain an even and solemn countenance so one does not disturb the peaceful air around one with an overabundance of chatter or laughter. Both sins I find need to confess much too often."

She pulled open one of the drawers in the chest and lifted out a dress and underclothing. "And now is a time for solemn attention to the task at hand so we won't miss the midday meal." She handed Charlotte the clothes. "If you need assistance with your collar and cap, I can supply that after I fetch you some shoes."

"Why can't I wear these?" Charlotte lifted her skirt to show her feet clad in the sturdy side-laced shoes she wore when riding.

"You will feel better wearing the same as all the sisters."

"Can I keep these here in my room?"

"Nay, such would only be undesirable clutter. Those of the Ministry will store them for you if you feel an attachment to them. It is the Shaker way." She spoke kindly, but there was no room for argument as she pointed Charlotte toward a small dressing room that opened off the sleeping room. "I will gather up your worldly clothing after you change."

Charlotte stripped off her gray riding habit and laid it aside with some regret. She was tempted to leave on her own underclothing, but she had agreed to abide by their rules. She untied the ribbons around her waist and let her pantalettes fall to the floor in a soft cloud of silk before quickly pulling on the plain white cotton drawers with no bit of lace anywhere on them. She had not worn a corset over her camisole, and she was relieved to see there was none in the clothing Gemma had handed her. At least she'd be able to breathe while pretending to be a Shaker. She shed her camisole with its lace and ribbons and pulled the shiftlike undershirt over her head.

The fabric of the dress was sturdy but soft and faded to a light blue from many washings. It was too large for her, but once she lapped the white collar across her front and tied on the apron, it didn't much matter that several inches of the waistline were folded under. A mirror not much bigger than her hand hung on the wall. She peered into it as she stuffed her hair up into the cap.

When she was finished, she stared at her reflection a moment longer as though staring at someone she didn't know. Had she lost her identity so easily? Just by shedding a few clothes the way a butterfly broke out of a cocoon? But this was not a transformation to beauty. Rather in the opposite direction. From the active pursuit of beauty in every facet to plainness. There would be no party dresses she could not unbutton here. No jeweled combs in her hair. No glittering necklaces or rings. No one would care if freckles appeared on her nose or if her hair curled or hung straight. No one would see more than a glimpse of hair under the cap.

She suddenly smiled as she spoke to the reflection in the mirror. "Good morning, Sister Charlotte. I do hope I can learn to get along with you for a few weeks."

Then she laughed softly as she thought that Adam Wade would have little desire to steal a kiss from the new Charlotte. But it wasn't the artist she needed to think about. It was Edwin. Perhaps this plain sister would not be so intimidating to him. Perhaps he would look at her and regret the thought of giving up their plans. It was beyond her understanding how he could even consider surrendering the Hastings land to the Shakers. Land passed down from his grandparents. Whatever that Elder Logan had told Edwin, it certainly wasn't true that Faustine Hastings would have approved of that. She was no doubt turning over in her grave.

As surely Charlotte's own mother was. Charlotte took one last peek in the mirror and twisted her mouth to the side to hold back another smile at the glimpse of Charlotte Mayda Vance as a plain and simple Shaker sister. Not the heiress to Grayson. Not the senator's daughter. A Shaker sister.

The thought wasn't nearly as distressing as she might have supposed it would be. Of course it was only temporary. She ran her hands down the long white apron so like Aunt Tish's, tucked a stray hair up into her cap, and pushed open the door just as Gemma came back in the sleeping room carrying Charlotte's new shoes. They bore little resemblance to any dancing shoes she'd ever seen, but everyone knew the Shakers danced in worship. A dance she was prepared to learn.

13

"It won't last three months. Once a few shots are fired, those Johnny Rebs in the South will see the futility of their position and come back into the Union like whipped dogs with their tails between their legs." Sam Johnson sounded sure of his words.

Adam watched Sam pace in front of him as he spoke. Tall with a bony frame, the man was rarely still in spite of an old knee injury that caused him to limp badly. He claimed to be able to think better on his feet. The pain of movement was incidental. Actually sharpened a man's thinking, Sam claimed. A mind lacking agility, that's what should worry a man. Not a crippled knee. Sam had no problem carrying dozens of story ideas for *Harper's Weekly* in his head all at once, and he often jumped between them without warning.

Something he did now—to the chagrin of his secretary whose charge it was to record whatever was said if Sam deemed it important. The only problem for the long-suffering man with the pen and paper sitting across the room at a little desk was that Sam never indicated which words he might later deem important enough to recall. So his aide found it necessary to record everything.

Sam stopped in front of the table where

Adam's sketches were spread out for his view. As he pushed them to and fro searching through them, Adam had to force himself not to lean forward to rescue them from the man's impatient hands. Sam had summoned Adam to meet him in Washington, D.C., and hear his new assignments now that war clouds were looming on the horizon. That didn't mean he'd forgotten Adam's old assignments.

"Where's that Shaker staircase? I told you we needed that."

"You want a staircase? Now? With war breaking out?"

"Not any old staircase. The one that people say rises straight up in the air curling around the wall like it's attached with glue or something. They say if you stand at the bottom and stare straight up that it's a good chance you'll get dizzy from those stairs telescoping away from you." Sam made a telescope shape with his hands and looked through them toward the ceiling. "Up. Up. A marvel of engineering. Shaker engineering. I've heard people say they were almost afraid to step on the risers since they didn't see how the whole contraption held to the wall. Didn't trust the glue, I guess. What about you?" Sam lowered his telescoped hands to peer through them toward Adam. "Did you climb up it?"

"No, I didn't even see it."

"Didn't see it? That's why you went down

there." Sam's voice cranked up a couple of levels as he dropped his hands and frowned at Adam.

Adam didn't bother pointing out to Sam that he hadn't gone to Kentucky on assignment for *Harper's Weekly*, but on his own. The Shaker staircase had simply been a suggested side venture, but it never did to contradict Sam. Instead he mumbled, "Sorry, boss."

Sam waved away Adam's apology as if he no longer cared about any of it and turned his attention back to the sketches. "Whew! Guess Dickens was right if all the women look like her. He visited one of their communities in the East when he came to America, you know." He snatched up the sketch of the old sister Adam had seen on the pathways at Harmony Hill and held it out away from him for a better look. "No feminine charms, he said. Not one. And very few red-blooded men are beyond wanting to see a few feminine charms. Right, Adam?"

"Absolutely, sir." Adam pushed the words out quickly before Sam took off on a new tangent. The secretary scribbled frantically on his pad of paper. Adam shifted to a more comfortable position on the settee in the editor's hotel suite. At first it had bothered him to be seated when the editor was pacing and ranting, but he'd grown used to it. Now he just listened and tried to pick out the directions the editor most wanted to travel in his weekly newspaper.

The editor turned to pin Adam to the brocaded back of the settee with his sharp eyes. "I haven't been hearing about any female problems about you now, have I?" He didn't wait for Adam to answer. He threw the sketch back down on the table and began pacing again. "You've got to keep your mind on business. No time for women. Leastways the kind who want to tie the knot and commence to having a pack of children. You'll have to wait for that pleasure, my boy. Especially with those Secessionist states stirring the pot. Of course a little bit of war is sure to up circulation. If you find the pictures we need. People like pictures. Nothing but words bores them to tears."

"Pictures can bring them to tears too," Adam said.

"But those are the tears we want, my boy. Pictures that yank on their heartstrings and open up their purse strings. Open purse strings. That's what we're after." He paused a moment and shot Adam a look. "That and that staircase. Didn't you say you were within a stone's throw of the place? There's that atrociously ugly woman to prove it." He threw out his arm to wave at Adam's sketches. "And who's the girl?"

He pulled the drawing of Charlotte on her veranda out of the pile, pausing his pacing for a moment to give it consideration. "Why didn't you draw her face? Nobody cares about a

169

woman's backside when it's hidden under all those hoop-de-doops. Looks like an upside-down mushroom." He peered closer at the sketch. "Can't even be sure there is a backside under there but the shoulders and neck are quite enticing." The older man turned back to Adam with a grin that hinted of lechery. "What about it, boy? Can you vouch for her backside?"

"Now, Sam, she was a lady."

"When did that ever stop you? I hear you've left a string of broken hearts from here to California and back."

"I just draw their pictures, Sam. That's all."

The old man laughed and shook the sketch at him. "Then draw their front sides."

"But I wanted you to see the posture of her pensive longing for peace. Can't you sense her worry about whether the war is going to tear apart her world?"

"You're making that up on the spot," Sam said with another laugh. "That's why I like you, Adam. You're quick on your feet. You're going to have to be to stay out of the fray and bring home the scenes we need. Lincoln's plan to blockade the Southern ports has got them stirred up if their newspapers are any indication. The gentry down there are equipping regiments. Out of their own pockets. Got to have some deep pockets for that, but what is it they say? Cotton is king. Pockets might empty out if they can't get around

Lincoln's ships. Rich men's soldiers won't get that cotton to the English factories. Their army will turn out to have a thousand arms flailing against the wind with no head. Probably end up shooting each other instead of us Yankees."

"That sounds good for us."

"For me. But you'll have to duck bullets to draw it happening. And no yearning backside pictures." He flipped his fingers against the picture of Charlotte Vance before he dropped it back on the table. It slid off on the floor, but he didn't lean down to pick it up. "We want to see the gritty truth. If men are fighting, men are going to be dying. Our readers will want to see it all."

"I think I'd rather do the yearning for peace ones." Adam leaned forward and rescued the picture before Sam could step on it.

"Dead men don't move. They'll lay right there and let you draw them however you want." Sam had the grace to let a flash of sorrow cross his face as he slowed his pacing and sighed deeply. "I'm not saying I'm glad for this, but it's going to happen. We're going to have to march an army down there into Virginia, take Richmond back, and let those Rebels know they can't just up and leave the Union whenever they take a notion. The President never once said he was going to take their slaves away even if that's what he should have said. No place for slavery in this modern-day world. Those old boys down south are jumping to conclusions without the first thought of wanting peace. So it's history in the making, my boy, and our job is to capture that history and send it out to the people."

"Yes sir." Adam wasn't exactly sure what he was agreeing to, but those were the words Sam expected to hear. And he did want to be there to record history in the making while drawing down pay for it. He stood up to leave. He had learned to sense when Sam was through even if he didn't always know what Sam was through telling him.

"Best get to it, Adam," Sam said. When Adam reached down to straighten his sketches and put them back in the portfolio holder, Sam waved him away from the table. "James will pack those up. Some of them might do."

"Good to hear," Adam said. He was still holding Charlotte's veranda picture. He didn't seem to want to drop it down on top the others and surrender it to Sam's careless hand.

He had other sketches of her back in his hotel room. He must have drawn her from memory at least a dozen times since he'd left Kentucky to come to the capital. Every time he drew a crowd scene, he put her face there. But this was the very first time he'd captured her likeness. He could almost feel the soft curve of her shoulder under his hand when he looked at it. He turned toward the hotel room door carrying the sketch with him.

Sam stopped him. "Where do you think you're going with the yearning backside picture?"

Adam turned back toward him. "You said you didn't like it."

"Artist ears! Always perked up for criticism in everything a man says." Sam shook his head. "What I like don't matter a penny's worth. It's what our readers like."

When Sam reached for the picture, Adam surrendered it reluctantly.

"Who is she?" Sam asked.

"A Kentucky senator's daughter. There's no need to print her name."

"Protecting her, are you?" Sam looked up from the picture at him. "From what? Most young ladies would be thrilled to see their picture in *Harper's*."

"Without a name she can represent a hundred Southern belles."

Sam looked back down at the sketch. "True enough." Then he was eyeing Adam with a knowing smile. "I think this Southern belle's charms caught your eye, young Adam."

Adam smiled back to try to negate the bit of color climbing into his cheeks. "She was very pretty. Red hair and green eyes. Not your usual fainting belle."

"I knew a redhead once. Quite a woman. Would have married her except she found a man with more money."

"A mistake I'm sure she rues to this day," Adam said.

"He invested in railroads, so I doubt it. She was dripping in diamonds last time I saw her, but the red had turned gray. Old gets us all."

"If a bullet doesn't get us first," Adam said, turning toward the door again.

"You stay out of the crossfire, boy. We need pictures, not dead illustrators."

"I'll do my best."

He was almost out the door when Sam called after him. "No bullets are flying yet, so go on back down there and get that staircase. You keep dragging your feet, somebody's going to beat us to it. I'll print it right beside the old Shaker cow you drew. Make a good contrast. Heaven knows why, but readers want to know about those crazy Shakers. But do it fast. Armies are gathering and you don't want to miss the war."

That's how everybody in the capital was talking. As if the war might only last a few days, weeks at the most. While men were lining up to volunteer to preserve the Union, nobody thought it was going to take much effort. A show of cannons. A few rounds of ammunition. Adam had sketched some of the new recruits gathering in the Army of the Potomac. Young. Fresh.

With no idea of what they were heading toward.

Adam didn't know either. He'd never been in a war. But he'd read history. His grandfather had insisted that the only way to be ready for the future was to know the past. Plus Adam had talked to Mexican War veterans. Some of them were lining up to volunteer again alongside the fresh-faced kids. The old warriors had a different look. While they weren't shying away from the conflict, they were going into it with a stoic knowledge that fighting and dying went hand in hand in a war. And this time the face of the enemy wouldn't be foreign. This time they would be fighting their brothers and cousins and some of the men who had lined up beside them to fight the Mexicans.

That was the story he needed to be finding. Not some winding staircase at a Shaker village in Kentucky. His interest in the Shakers had been shoved aside. They'd be there living their strange beliefs after the conflict ended. Now he needed to be where the armies were massing. Where men were choosing North or South.

Then again it might be good to be back in Kentucky. If ever a state was divided, Kentucky was. Their governor leaned toward Secessionist, but most of the other political leaders waved the Union flag even while they had nothing good to say about President Lincoln. They wanted to ignore the war. Keep trading with the

North and living like the South with slaves working their land. Governor Magoffin saw no problem with sitting on the fence. Something it seemed both sides were willing to go along with as long as they could set up their recruiting camps just across the borders to the north and south. The last news report Adam had read said plenty of Kentucky men were walking out of the state in both directions to sign up to fight.

So maybe Kentucky wouldn't be a bad place to be. There would be scenes aplenty to keep him busy while the armies were gathering. And he could do that ethereal staircase Sam was so determined to show his readers. It was good to keep Sam happy. Or as happy as was possible.

Adam smiled a little. A side trip to Grayson might not be out of the question on his way to the Shaker village. Another stolen kiss before he went off to war. He couldn't remember a girl so haunting his thoughts, but the senator's daughter was different. He might consider propping his feet up in front of a fire that she was tending. He hoped that pantywaist from next door had gone to the Shakers so Charlotte would forget the asinine idea of marrying him.

Not that Adam was ready to propose or anything. The word even surfacing in his mind was enough to bring him up short on the street outside the hotel. His sudden stop caused the man walking behind him to bump him a little before he veered to the side to pass him with some angry words. Adam muttered an apology without really hearing what the man said.

What was the matter with him? Charlotte Vance was a mere diversion. That was all. So what if her lips had been sweet? So what if he couldn't stop drawing her face and seeing her in his dreams? That didn't mean anything. Nothing except the artist in him admired a perfectly aligned face.

It was the war. That was what had made him consider the unthinkable. A man faced with the prospect of being in front of a bullet with his name on it wanted to leave something behind. Wanted to know someone would grieve his passing. Wanted to leave his seed so that a child might carry his spirit forward. The sound of war drums gave Cupid a whole quiver full of arrows. That's all it was.

He'd have to rein in his emotions and not get carried away. He hadn't ever seriously considered proposing to Charlotte Vance or any other girl, no matter how entrancing. Of course it wasn't just beautiful women who posed a danger when the sabers were rattling. Many men and boys jumped into the recruiting lines to prove their courage.

Adam touched the pocket of his coat where he'd stuck Phoebe's telegram. Her words were to the point. *Jake dropped out of school. Joining the Potomac Army. Too young. Do something.*

So before he could head to Kentucky to draw Sam's staircase, he'd have to search through the Potomac Army to send Jake home. The boy had always been ready to fight at the slightest provocation. No sense of self-preservation at all. Phoebe was right about this one. Adam did need to do something. And Sam would take the army scenes and sell more newspapers with them than with any staircase.

But first Adam wanted to go back to his room and sketch that picture of Charlotte on her veranda from memory. The same as he'd done the first time. He assured himself it wasn't because he wanted to keep the picture of Charlotte necessarily. It was the idea of yearning for peace. That was what he wanted to keep.

14

Once Charlotte had put on the Shaker costume, the pretense was easy. It was as if, along with the new clothes, she donned a new identity. The other Charlotte, the real Charlotte, was hovering somewhere in the shadows of her mind waiting for the right moment to step back into her life, while this new Charlotte—Sister Charlotte—was following after Sister Gemma meekly, learning to say yea and nay, to bend her head and watch

178

the path in front of her instead of the sky. At least some of the time.

The new Charlotte was acting a role in a play. One that she had set in motion herself, for she had come voluntarily to this place. But once at Harmony Hill, the next act wasn't as easy as she'd imagined. No matter how she searched the pathways, furtively peering up from under her cap at each Shaker brother who came near, she saw no sign of Edwin. He was there. She was sure of that, but she could hardly search through the men's quarters for him. Not with Sister Gemma or Sister Altha constantly by her side to teach her the Shaker way. So as the week passed, the ending began to stretch far in the distance. At the same time, she saw no way to step out of the role and go back to Grayson. For her or for Mellie.

She missed Mellie. Not because of the way she'd helped her dress back at Grayson. It was a welcome novelty not having to be concerned about what she wore or how she looked. She certainly didn't miss the constricting stays squeezing her waist fashionably small for the party dresses or the hoops that had to be scooted sideways through doors. But she did miss Mellie plaiting her hair at night. Not because she couldn't weave the plaits herself, but because that was when she and Mellie had talked and laughed.

While the Shakers spoke of being loving sisters, idle chatter among these sisters was frowned upon. Silence allowed one to concentrate on one's duties. A loose tongue was reason for confession, Sister Altha instructed before she pinned her sharp eyes on Charlotte as if waiting for her to voice that confession. Not because she gossiped but because she couldn't keep from questioning the why behind the Shakers' many rules. So Charlotte did ask forgiveness for her curiosity, then could not keep from following it up with another question. "But shouldn't a person try to make sense of rules?"

"Understanding is not necessary. Obedience is necessary. That is what the Eternal Father asks of us. Obedience." And then she had looked at Charlotte as though she should make another plea for forgiveness.

Perhaps that was why Sister Altha saw to it that Charlotte and Mellie were separated. To make obedience to the rules come easier for both of them. When Charlotte had asked about Mellie, Sister Altha frowned and said, "Worldly relationships are the cause of much stress and loss of peace. Especially that of husband and wife or slave and master. The Scripture clearly states, 'Be not ye servants of men.' For Sister Melana's spiritual growth and for yours, it is best if you break loose from the sinful ties of the world."

Charlotte bit back the arguments that sprang to her mouth. While she was playing this role, she had little choice but to do as Sister Altha said.

Her pretense of obedience didn't keep Charlotte from looking for Mellie among the Shakers with the same diligence as she searched for Edwin. Relief swooshed through her when she finally spotted Mellie on a pathway between the buildings on the third day and saw that she no longer looked frightened. Instead Mellie raised her eyebrows high and shrugged her shoulders the barest bit before flashing a smile as if this whole thing with the Shakers was some kind of farce they had planned together as an escapade of sorts. Then without the chance to exchange a forbidden word on the silent walkways, she had rushed off to keep up with her Shaker guide, Sister Cora.

When Charlotte had taken a step after her, Gemma placed a restraining hand softly on Charlotte's arm. "Come, my sister. Our work duties lie in another direction."

"But I only wanted to speak with Mellie for a moment."

"Sister Melana," Gemma corrected.

"Sister Melana then," Charlotte said looking after Mellie. "I just want to ask her if she's all right."

"She appears in good health," Gemma murmured before she turned and began walking again the opposite direction toward the workshop where they were filling the seed packets. Charlotte had no choice but to follow her. She had no idea what they had Mellie doing.

So it was with some surprise she found herself actually seated beside Mellie in the meetinghouse on Sunday morning.

A bell had summoned them to meeting. Bells were always ringing in the village, summoning the Shakers to do something—get up, go to work, take meals in total silence in what to Charlotte's amusement the Shakers called the biting room, go to bed. It seemed every moment of the day was regimented by the ringing of bells.

Charlotte hadn't known what to expect when the bells sounded to call them to meeting. They had returned to their sleeping rooms after the morning meal for a time of meditation that Gemma said would properly prepare their spirits for meeting. Charlotte had been on her knees more in the few days she'd been with the Shakers than her whole life. A Shaker knelt in silent prayer upon rising. A Shaker knelt in silent prayer before and after every meal. A Shaker knelt in silent prayer before lying down at night on the narrow, uncomfortable bed.

Each time Charlotte knelt, bowed her head as instructed, and listened to the silence. She could almost feel the devout prayers rising from the sisters around her as her own thoughts jumped hither and yon from prayer words she'd learned as a child to the sweet memory of Adam Wade pulling her close against him for a kiss before he raced out of her life.

With effort, she would push thoughts of Adam aside and dwell only on the plans she'd made that were the reason she was kneeling among the Shaker sisters. She'd find Edwin and convince him of the error of his ways. With proper remorse, he'd come away from the Shakers with her. Or her father would see the terrible mistake he had made marrying Selena and beg Charlotte to return to Grayson so everything could go back to the way it used to be. Then she would remember Fort Sumter and despair would darken her thoughts. Nothing was happening as it should. And she didn't know what to do except to keep walking this strange path she had chosen until a better way presented itself.

With the bell still tolling, Gemma led Charlotte out into the hallway to line up with the other sisters for the march down the stairs, out the door, and to the meetinghouse. The brethren were making a parallel line down their own set of stairs. Outside one voice began and then others joined in singing what Gemma said was a gathering song as they walked. The unity of spirit was palpable as the streams of Shaker men and women converged on the meetinghouse from all directions.

Each person fell silent as they entered the white frame building, while outside the voices continued, growing less clear as more of the Shakers came inside. The sisters and brothers silently found their seats on backless wooden benches arranged in two sections facing one another, the men on the east side, the women on the west. Charlotte was ushered over to sit beside Mellie on the end of the front sisters' bench so Eldress Sadie, who seemed to be filling the role of preacher for the morning, could introduce them to the assembly. Charlotte couldn't imagine what a stir a female preacher would cause in the church she normally sat in on a Sunday morning.

Sister Altha had spent much time in the days Charlotte had been at Harmony Hill in trying to open Charlotte's mind to the truth of the Believers. "The Eternal Father created both man and woman in his own image, and how can that be if there is no feminine form of God?" She hadn't expected Charlotte to answer, only to listen. "I assure you such cannot be. That is why it was necessary for Mother Ann to come into the world. Doesn't the Scripture speak of a bride coming? Not in the physical sense of the world, but in a spiritual sense. The Eternal Father revealed that truth to Mother Ann, and because she accepted the truth of his calling for her to be the Second Coming, she was persecuted and maltreated. There is much evil in the world. So those who sought and embraced the truth withdrew from that world to establish our islands of peace and harmony onto which we invite all to come and share in the true way."

Sometimes after a couple of hours of Sister Altha's words beating down on her, Charlotte had no idea what she actually believed. She had always attended church faithfully when her father was at Grayson and occasionally when he was not if the weather was favorable for a carriage ride. And Aunt Tish had preached Jesus to her ever since she was big enough to remember Bible words.

She knew what Aunt Tish believed. Now she heard the belief in Sister Altha's voice, even though much of what she said seemed contrary to words Charlotte had heard preached from the pulpit in the town church. But when she peered down into her own spiritual heart, she knew not what was there. Perhaps nothing. Perhaps that was why her prayers only circled around her own head and never rose to heaven.

She could speak the words, *Our Father who art in heaven*, but as Aunt Tish had often told her, it wasn't the words that mattered. It was the feeling behind the words. "You got to lean on Jesus, chile. Once you does that, everything comes clear."

But Charlotte saw no need to lean on anybody. It was up to her to make things happen the way she wanted them to. Didn't everybody say the Lord helped those who helped themselves? So what if those words weren't actually written in the Scripture. They were still true. Even the

Shakers seemed to believe so, or else why would they go about their assigned duties with such diligent industry? Charlotte had heard as much about the work of the village as the spiritual beliefs in the days she'd been there.

Sister Altha spoke one line so often that it echoed in Charlotte's head like a tune caught there sounding over and over. *Put your hands to work and give your heart to God.* The older woman told her with great assurance that if she managed to do that, all else at the village would be easy.

"All can believe who so will," Sister Altha said before she shook her head a bit and fastened her eyes on Charlotte. "It is a sorrow that not all wish to pick up the cross and carry it. In many there is a lacking of proper spirit."

It was obvious she judged Charlotte to be one of the unwilling ones in spite of Charlotte's best efforts to do all she was told. Under Gemma's kinder guidance, Charlotte had carefully counted the bean seeds and sealed them into the packets. She had hung the chairs on the blue pegs and swept the bare wide-planked floors. She had pretended to bend her spirit while continually watching for some sight of Edwin.

She hadn't seen him until the Sunday morning meeting. Then he looked so different lined up with the other brethren, dressed in his gray trousers and round-collared cotton shirt with his hair combed in bangs across his forehead that she almost didn't recognize him.

But it was more than the clothes. Something else was different. Something she couldn't quite put her finger on until she realized he was sitting without a slouch even though he was a head taller than the two men on either side of him. She had never seen him sit so tall. His posture didn't change when Eldress Sadie spoke Charlotte's name. If anything, he appeared to square his shoulders even more, almost as if with pride as he looked directly at Charlotte with something akin to joy on his face. It wasn't a look that gave Charlotte any hope he was regretting his decision to come to the Shakers. Rather it was a look celebrating her joining him there. As a sister.

Charlotte and Mellie returned to their places on the bench as Eldress Sadie continued to talk. She was a little woman, barely taller than a half-grown child, but she seemed to radiate energy as she moved about in front of the Shaker believers perched on the hard benches.

There were no adornments in the building that might suggest this was a house of worship. Instead, ringing the walls were hats and cloaks hung on the same sort of blue pegs as in every other Shaker building. There was no pulpit for a preacher to place his Bible or pound out a warning of damnation, no offering plates, not even a table for the Holy Communion cups and unleavened bread. To Charlotte, the large open room more resembled a barn than a house of worship.

That didn't seem to matter to those gathered in the building as they listened to Eldress Sadie's words with rapt attention and hushed reverence, even though she was speaking more of the business concerns of the village than of any spiritual matters. With each of her words, a feeling of anticipation trembled a bit more vibrantly in the air. Charlotte studied the faces around her and decided it wasn't what the woman was saying but rather what her words were leading up to that was exciting the congregation. They wanted to dance.

At last Eldress Sadie spoke the words the assembled Shakers had obviously been waiting to hear. "Let us go forth and labor a song to bring down the joy of the spirit upon us."

The men and women stood in unison and began carrying the benches to the ends of the room in an orderly fashion. Charlotte and Mellie moved awkwardly out of the way. Sister Altha appeared in front of them to lead them to the benches where a few older Shakers were sitting.

"In a few weeks, you might be practiced enough to take part in laboring the songs, but for now it will be well for you to watch and open your minds and hearts to the words of the songs." She let her eyes settle on Charlotte's face. "I asked the singers to do this first song for your ears, Sister Charlotte. It's an old hymn of humility."

Charlotte bent her head and studied her hands in her lap. Silence was often the easiest answer. Beside her, Mellie's surprise at her submissive posture was almost tangible. Charlotte waited until Sister Altha turned away and the singers began their song before she peeked over at Mellie with a sideways grin. Mellie covered her mouth quickly to hide her answering smile.

One of the sisters had stepped forward to begin the song.

> I want to feel little.
> I want to feel small.
> The last of my Brethren,
> The least of them all.

Other voices joined her clear voice.

> That I may inherit that pure gospel spirit.
> The spirit of Christ and of Mother.

Charlotte scooted closer to Mellie. She glanced behind her, but none of the older Shakers were paying any attention to them. All eyes were on the singers, and then others began to move out into the middle of the floor to form lines to begin the dance. She didn't look at Mellie as she said, "I don't think Sister Altha believes I can humble my spirit."

"You appears to be humbler than I ever thought to see you." Mellie's voice was not much above a whisper, but there was little chance anyone would hear them now, with the dancers shuffling back and forth across the wooden floor while the singers continued. There was no music except the sound of the voices in unison.

> I want to feel humble
> And simple in mind.
> More watchful. More careful.
> More fully resigned.
> That I may inherit that pure gospel spirit.
> The spirit of Christ and of Mother.

"I'm trying, Mellie," Charlotte said.

"It ain't so bad, Miss Lottie. You just do whatever they tells you. Instead of Mammy or you doin' the tellin', it's Sister Cora." Mellie frowned a little as she studied Charlotte's face. "Course I guess as how it's harder for you. You ain't never had nobody tellin' you what to do all that much. You sorry you came?"

"Things aren't happening the way I planned," Charlotte admitted.

"You had a chance to talk to Mr. Edwin?"

"No, I was never alone to look for him,"

Charlotte said. "Only laid eyes on him just now."

"He don't look the same in them Shaker clothes. That's for sure." Mellie looked toward the men dancing in front of them. Edwin moved past them in step with the other Shaker brothers. He didn't look their way but kept his eyes on the floor as if searching for something. Mellie's voice held a touch of wonder. "Can you believe that? Mr. Edwin never even liked to dance, did he?"

"I guess worship dances are different," Charlotte said as she watched Edwin shuffle away from them across the floor. The dances were precision forward and backward motions and turns such as a company of soldiers might practice. "Everything is different. We probably look as different as he does."

"Ain't that the truth. What with these long-eared caps." Mellie pulled on the flap of her cap that hung down by her left ear. "Especially for you with your pretty hair covered up. But Mr. Edwin looked right happy to see you."

"In Shaker dress. As his sister."

"Better his sister than his wife. I've been tellin' you that forever. You just need to get out of here and be glad to be shuck of the likes of him. You need a real man. Somebody like that artist feller."

The singers started in on a new verse.

I want to be holy.
More perfect in love.
I want to be gentle
And meek as a dove.

Meek as a dove. Was that what she was becoming? Charlotte Mayda Vance. No, the meek as a dove Charlotte was the new Sister Charlotte. Not really her at all. Just a role she was playing while she figured out how to make things happen the way they had to. And in spite of the way her heart jumped at the thought of Adam Wade, he played no part in her future. None at all.

"He's gone," she whispered to Mellie.

"For now. But could be I was just happenin' to be lookin' out the upstairs window when he come back to tell you goodbye in the garden. A man kisses a woman like that, he's intendin' on comin' back."

"Even if he did, he wouldn't find me now." Charlotte wasn't quite able to keep the tremble of sadness out of her voice.

Mellie scooted her hand over under their skirts to squeeze Charlotte's hand. "You don't have to stay here, Miss Lottie. Go on home. It ain't a far walk even if they don't let you have your horse back."

Charlotte stared out at the Shakers moving back and forth in orderly formations. The men stayed in their lines as they passed through the lines of sisters. No one touched shoulders or hands. Then as if on a signal only they could hear, the lines turned and began marching in the opposite direction. The singers were repeating the words of the song, but the tune was getting livelier. The dancers began stepping higher and quicker until their feet on the floor were like the beating of drums.

All at once all the dancers and singers clapped and the sound exploded like the blast of a gun. Both Charlotte and Mellie jumped. The singers changed songs. Some of the dancers continued the orderly marching while others began leaping and jumping as the singers sang.

Hop up and jump up and whirl round.
Gather love, here it is, all round.

All the dancers began to jump and whirl until Charlotte thought they would surely fall from dizziness. Several young girls hopped up and down while holding hands. Some of the women began to reach up into the air as though plucking fruit from a tree. Sister Cora came over to where Charlotte and Mellie watched.

"Have some pomegranates, Sisters. Mother Ann has sent them down to us." There was a glow on the older sister's face as she held out her cupped hands toward them. "Eat these and love will flow through you like a river."

They both just stared at her. She pushed her hands toward them. "Take it. You'll be glad you did."

Mellie lifted her eyebrows, but she reached out and pretended to take something from the woman's empty hands. Charlotte did the same while all around them the other Shakers were whirling and chattering and laughing. It was hard to hear the singers.

"I ain't never ate a pomegranate. They ain't poisonous, are they?" Mellie said as she frowned down at her hand as if she actually saw something there.

"Oh no, my sister. Mother Ann only sends down good gifts. The fruit she sends us is sweet as honey and like none you will ever taste anywhere else," Sister Cora assured them.

Mellie and Charlotte lifted their hands up and pretended to take a bite. Sister Cora smiled and spun away back to pick more fruit.

"These people done crazy as loons." Mellie shook her hand as if getting rid of the remains of the imaginary fruit.

Charlotte couldn't deny that as the Shakers began to form lines and march in orderly fashion again. "Sister Altha says we should be open to the spirit."

"The' ain't nothin' real wrong with that, but Mammy would say you'd better be sure you isn't lettin' in no wrong spirits. We'd best keep our eyes fastened on Jesus till we know more about this Mother Ann and her spirit fruit." Mellie warily watched the dancers as if worried some other Shaker was going to spin away and offer her fruit she didn't want to eat. "And you need to just go on back to Grayson before that Miss Selena messes everythin' up."

"Have you heard something?" Charlotte turned her head to look at Mellie.

"Best look back out toward them dancers. Sister Cora told me nobody was supposed to do no talkin' much at meeting. They's apt to move us apart."

Charlotte looked forward quickly, and they both sat in silence as they tried to see if anyone had noted their inattention. "Nobody's watching," Charlotte said after a moment.

"Sister Cora says they has watchers that you don't never see. Peephole watchers." She barely moved her mouth as she went on. "Nate says that woman is gonna sell them all down the river."

"Father won't let her do that."

"Not in his right mind, but that woman has done spun his head around like these here Shakers were spinnin' a couple minutes back. Besides, Nate says Massah Charles ain't even there. He's still in the capital tryin' to stop the war a comin'."

"You saw Nate? When? And how?"

"Ever'body's got to go to the necessary room from time to time. Sometimes right in the middle of the night. But it don't matter all that much when I saw him. Just what he tol' me."

"But what can I do? She said Father gave her full rein to do whatever she wanted at Grayson."

"She said. You ain't knowin' for sure what he said or what he might know or not know about what's goin' on."

Mellie was right. Her father did need to know. "I'll write my father in the morning."

"A letter?" Mellie seemed to forget her worry about the watchers as she turned and looked directly at Charlotte. "What's the matter with you, Miss Lottie? I ain't never seen you act scared. That woman can't send you down the river. Grayson is your home."

"Nothing's working out the way I thought it would," Charlotte whispered. "The way I planned."

"Then maybe it's time to think on a new plan."

An old sister whose back was bent from years of work appeared in front of them. Her wrinkled face was not condemning, but rather full of kindness. "If we cannot dance or sing, we must meditate and ask the spirit to fill our souls with love and joy. Let me sit with you to help you properly meditate on the gifts of the spirit."

"Yea, Sister." Charlotte used the Shaker yes to try to make up for her and Mellie's lack of proper behavior as she scooted over to let the woman sit between them.

"I'm Sister Martha." The woman groaned softly as she lowered herself to the bench, and then lightly patted both of their legs. "Forgive me. My spirit is willing. Would that I could still get out there and dance down glory, but the old bones are weak."

"Is that what they're doing? Dancing down glory?" Charlotte asked.

"I suppose that sounds strange to you," Sister Martha answered with a gentle smile. "Never fear, you will learn our ways. But first you must free yourselves from thoughts of the world. Whatever worries you had there are no longer important. You have left that life for a better life here with us where there is only peace and harmony."

Peace and harmony. Charlotte wondered if such was even possible with the nation split and shots already fired at Fort Sumter. The news received at the Shaker village since then didn't hold out much hope for peace with the threats of blockades of the Southern ports and the call to arms by both sides. The situation seemed to be totally out of control. The same as Charlotte's life.

A few days ago it had seemed reasonable to follow Edwin to the Shaker village to convince him he was wrong to want to be a Shaker. A few days ago she had believed she would be able to hang on to Grayson. To go home again and sit in the peace of Aunt Tish's kitchen. Her kitchen.

But now she was sitting in a church without an altar, watching men and women whirl until they collapsed from the effort, eating imaginary fruit while people watched from peepholes to be sure she was obedient. Reason was lost.

15

It took Adam the better part of the afternoon to find Jake. Rows of tents were popping up on any bit of open ground in and around Washington, D.C., as regiments and companies from all across the Union answered President Lincoln's call for troops to enforce the laws of the land. Some of the volunteer companies came in with proper supplies and like uniforms, but others showed up with no hint of military bearing or dress, carrying hunting guns that had probably never been fired at anything bigger than a raccoon.

Just outside the city across the Virginia border, the same mustering in was going on as reports came in that men of the South were navigating to Richmond, the new capital of the Confederate States. When Fort Sumter fell, taking with it the last faint hope of a peaceful compromise between the two sides, Virginia, Arkansas, North Carolina, and Tennessee had seceded to join their sister Southern states. It was also being bandied about that Robert E. Lee had been offered command of the whole Union army, but instead of answering the President's call, he had resigned his commission and gone south to line up against the Union.

Sam Johnson had already offered Adam a bonus if he could get a sketch of Lee in his Confederate gray leading his troops into battle. When Adam asked how he was supposed to keep the Rebels from shooting him as a Yankee spy while he was doing such a drawing, Sam had waved his hand in airy dismissal. "You'll find a way. You always do."

And Sam was right. He would find a way. If it was a face or scene that mattered, Adam wanted his name to be the one scribbled at the bottom of the illustration. While it might not be the best time to be a Northerner in the South, that didn't mean it couldn't be done.

Adam pushed that problem aside to concentrate on the task at hand as he rode his horse slowly through the camps, pausing now and again to ask if any companies from Massachusetts had marched in. Everywhere he turned, patriotic feeling was at a fever pitch. The soldiers nearly to a man carried a spirit of revelry as if the whole idea of war was some kind of frolic the President had organized for their sole enjoyment.

Adam left his pencils in his bag and didn't pull out his sketchbook even though scenes all around him begged to be captured. On one side a baby-faced soldier who didn't look a day over fifteen caressed the barrel of the Springfield rifle just handed him by his captain. Down the block a plump lady in a feathered hat climbed down from a carriage to offer a basket of food to a circle of soldiers around a campfire. A mournful-looking black and tan hound rested his head on his master's leg as the man read a letter from home.

But Adam wasn't on a work mission. He was on a Phoebe mission. Something he seemed to be doing way too much in the last few weeks. First Selena Vance. Now Jake. But Phoebe was right about this mission. Jake shouldn't be here straining at the bit to go to war. He was only nineteen and a young nineteen at that. It would destroy their mother if something happened to him. She doted on Jake and William.

"I'm almost twenty," Jake said with fire in his eyes when Adam at last found the 5th Massachusetts Regiment and confronted him. "Besides, who are you to tell me I'm too young? You left school even younger."

"But not to play at going to war."

Red flooded Jake's face as he balled up his fists. Adam stared him down before he could swing a punch. Adam was still the big brother, the one who had always bested Jake in any confrontation and then cleaned up his bloody nose before their mother could see. Adam wasn't sure if it came to it that he could best Jake anymore, but luckily for both of them, Jake wasn't anxious to take the chance there in front of his fellow recruits that Adam might still be able to whip him.

The boy had grown another inch or two taller since Adam had last seen him, and his shoulders were broad under the blue Massachusetts Regiment uniform. There was no mistaking he and Adam were brothers, but where Adam tamped down his emotions and rarely let anybody know what he was thinking, Jake hid nothing. He did everything to the fullest, whether it was fighting or racing horses or loving. He'd already suffered a severely broken heart thanks to Phoebe, who claimed if not for her diligent watch and timely action, Jake would have been trapped in a disastrous marriage that would have brought nothing but embarrassment to the family.

But an unfortunate marriage might be less dangerous than a battlefield. Embarrassment was rarely fatal. A battlefield could be. That's why Adam had tracked him down. To try to slow Jake's headlong rush into yet another disaster.

Adam threw his arm around his brother's stiff shoulders and tried to defuse his anger. "Sorry,

Jake. I shouldn't have said that. It's just that Phoebe is worried about you." He didn't add that so was he. Better for Jake to feel the two of them were taking sides against Phoebe as they had so often in their younger days. "You know how Phoebe is."

Jake's muscles relaxed as he uncurled his fists and shook his head. "I should have known she would sic you on me."

Adam guided him away from the curious eyes and ears of the other men lolling about. They had been eager for the diversion of a fight to break the monotony of the camp. "She sent word you had signed up."

Jake hung his head a little. "Yeah, she isn't very happy with me. Says Mother weeps every time anybody mentions my name. I feel bad about that, but I still had to sign up. What else could I do?" He looked back up at Adam. "A man has to step up for his country at a time like this. You're joining up too, aren't you?"

"I'm not planning on it anytime soon."

Jake stared at him with wide open eyes that were a truer blue than Adam's. His never faded off to gray. "You're joshing me, aren't you?"

"Sorry to disappoint you, little bro, but no, I'm quite serious. I'll be there but not carrying a government-issued rifle."

"Drawing." Jake spat on the ground in disgust. "What good will that do?"

"More good than being cannon fodder." Adam stared straight at Jake until his brother shifted uneasily on his feet and looked down. "No need in you being cannon fodder either. Go back to school and finish out the year. Then you can be commissioned an officer if you're still determined to go to war."

"The fighting could all be over by then."

"We can hope," Adam said. *And pray.* He heard Edwin Gilbey's servant's words echoing in his head. Redmon. That was the man's name. If Adam went back to Kentucky and saw him again, he'd tell him to forget about those prayers for him and just pray for Jake. And others like him. Young. Foolish. Too ready to die for their country. Or maybe too sure they couldn't die.

Adam was only five years older than Jake, but in some ways he'd been older than Jake was now since he was twelve and their father left to seek his fortune. With his father gone, Adam had no choice but to leave boyhood behind. If he wanted something done, then it was Adam who had to do it. Nobody was going to step in and be a buffer between him and the realities of the world. But Jake and Harry had Adam ready to step in the gap for them and protect them as much as he was able.

Now it appeared Jake was determined to break through the gap and be his own man as he planted his feet on the ground and stretched up to his full height. His eyes were level with Adam's. "I won't leave the regiment. I'm not sitting on the sidelines. If you try to make me, you might as well just shoot me between the eyes right now, because I couldn't live being branded a coward." Jake's voice rose with each word until a couple of the men back at the camp lifted their heads to look out toward them.

Adam kept his voice quiet, almost pleasant. "Is that the iron you're branding me with, Jake? A coward's brand?"

Another flush reddened Jake's cheeks before he dropped his eyes to the ground. After an uncomfortable few ticks of silence, he mumbled, "You know I don't think that, Adam. Not really. You just look at things different than me. The artist in you, I guess. You've always been an observer. A watcher. But that's not me. I can't sit on the side and watch. I've got to be in the middle of making it happen." He raised his eyes back up at Adam. "It's time you and Phoebe realize that and let me be my own man." He was the little brother again beseeching Adam for permission to do something that would horrify their mother or Phoebe.

Adam stared at him for a long moment before he let out a sigh and shook his head. "I don't know what I'm going to tell Phoebe. Or Mother."

Jake smiled like a kid getting a puppy on Christmas morning as he bounced up on his toes and down again. "You can tell them you think I'm a man now. You do, don't you?"

Adam frowned at him. "I think you're headstrong and foolish." He let his frown fade away as he put his hand on Jake's shoulder. "But way too big for me to knock any sense into. Just remember it's war, Jake. Real bullets. Be brave but don't be stupid."

He went back over to the campfire with Jake and let him introduce him around to his buddies. All young. All burning with the war fever. He sat with them until dark fell, sketching their faces, hearing their blustering talk, wondering what he was going to tell Phoebe.

He took the easy way out and didn't go back to Boston before he caught a train to Kentucky. He sent a telegram. *Jake won't listen. Matter of honor. Pray war short.*

Adam could only hope Phoebe's response wouldn't find him until after the shooting stopped and Jake was safely home. As he watched the colors of spring bursting forth in the fields outside the train window, it seemed impossible that American men were gathering to shoot at other American men and that the only difference in the enemy would be the color of their uniforms. There'd even been stories in the papers about brothers shaking hands and marching off in opposite directions. To his chagrin, some other artist had beaten him to that illustration, but who knew what the coming weeks would bring? Cannons might be exploding in these very same green fields rolling so peacefully away from the train tracks, or the trains themselves might be derailed. If so, commerce in the nation could grind to a halt. That's what President Lincoln was hoping would happen in the South when he ordered the blockade of their ports.

Adam felt as ambivalent about it all as Kentucky was. It hadn't bothered him that Jake thought he lacked courage. He wasn't a coward. He had no need to prove himself on a battlefield except to draw the scenes that would tell the battle's story. That was the greater need. To record the conflict for history.

It seemed a waste of time heading back to the Shaker village in Kentucky just to draw a staircase. Sam had to be losing all sense of what was important. But Sam was the boss, and like he said, no cannons had lined up yet. As best Adam could tell from what he had heard in Washington, as many battle plans as there were regiments were being bandied about. If Lincoln didn't find a way to pull all the units together, who knew what might happen or when? So he supposed there was time for Sam's staircase. Plus time to swing by Grayson first. A slaveholding landowner trying to straddle the fence while waving a Union flag had to be a picture Sam Johnson could use. And could be he might convince the senator's daughter to pose for him in the garden. That would be one to add to his private collection.

But the senator wasn't there. Nor was the senator's daughter, according to the very proper black butler who answered the door and escorted him to the receiving parlor before going to inform the senator's wife she had an unexpected guest. Gibson, the old butler who had quaked so visibly under Selena's tirade in the parlor that day, had obviously been replaced. After cooling his heels in the small room for the better part of an hour, Adam decided to go see who he could find on his own to tell him when the senator's daughter might be in.

The house was being transformed. The sound of hammering drifted down from the upstairs floor while in the main parlor two black men were scraping paint off the woodwork. They paid scant attention to him as he stepped into the room and looked around. The furniture was covered in sheets and all the paintings removed from the walls, so at least Adam's eyes didn't have to be assaulted by his too-pretty portrait of the new Mrs. Vance. Outside the window the garden was no longer a peaceful retreat as a swarm of workers was cutting and trimming and tearing out the old plants and bushes. No chance of a quiet encounter with the beautiful Charlotte there now, even if she had been home.

He turned toward the kitchen. The cook had been friendly to him when he was here before. What was her name? Something odd. Aunt Tish. Latisha, according to Redmon when he saw the sketch Adam had drawn of her. Adam still had that sketch, along with the one he'd redrawn from memory of Redmon holding his horse. Someday Adam hoped to find a backer to help him publish a book of the many faces of America.

"Who are you?" a young voice asked as Adam stepped into the dining room that as yet was untouched by the bevy of workers.

Adam looked around the empty room. "Am I talking to a Grayson ghost?" he asked. "If so, I demand you introduce yourself."

A boy of five or maybe six poked his head out from under the table and giggled. "I'm not a ghost."

"What a relief." Adam put his hand over his heart and let out an exaggerated breath. "But if not a Grayson ghost, who are you?"

"I asked you first."

"So you did. Adam Wade at your service." Adam bowed a little from the waist and then crouched down to be eye level with the child. He surmised the boy must be Selena Vance's son, even though his small round face little resembled his mother as it shone with an innocence quite foreign to hers. "Is some sort of attack imminent? Should I ask you to make room for me under there with you?"

The boy giggled again, his dark eyes dancing under a mop of curly hair. "You're too big to hide under here, but I doubt you need to. Miss Pennebaker won't be chasing you to make you form your letters on the slate until your fingers won't uncurl from the chalk." He flexed his fingers as his smile disappeared. "Miss Pennebaker has no fondness for fun. If she catches me, I'll have to stand with my nose in a circle on the schoolroom wall for hours."

"How irksome for you, young sir. Can your mother not intercede for you, Master . . . ? I don't believe you gave me your name."

"Landon. Landon Black, and Mother gets even angrier than Miss Pennebaker when I run off and hide." The boy's eyes got bigger as he shrank back under the table a bit. "The last time she said she was going to tell my new father to give me a whipping. But he hasn't come back from wherever he works. Do you know him?"

"I do know him."

"Is he very mean?"

"He didn't seem so, but perhaps you should do what Miss Pennebaker tells you so you won't have to find out about that."

"I suppose I will just have to take my punishment then." The little boy sighed heavily. "A whipping is better than staying in the schoolroom all the day long. Mother says I have to learn to be a gentleman, but I don't want to."

"What do you want to learn to be?"

"A sea captain. I want to smell the sea air and harpoon whales." The little boy crawled the rest of the way out from under the table. He stayed on his knees but stretched his head up in the air. He was so thin that Adam thought a stiff sea breeze would surely bowl him over. The child peered at Adam and asked, "Have you ever seen a whale?"

"Only in drawings."

"Drawings." Landon frowned. "That sounds like schoolwork."

"Not to me. To me it's an adventure every day as I chase the unexpected the way a sea captain chases whales."

"But you can't harpoon whales unless you're a sea captain. Harpoons are heaps more fun than drawing pencils." The boy raised his arm and pretended to throw a harpoon before he shook his head sadly. "But Mother says I have to be a gentleman because all this will be mine some-day."

"What about Charlotte? Where is she?"

"Charlotte. That's my new father's daughter. Mother says I'm my new father's son, so that would make Charlotte my sister, wouldn't it?" The child didn't seem to expect Adam to answer him as he went on. "But she's not here. She's somewhere in Virginia. Mother says she had to go there to learn to be a lady before I came here."

"Virginia?"

"That's a state. Miss Pennebaker says they seceded from the Union, and we'll be shooting people from Virginia now, so I might never get to meet her. My sister, I mean. I had a father." The boy's lip trembled as he went on. "He had to go to heaven to see God. So I don't need a new father even though Mother says I do, but I've never had a sister. A sister might be fun. If she knows about seas and such, but Mother says to forget about having a sister."

"Oh? Why is that?"

Landon started to answer, but the sound of female heels clicking on the wooden floor and coming closer stopped his words. "Mother's coming. I'll harpoon you if you tell her I'm under here." He scooted back out of sight under the tablecloth.

16

Adam stood up and stepped away from the table a bare second before Selena Vance came into the room. He pushed his lips up in a smile as he greeted her.

Her return smile looked every bit as fake as his

211

felt. "Adam, how delightful to see you again. But James said you were waiting in the receiving parlor."

"So I was," Adam said. "But it was a long ride here and the day was warm. I hoped to impose on your housekeeper for a drink of water."

"You poor man." She pulled her mouth down in a sympathetic look. "I should have had refreshment sent to you at once. What a regretful lapse of proper hospitality! I fear I've been in quite a spin trying to correct years of neglect here and simply got distracted. Let me ring the bell for tea."

She hardly seemed dressed for work, with her waist pinched small as a wasp's above the shimmering rose-colored skirt, fashionably plumped out by multiple petticoats. As she brushed past Adam toward the sideboard, the skirt's silky material rustled softly against his legs.

"That's kind of you, but you don't have to bother with tea on my account," he said. "A glass of water, then I'll be on my way. I only stopped by to have a few words with the senator, but your servant says he's not here."

"No, I fear he's still in Frankfort. The war news is causing so much division that he doesn't know when he might be able to return. Plus of course, the election looms next summer." She studied Adam as if trying to figure out why he would need to speak with the senator. "Was there some difficulty with your payment for the portrait? I have come to realize that sometimes mundane business matters very often escape Charles' notice when he is up to his ears in political maneuvering."

"No, no difficulty. Actually it was politics that brought me here." Adam told the partial truth. "I hoped to speak with him about the local political mood. And to see if he might be willing to allow me to do a sketch of him for the newspaper. A Kentucky senator trying to hold on to the peace here in the state." Adam held his hands up as if framing the caption.

Her face changed, became more welcoming. "I'm sure he'd look on that with favor. You really must stay for tea so that we can chat about your work." She picked up a small bell off the sideboard and rang it.

"Will Charlotte be joining us?" Adam asked as if the butler and the child hiding under the table hadn't already told him she wasn't there. "I do hope she is well."

"I'm sure she is quite well." Selena carefully set the bell down to keep it from tinkling again and ran her fingers along the tatted lace edge of the cloth on the sideboard before she turned to look at Adam. "But Charlotte's not at Grayson right now. She's gone to Virginia."

"Virginia? With war imminent, do you think that is wise?"

"Charlotte is a very determined young woman.

What she decides to do, she does." Selena held out her hands in a gesture of helplessness. "Charles warned me she was thus before we married."

"I'm surprised she would decide to leave Grayson. She spoke so fondly of her home here." Adam watched Selena. Something seemed amiss in what she was telling him.

"Young women can be quite unpredictable." Selena shook her head slightly with a look of amused wonder. Then her eyes sharpened on Adam. "She is very attractive in spite of those unfortunate freckles. Were you smitten by her?"

A young female servant answered the summons of the bell and saved him from having to come up with a suitable response.

"We'll take tea in the receiving parlor," Selena told the girl.

"Your offer of tea is very kind, but I really must be on my way," Adam said quickly. He had no desire to be trapped into an extended visit with this woman. But he had pretended thirst, so he added, "However, a glass of water and perhaps one of Tish's apple tarts would be more than welcome."

Selena shooed the servant girl back to the kitchen with no change in her orders before she turned to smile at Adam. "We have a new cook now. One I brought down from Boston. Unfortunately a skill for finer cooking seems to escape our Southern Negroes."

"Oh. And where is Tish? I had the feeling that she had long been part of the household."

"So she had, but you needn't dredge up any of your Northern sympathies for her. I haven't sent Tish away, merely moved her to the slave quarters to cook there. Perkins says she's quite happy. How altruistic of you to be concerned for her." Selena's bland smile grew even wider.

"None of my business, of course," he said in what he hoped was a pleasant tone. "I was just a bit surprised to hear the senator would agree to change cooks. He seemed fond of Tish."

"My dear Adam, all things change. You surely know that. Think of how our Charlotte found it necessary to make new plans after the disappointment of her broken engagement. You did know of her disappointment, didn't you?" She pulled a sorrowful face and went on with no pause for him to answer. "And so we all find it necessary to make changes. Grayson was sinking under my husband's misguided kindness and distracted management. That is being corrected."

"I see." Adam gave up on pretending politeness.

His frown seemed to make her smile more genuine. "Perhaps you do," she said as she once more picked up the bell. "I'll have James show you out."

"Don't bother," Adam said before she could ring it. "I can find my way back to the door."

"I daresay you can." Her smile didn't waver as

she replaced the bell without letting it make a sound. "Would you like me to send your regards to Charlotte when next I write?"

"Certainly. *If* you write."

"Oh, I have written her. It's the least I can do for Charles, since he is much too busy himself to worry with such correspondence."

She reminded him entirely too much of Phoebe, who continually arranged and ordered the lives of everybody around her, but at least he could usually believe Phoebe was driven by love to push her family to do whatever she determined was best for them. In Selena Vance, Adam glimpsed no redeeming core of love. Marriage to the senator had given her position, prestige, and power, and those were the whips she was using to bring the world around her to its knees. There would be no peace at Grayson for a long while. As Adam turned to go out, he felt a rush of gratitude that he'd never allowed himself to be caught by such a woman.

He was almost to the door when a frazzled-looking middle-aged woman passed him in the hall without seeming to note or perhaps care that he was a stranger. "I have lost young Landon again. If you've seen a small boy of six, I would count it a great favor if you would point me in his direction."

Adam was saved from answering by Selena's firm voice in the dining room. "Landon Harley

Black, come out from under that table at once and go do as you're told by Miss Pennebaker. There are consequences to pay."

As if the consequences were payment due from her instead of Landon, the unfortunate Miss Pennebaker looked near tears as she hurried on toward the dining room.

Poor Landon had little chance of ever harpooning his whales. Not with Selena calling the shots. He would be a gentleman or else. Then again, the same might have once been said about Adam's chance of being an artist with his grandfather so set against it. Of course Adam hadn't had the added burden of being a gentleman on his shoulders. The son of a shopkeeper and the grandson of a schoolmaster didn't have quite as much to live up to. No Graysons in his future. Thank the merciful heavens.

And what of Charlotte's future? She had seemed so set on coercing her young gentleman friend into marriage. As he had eavesdropped on her and Gilbey in the garden the night of the party, she had shown signs of Phoebe's and the new Mrs. Vance's determination to shape life to suit them. That should have been enough to make him run from any contact with her, but instead he had stepped out of the shadows to confront her. He still wasn't sure why. Perhaps because of the innocent vulnerability he'd glimpsed behind her smile when the senator had escorted his new wife into the house. Perhaps simply because he was a man and she was a woman. He had thought to merely offer her a few kind words, but she was so lovely and her lips so inviting.

Even now as he rode away from Grayson, he could shut his eyes and bring up the exact image in his mind of how she had looked in the moonlight. Her skin soft under his touch, her eyes brimming over with fearful desire, her lips begging to be kissed. He had drawn her face many times since then, but not that image. If he kept it only in his head, then he might still convince himself that she was only another beautiful woman who had allowed him to steal a kiss from her in a weak moment. He could forget his disappointment when she pushed him away in the graveyard and assure himself that the kiss before his leave-taking the next day was nothing more than the last move in a game they had been playing with their emotions. His winning move.

But if that was true, why did he feel so much the loser now that he hadn't found her at Grayson? He had expected her to be there. He had pictured her there, if not exactly waiting for him, at least remembering him the way he was remembering her. As some unexpected twist in the road with entrancing possibilities glimmering in the distance. Obviously her plans with young Gilbey had gone awry. Perhaps that had been a disappointment she had run from as Selena Vance had suggested. But into the direct path of the war? The senator should have known better than to let her go to Virginia where both armies were lining up to fire the first salvos of the conflict. Each thought to take the other's capital and end the war in one brilliant maneuver.

Adam wished he had asked where in Virginia. But if Charlotte had gone to a finishing school as Landon said, Adam could find her. It wouldn't be that much of a challenge. The challenge would be in not getting shot as a Yankee spy.

He reined in his runaway thoughts as up ahead he caught sight of the buildings of the Shaker village rising into the sky. It was better that he didn't know where Charlotte was. He had no time to be chasing after her, no matter how she haunted his thoughts. Her father would undoubtedly send for her before the war advanced to any place near her. She wasn't Adam's responsibility. So what if she had touched something deep inside him that no other girl had ever even come close to touching. That didn't mean it was something that wouldn't fade into forgetfulness after a few months in spite of how memories of her pulled at his heart now. He had pictures to capture, and the first one was this confounded staircase Sam Johnson was so determined to have.

But since he was there, he might as well look around for more faces and scenes to draw. The next day was Sunday. Perhaps they would allow him to attend their morning meeting to observe the Shakers' dancing worship that sounded so odd to him. Dancing had no place in the religion his grandfather had shoved down his throat. In his grandfather's place of worship, a person sat on hard benches and listened in total silence as a dark-clad preacher threatened the Lord's punishment on any man, woman, or child who let his thoughts wander away from the preacher's words.

While the Lord had never sent down a lightning bolt to strike Adam down as the preacher sometimes warned might happen to those who didn't take the message of the Lord seriously enough, Adam's grandfather had been more than ready to pick up the rod on the Lord's behalf to keep Adam's spirit in check. Adam hadn't been in a church building since he left his grandfather's house.

It wasn't that he didn't believe there might be a God. The beauty of this very spring day seemed to suggest some higher power had set the world in motion. Even more than the beauty of nature, Adam couldn't dismiss the strong belief of a man like Redmon who offered to pray for a white man he barely knew while enslaved to another white man. And the man clearly believed his prayer would be heard and attended to. Yet if that was so, why was Redmon still a slave? If what the Bible said was true and nothing was impossible with the Lord, why hadn't that most powerful God set Redmon, a man who loved him, free?

While Adam hoped Redmon's prayers brought him comfort, he couldn't imagine a most high God leaning down to pay attention to any petitions he, Adam, might offer up. Perhaps the Lord had lent his ear to the first Adam in the garden or helped the disciples catch fish the way the Bible said, but a lot of years had passed since then.

And now soldiers were lining up to go to war, and on both sides men were praying to God for victory. What happened then? Wouldn't it be better if the prayers of men of peace were answered and there was no war?

The Shakers believed in peace. They had shut out the world in order to establish a community of perfect peace. A few days immersed in their peace might be good before he had to go back east where the armies were massing and the voices of those calling for peace had been drowned out by the beat of war drums.

17

The letter from Grayson came the first week of May. Spring had spread its blooms from one end of the village at Harmony Hill to the other, but when Charlotte paused to admire the white clouds of apple blossoms in the orchard, Gemma had mildly taken her to task.

"We don't look at the fleeting beauty of the bloom. It is the beginning of fruit that we see," Gemma told her.

"But what is the wrong in enjoying the flowers first? Don't you think the Lord created such beauty for the eye to behold?"

Charlotte was trying to understand the Shakers. Not because she planned to stay with them, but merely as a puzzle she needed to figure out. She had asked so many "why" questions that Sister Altha finally forbade Charlotte to speak the word in her presence. A novitiate's place was to listen and learn and not to question why. Sister Altha said the why had been answered many years ago by Mother Ann through the visions she had received from the Eternal Father. There was no need to question the Believers' truths given in such a sacred manner nor should one doubt the decisions of the Ministry who were even now led by Mother Ann's precepts and spirit.

More patient with Charlotte's questions, Gemma stared out at the blooming trees as she explained, "The beauty in anything is in its usefulness. It is wrong to celebrate beauty for beauty's sake, but with our bees' help, these blossoms will become apples to supply our needs for nourishment and for produce to sell to the world. That is what we celebrate. We can ever be thankful for the bounty of nature."

But the whys still sat on Charlotte's tongue.

Why couldn't they breathe in the beauty of the blossoms and still celebrate the apples? Why? Why? The questions circled in her head and always ended with the same ones sitting down to stay with her. Why was she still here? Why hadn't she gone back to Grayson the way Mellie had told her she should on that first Sunday?

Perhaps she needed to forbid her mind from thinking the word *why,* for she had no answers. She had always had answers. From the time she was a small child, she'd been able to see the path of her life clearly before her, but now the path she'd been so sure of was fading from sight. Selena had taken over her beloved Grayson, and Edwin showed no inclination to return to the "world," as the Shakers called all that lay outside the borders of their villages. He was cut from the same cloth as the most devout of the brethren.

When at last she had been able to speak with him face-to-face, she had never seen him so animated as he told her how anxious he was for his birthday in December when he would be of the proper age to officially sign the Covenant of Belief and hand over Hastings Farm to his new family. She stared at him and did not know him. Arguments rose in her mind, but she couldn't seem to bring them to her lips with Sister Altha beside her and Elder Logan beside Edwin as they supervised their meeting.

She had been surprised when Sister Altha suggested she talk with Edwin. Charlotte hadn't requested to do so, even though she had almost given up meeting Edwin in some unsupervised place. There were no unsupervised places at Harmony Hill. Even the shadows seemed to have eyes and ears.

Very aware of Sister Altha's stern eyes upon her, she looked at Edwin and finally got out the weak question. "Are you sure?"

"I have never been surer of anything in my life, Charlotte." When he forgot to call her "sister," Sister Altha frowned and he quickly amended his words. "Sister Charlotte. The brotherly love here surrounds me until I feel as if I'm resting on a pillow of peaceful purity. This is the way the Lord wants us to live. Staying pure of worldly sins of the flesh, listening to him and working to make his way our own. Mother Ann instructed us to let such be our inheritance, our treasure, our occupation, our daily calling. Isn't that right, Elder Logan?" He looked to the man by his side for approval. They sat in two chairs facing Charlotte and Sister Altha with a good distance between, as if even the air the brothers and sisters breathed should not be mixed.

"It is as you say, Brother. Our sister may come to know the same treasure if she bends her will and opens her heart to the teachings." Elder Logan's face was lined with wrinkles that seemed to speak of kindness and understanding. His hair was as white as the stones that made up the impressive exterior of the building they were in. He sat straight in the chair with his open hands resting lightly atop his knees. Edwin sat exactly the same, a head taller than the elder.

"I have often told her so in the time she has been among us," Sister Altha put in. "Have I not, Sister Charlotte?"

"Yea," Charlotte agreed, using the Shaker word. She was tempted to add that Sister Altha always made it sound as if it was a treasure Charlotte had scarce hope of finding, but she held her tongue. That hardly mattered, since the Shaker way was not a treasure she had ever thought to seek. It certainly wasn't the reason she was sitting in a Shaker room looking across at Edwin, who had donned the Shaker spirit along with his Shaker clothes. The Hastings land no longer mattered to him. He had found his place among the brethren. Perhaps for the first time ever, he looked comfortable in his own skin.

Charlotte had never been one to hide from the truth. Hadn't she knelt by her mother's body on the garden path and looked death in the face without pretense? She had looked on her arrangement with Edwin with the same direct honesty. She had realized early on that the two of them might never share any sort of bond other than the love for their land, but she had believed that would be enough. Now she knew it was not. And yet she stayed hidden among the Shakers, waiting for some word from her father that she could come back to Grayson. She needed the loving assurance that, even with Selena attempting to push her out the door, he—her father—would always make a place for her there.

She had sent a letter to her father on that first Monday with the Shakers the way she had promised Mellie she would. Gemma told her she was free to write what she willed to her father, but that the Ministry would read her words before the letter was posted to be sure she had written nothing too worldly or improper. So she had carefully considered each word she penned.

Dear Father,

Please forgive me for leaving and coming here to Harmony Hill without talking to you first. I tried to explain my reasons in the letter I wrote to you before I left Grayson, but sometimes it's hard to tell everything in words on paper. As you may already know, Edwin has decided to join with the Shakers and become a Believer. Thus there will be no wedding in May and no joining of the Grayson and Hastings farms as we had once hoped and dreamed.

I followed Edwin here at his invitation in hopes of finding a new plan for my life. I brought Mellie with me and she is now a free sister among the Shakers. She has heard some disturbing news from Grayson that Selena has no awareness—as is understandable since she is so new to our home —of our commitment to our people. Our Negroes have long been loyal to us at Grayson. I know you feel the same sort of loyalty back toward them and will want to protect them from the great sorrow of being forced to leave the only home many of them have ever known. I can't believe you would approve of such a course of action and trust you will do what needs to be done to make things right again. For all of us.

Your loving daughter,
Charlotte

As Sister Altha read through the letter, the frown lines deepened between her eyes. But she made no comment for or against any of Charlotte's words when she handed the sheet of stationery back to Charlotte. "Address the envelope," she ordered. "I will have to post it for you."

Charlotte dipped the pen nib in the inkpot and stared at the blank envelope, not sure which address to write. She could post it directly to Frankfort, but then what if her father had returned to Grayson? It had been her experience in the past that letters sent to him in Frankfort often were lost if he wasn't still in the capital city to receive them.

"You surely know your own address, Sister Charlotte." Sister Altha blew out an impatient sigh as she tapped her toe against the wood floor.

"Yea, of course, Sister Altha."

"Then let's be done with this. We cannot neglect our duties overlong."

Finally Charlotte wrote her father's name on the letter and sealed it with a bit of wax before slipping it into the envelope. Quickly she addressed the envelope to Perkins, the overseer at Grayson, with instructions on the back to forward her letter to Frankfort if her father wasn't expected home. Perkins might be taking orders from Selena, but his first loyalties would surely be to Grayson and her father. He would see that the letter was delivered into her father's hand.

"I hope you are not planning on writing many letters, Sister." Sister Altha snatched the envelope from Charlotte before the ink had time to dry. "Now Sister Gemma is waiting to take you to your work duties. It is good to dwell on the truth that a Believer has no time to waste."

Days passed and became weeks as Charlotte anxiously awaited an answer, while at the Shaker village she continued the mind-numbing cycle of work and listening to Sister Altha's instruction in the Shaker way. With the seed packets all sealed and ready to be marketed in the world by the Shaker traders, she followed Gemma to a new duty in the pressing room on the third floor of the Gathering Family House.

It promised to be hot and tedious work. A fire in the small round stove in the center of the room kept the irons hot—and also the workers, whose faces glistened with sweat in spite of the windows open to the spring breeze. As she followed Gemma into the too warm room, Charlotte longed to fling off the worrisome cap and let her head feel the air, but she knew Gemma would simply fetch the discarded cap and pleasantly tell her to put it back on. Nothing she did upset Gemma, who seemed to float on a peaceful sea with no storm waves ever. But at the same time, she never allowed Charlotte to lag.

When she noted Charlotte eyeing the overflowing basket of bedclothes beside the ironing board assigned to her, Gemma laughed. "We have need of many beds for our sisters and brothers, but do not despair, my sister. We also have many hands to get the work done. You are not expected to do more than your share."

"That is good to hear, but you'll have to show me how," Charlotte said as she watched one of the sisters pick up an iron from the stove and moisten the tip of her finger to give its flat side a quick touch. Obviously satisfied with the heat she felt, she moved back to her board and began smoothing the skirt of one of the Shaker dresses. "I've never used an iron."

"Never?" Gemma looked surprised. "Did you wear your clothes wrinkled?"

"Oh no." Charlotte almost laughed at the idea. Her mother had taught her that a lady had to maintain the proper appearance at all times. "That wouldn't have been allowed."

A sister plain of face and looking to be in her middle years looked up from her steady pressing strokes. "Our new sister was a lady, Sister Gemma. Remember? Ladies have servants to do such common chores. I've even heard they have servants to dress them. That all they do is hold up their arms and turn and stand like a china doll while a servant tightens their corsets and does up their buttons. Is that true, Sister Charlotte?"

The other sisters in the room held their irons up away from the fabric spread on their ironing boards and looked at Charlotte as they waited for her to answer. None of them had probably ever had a servant do up their buttons or tie the laces on their pantalettes, but Charlotte sensed no animosity, only interest in what her answer might be.

"At times," Charlotte said. "For fancy dresses and such. A lady's waist must be fashionably slender and so the stays must be pulled as tight as possible. Tighter than one can do on her own. And then the buttons are completely out of reach on those dresses and they have no wiggle room. Not like these dresses at all." Charlotte smiled and pulled the loose fabric of her dress out away from her waist.

The other women looked at her with unbelieving eyes as if hardly able to imagine such a life where somebody else fastened one's buttons. One of the older sisters returned her iron to the stove and picked up a new one. When she spat on it, her spit sizzled on the hot surface before she turned toward Charlotte. "Did you not like being a lady, young sister? Or did your family's fortunes change?"

The woman's look was sharp, and Charlotte thought that, not only would she know if Charlotte did not speak the truth, she would be sure to report such a lapse of honesty to Sister Altha. So she simply said, "At times I felt trapped in dresses I could not unbutton."

She might have said more, but one of the younger sisters spoke up. "I wore such a dress once. My wedding dress had tiny pearl buttons with fabric loops to hold them. My dear mother fastened them for me. She'd worn the dress when she married my father years before."

"And did you feel trapped in it the way our new sister says?" the older sister asked.

"Nay. I felt beautiful and happy on my wedding

day." The girl's face softened as if she could still see herself the way she had looked on that day.

"Such feelings of vanity are a sin, Sister Dulcie," the older sister warned.

"Yea, Sister Erma." The young woman lowered her eyes to the floor. "I will confess my sin at the first opportunity."

"You are married?" Charlotte looked at the girl in surprise. "I understood marriage was not allowed among you here."

Gemma answered before Dulcie could. "Many come among us with the need to shake free from the sin of matrimony before they can begin living the true way."

"And how does that happen?" Charlotte asked. "Aren't the vows of marriage sacred? Doesn't the Bible speak of forsaking all others and cleaving to your husband or wife?"

Gemma smiled. "Sister Altha is right. You do have many questions and little understanding of our ways. Here in our community we demonstrate the practical love that is asked of believers in the Scripture. 'By this shall all men know that ye are my disciples, if ye have love one to another.' The selfish love of husband and wife and children cannot satisfy that commandment of the Lord. Such selfish unions bring naught but sin and stress into one's life. But the peaceful, all-encompassing love we practice here for all our brethren enables us to live the perfect life at

Harmony Hill. Is that not right, my sisters?" Gemma swept her eyes around the other women in the room.

"Yea," they echoed one another, but Charlotte noted some of the voices sounded less enthusiastic than the others. Dulcie's yea was barely above a whisper.

"Good, we are all agreed as how it should be. We have no ladies here, only sisters," Sister Erma said with another sharp look toward Charlotte before she began plying her iron again. "Now it will be best if we stop our chatter and attend to our labor. The irons do not smooth the wrinkles without our arms pushing them."

Again the sisters answered with a chorus of obedient yeas as they turned back to their ironing boards. Dulcie stepped over in front of Gemma. "If it pleases you, Sister Gemma, let me show our new sister how to iron the sheets. I have not learned much well enough to teach it while I have been here at Harmony Hill, but I know well how to do this duty. And there is an open ironing board here beside me."

"That would be good, Sister Dulcie. Sister Altha has asked me to write some letters for her since her arthritis is making writing difficult, so this will give me the opportunity to tend to those duties. Plus I must confess ironing is not my favorite duty." Gemma flashed them her smile before she headed for the door.

18

Dulcie watched Gemma leave and then shook her head slightly. "Sometimes you want to pinch Sister Gemma just to be sure she is a flesh-and-blood sister and not an angel in Shaker dress. Have you ever seen her the least bit perturbed?"

Charlotte thought a minute before she said, "Not that I can remember. Even my many questions don't seem to bother her. She always answers me kindly. Unlike Sister Altha who tells me such mindless curiosity will surely lead me down the devil's path."

Dulcie made a sympathetic face. "Yea, Sister Altha does greatly desire to keep us off that path. But engaged in our duties, we won't be tempted to stray. Come, let me show you how to do this ironing duty."

She pulled the basket of sheets over to the side and showed Charlotte how to sprinkle water over them and then roll them up tightly so the fabric would be damp enough for the irons to smooth more easily.

The hiss of the heated irons against the damp cloth, the clank of cooling irons being set back on the stove, and the rustle of the fabric being shifted and straightened on the ironing boards made it impossible to hear any words spoken except by someone standing very near. Charlotte peeked over at Sister Erma to be sure she wasn't looking their way before she asked Dulcie, "So how come you to be here if you were married?"

Dulcie kept her voice as low as Charlotte's. "My husband was converted by a Shaker brother selling garden seeds. Our farm was rocky and the ground so poor we could barely grow enough corn to feed our children."

"Children?" Dulcie looked too young and too slight to have ever borne a child. "You have children?"

"We had three. Two girls and a wee boy. Then the wee one, our sweet little Willy, got a fever and died. I could have overcome the sadness, but my William felt it was a direct punishment from the Lord for what he called our sins of lust." Dulcie kept her eyes on the tightly rolled dampened sheet as she placed it back in the basket. "Brother Joseph, the Shaker man, said the Lord had revealed that truth to William, and the only way to protect our girls was to come to Harmony Hill. So we did." She stood up and together they carried the basket of dampened bedclothes back to the ironing board.

Charlotte shook out a pillowcase and laid it on the board as she saw a sister doing across the room. "Are you sorry to be here?"

"We don't go hungry and Shaker children rarely get fevers." Dulcie handed Charlotte an iron. "Careful. You can burn yourself," she

235

warned as Charlotte set the iron down on the pillowcase. There was a slight hiss as steam rose up around the hot iron.

"Keep it moving or you will scorch the fabric." Dulcie took the iron from Charlotte and moved it back and forth with just the right pressure to smooth out the wrinkles. "A very hot iron works best, so when this one cools you must put it back on the stove in the iron holder and take a newly hot one. When you need to adjust the material, you can set the iron down on its heel." She propped the iron up on the end of the ironing board.

"It looks easy when you do it," Charlotte said as she picked the iron up to give it another try.

"I've had much practice. My mother had me ironing pillowcases by the time I was six."

While not as quick as Dulcie, Charlotte managed to smooth the wrinkles out of the rest of the case. She ran her hand over the warm cotton with satisfaction at its smoothness.

"Now fold it over and do the other side," Dulcie instructed. "We have no time to admire our work. There are many pieces to iron." She watched as Charlotte pressed and folded the pillowcase into a square that matched all the other Shaker pillowcases. Uniformity was desired in all they did. "Now lay it aside on the finished table and begin another until your basket is empty."

Charlotte looked at the basket heaped with

sheets and pillowcases. "I have to do them all? Today?"

Dulcie smiled. "I will take from your basket too and we will be finished before the midday meal. Sisters help one another here. That is a good thing." Then her smile faded as she reached down to lift a sheet out of the basket and hold it up against her bosom as if the bundle held a baby. "But I do miss holding my children against my heart."

Charlotte spread another pillowcase on the ironing board. "Where are they?"

"In the Children's House. They are well cared for and go to school."

"But does anyone hold them as you wish to?"

"Not like a mother. Only as a sister." Dulcie unfolded the sheet and spread it on her ironing board. She kept her voice low, barely loud enough for Charlotte to hear. "But they are not unhappy. They don't cry for me, and I manage to only weep on the inside when they call me Sister Dulcie." She ran her iron over the sheet for a moment before she said, "I shouldn't have burdened you with my words. Sister Altha will tell me it is a sin to speak of my unhappiness or even to feel such."

"Don't worry. I am far from perfect enough to share all I hear with Sister Altha. Our words are only about the ironing." Charlotte matched her quiet tone.

"Then, my lady sister, why are you here if you aren't searching for the perfect way?" Dulcie asked.

Charlotte looked across at the other sisters. None seemed to be paying the least attention to them. Even Sister Erma. "I thought to marry Edwin Gilbey before he came here."

"And you were so in love with him that you followed him here rather than live your life of comfort without him."

Dulcie looked at her with such dreamy eyes that Charlotte almost laughed. Put that way it sounded quite ludicrous, but was her way any less so? "I'm not in love with him."

A frown wrinkled Dulcie's forehead. "Then why would you think to marry him? And why did you follow him here? I don't think I understand."

"It seemed a good plan at the time."

"And now?"

"Now I don't know."

"You could leave the village and go back to your life as a lady, couldn't you?" Dulcie asked.

"I suppose, but there are complications. I'm waiting to hear from my father."

Dulcie paused in her ironing and looked at Charlotte a long moment before she asked, "Do you fear he is angry with you for following Brother Edwin here?"

"Perhaps." Charlotte carefully doubled over the pillowcase and pressed the iron down on it before she went on. "Or perhaps I am more worried that he might not care. Whichever it is, I seem to need his words telling me to come home before I can do so."

Charlotte smoothed the last fold of the pillowcase and laid it with the first one she'd done. With only a moment's hesitation, she pulled out a sheet and went to get a hot iron off the stove. Dulcie smiled at her courage to try the bigger piece and showed her how to fold the sheet to make it fit on the board. When Charlotte finally had the sheet ironed and folded and on the finished table with the other pieces, she felt a moment of pride. She had a blister on her thumb and a burn on her arm, but she had done it. She was capable. She wasn't a helpless young female who couldn't do up her own buttons or boil her own water for tea.

She'd read history books and studied politics at her father's knee. Such pursuits had not injured her mind as some were wont to think would happen when a young woman was interested in learning more than which flower denoted forgiveness or other such useless drivel. And now the Shakers had proven to her that she could accomplish necessary tasks. Her body was as strong and capable as her mind. She could go back to Grayson and begin her life anew.

Then Sister Martha brought her the letter after the evening meal during their time of rest before the families gathered to practice their songs and dancing.

"I have something for you." Sister Martha was so out of breath she could barely get out the words, and Charlotte quickly lifted down a chair from the pegs for her to sit. The old sister eased down on it gratefully as she put her hand over her heart and pulled in a few deep breaths before she was able to say any more. "The stairs get more difficult for me every day. Regrettably my advanced years render me incapable of performing most duties, but I can still help with the delivery of letters, though the task is easier if there are not so many steps to climb." She blew out a puff of air and reached into her pocket to pull out a letter. "This one is from your family in the world."

Charlotte took the letter from her. It wasn't her father's writing. She turned the envelope over to see that its seal was already broken. "It's open."

"Yea, the Ministry must be sure the words in any letter coming to those in our Society are not improper," Sister Martha said.

"Oh." She stared down at the neat, concise letters forming her name. The envelope had been addressed by Selena. Of course she could still believe the letter inside might be from her father as long as she didn't pull it out to see proof otherwise. "And so the words in this one were acceptable?"

"I so assume. I was not the reader. I was simply given the duty of carrying the epistle to you." Sister Martha sat quietly for a moment before she said, "If you have no wish to read it, I can carry it back unread. Some who come among us have no desire to glance backward at the world they left behind, and that serves them well."

"Nay." The Shaker word came easily to her lips as she sat down on the edge of her narrow bed. "I must read it."

"I always think that's best. To read and know instead of wondering. I did much wondering in my younger years."

"How old are you now, Sister Martha?" Charlotte looked over at her. The letter was almost burning her fingers, but still she delayed pulling it out to read. She had the unsettled feeling that reading it might be just another step to change her life forever.

Sister Martha didn't try to rush her even as a bell sounded to summon those in the Gathering Family to the upper room for their meeting time. The other sisters in the room began to file out, but Sister Martha made no move to rise from her chair. So Charlotte stayed seated as well.

Sister Martha waited until the room was empty except for the two of them before she answered. "I am well into my eighties. Perhaps as much as ninety. It's hard to keep an exact count of so many years. What are you? Seventeen?"

Charlotte smiled. "Not so young. I will turn twenty next month. I had planned to be married by then."

"Yea, it has been told us. You and Brother Edwin had such an arrangement. The sin of matrimony can cause many problems. It is good the two of you turned from such transgression and came to us unsullied."

Something in her voice made Charlotte curious. "Were you ever married? Before you became a Believer."

"I rarely bring to mind the early years of my life, but it is true that I was guilty of the sin of matrimony before I joined with the Believers when they first came to this place. My husband had left me and I thought him dead, but our worldly ties had caused us much misery. I have grown greatly in spirit since I came to Harmony Hill. As you can as well if you will put worldly desires behind you. Peace and love are the rewards of a faithful Believer."

"So you are happy here?"

"Happiness." The word was a soft sigh on Sister Martha's breath. She studied Charlotte before she asked, "Is that the reason you delay reading the letter? Because you fear it will not bring you happiness?"

Charlotte looked down at the envelope, then back at Sister Martha's kind face. "Perhaps."

"Ah well, then it is time you learned one of

our teachings. Happiness does not so much depend on circumstances as we think. Within our souls the foundations must abide."

"How do I build such a foundation?"

"Alas, it is not a foundation we can undertake to build ourselves. We must offer the building stones of faith and obedience to the Master Builder so that he can put that foundation in our souls." Sister Martha pushed up out of her chair and hung it back on the pegs before she turned back to Charlotte. "Now read your letter, my sister. You can overcome whatever it says with the help of the Master Builder."

Sister Martha lightly touched Charlotte's cheek before she smiled and shuffled out the door. Charlotte let the silence of the room fall around her. Above her head she could hear the sound of the other sisters and brothers in the house practicing their dances. There was no fury to the sound. The fury of the spirit seemed only to come in the meetinghouse on Sunday. Everything was disciplined and sedate in the practice hours.

She stared once more at Selena's writing on the envelope, and the one prayer she had been able to pray before she came to the Shakers whispered through her mind. *Lord, give me courage.* She took a deep breath, slipped the sheet of stationery out of the envelope, and unfolded it with trembling fingers. The letter was not from her father. At least not directly.

Dearest Charlotte,

It pains me to write this letter on behalf of your father, but he has demanded I do so and as a devoted wife I can do no less than honor his wishes. Charles cannot understand why you would leave the home where he has always attended to your every need as he has never had anything but your best interests at heart. Your irresponsible and ungrateful behavior in the face of that devoted caring has wounded him deeply. In time I feel sure he may be able to look upon this whole silly affair with more sympathy but until I am able to help him understand that young women sometimes make rash and foolish decisions they come to regret and persuade him to look more favorably upon you once more, he has ordered me to inform you that he has no desire to see you or correspond with you at this time. He feels you have deserted him and Grayson and so has washed his hands of you and states he no longer has a daughter.

Perhaps I should not have written that last, but I thought it best for you to realize the extent of the injury you have done him. And at a time when he needed your unfailing support as his staunch Unionist beliefs are causing some problems here at Grayson. It appears this area is quite overrun with those who sympathize with the South and do not see the same need to preserve the Union at all costs as Charles does. It is good he is not up for re-election this summer. Being cloistered in that strange village, you may not be aware of the division happening in families all around us. But at least you should be safe and I hear well fed. Be assured I will so inform you when I have convinced Charles to soften his stance. I trust young Edwin is well.

Your ever loving stepmother, Selena

Charlotte folded the letter and slid it back in the envelope. She sat without moving on the edge of the narrow Shaker bed and let the darkening air of the evening gather around her. Above her head the thumps of the Shakers' feet continued. She pulled off her Shaker cap and stared at its whiteness in her hand. What had she done? It had seemed the only way at the time, but now she could see no way.

What was it Sister Martha had told her? That the foundations of happiness had to reside in one's soul. But her foundations lay in ruins. The other Charlotte, the one waiting to pick up her life at Grayson, was lost. If only she could find

Mellie. Mellie would tell her the other Charlotte could yet be found, but Mellie was the same as lost to her too.

All she had left was this Sister Charlotte. Safe and well fed.

She crumpled the cap in her hand, but then very carefully smoothed it out again and put it back on her head before she stood up and went to the chest to pull the bottom drawer all the way out. She anchored a corner of the letter in the crack where the side and the back of the chest joined above the paper she had wedged there on the first day she was at Harmony Hill. Her fingers caressed that paper before she pulled it out. It was too dark to see now, but she unfolded the paper anyway and stared down at it. She knew the lines that were there. The lines of her face, the other Charlotte, drawn by the artist. By Adam. And instead of her face, she saw his as she wondered where his unexpected roads had taken him.

19

The double Shaker staircases were incredibly beautiful as they rose seemingly without support to the two upper floors. One side of the risers kissed up against the curve of the wall as the stairs wound up in a spiral, but the other side with its curling wooden railing seemed suspended in air. One stairway was for the men and the other for the sisters, stated the old elder with Adam. To Adam's surprise, the Shakers had not shown the least bit of hesitance to have part of their village featured in *Harper's*.

"We wish all to know the peace and serenity of our village, and if that peace can be felt by gazing on a drawing depicting our spiral staircases, then we have no desire to withhold sight of it from those of the world. Yea, we must do all the good we can in all the ways we can as often as we can to all the people we can," Elder Logan said as he stood back to allow Adam clear view of the stairways.

"Sounds like a good creed to have," Adam said.

"Not a creed. Simply our duty as Believers," Elder Logan corrected him mildly.

Adam went to the stairs and ran his hand gently along the curving cherry handrail. Sam was going to be happy. "Who came up with the design?" he asked.

"Some years ago, a young man in our Society, Micajah Burnett, demonstrated a gift for design. The Ministry sent him to school to develop his gift, and his dedicated work brought much good to Harmony Hill and to other Shaker villages as well. It is his design that allows the air to flow freely through our buildings and lets the unhealthy stale air escape through our roofs. Our rooms are full of light because he designed them so. That saves lamp oil and candles and improves our efficiency."

"But whoever designed these stairways surely had beauty in mind," Adam said as he stared up through the spiraling stairs to get their lines in his head.

"Not beauty. Utility and proper conservation of space. True beauty lies in an object's usefulness."

"Do the other buildings have such stairways too?" Adam asked.

"Nay. The more common staircases well serve the purpose in our family houses. If you desire to see them, I will take you there."

"Not right now." Adam stepped back and opened his sketchbook. "It's best I complete the task at hand, but before I leave I would greatly appreciate having a tour of your village." Adam looked over at Elder Logan as he added, "And I would like to also attend a worship meeting if outsiders are allowed to do so."

"At times in the summer we have open meetings for those of the world. While the spirit rarely comes upon our gatherings at those times, the watchers show great curiosity as we go forth to labor the dances. We once thought such open worships might be a way to bring converts into our Society, but history has shown that rarely to be the case. Most watchers from the world are simply curious. I doubt we will open our services to any this year with the unsettledness of the country and the threat of war." Elder Logan studied Adam for a moment. "And why do you wish to watch? Do you have an interest in learning the true Shaker way?"

"No. Only the same curiosity that you spoke of others having." Adam answered with honesty. "And the desire to draw your worship for others who might be curious as well."

"Is everything a drawing to you, Mr. Wade?"

"It is my work," Adam said.

"That is an answer we as Believers can understand. Work is as much a part of our worship here as the dancing that seems to so amuse the world. We believe the Eternal God is a part of any work we do, and therefore it is a grievous sin to do that work in a slipshod manner." Elder Logan peered over Adam's shoulder at the beginning lines of the stairway on his sketchpad. "You have been blessed with talent. Do you allow the Lord to guide your hand?"

Adam smiled and answered without looking up at Elder Logan. "I've always guided my own hand."

"And you prefer that thought?" Elder Logan asked but didn't wait for an answer. "I much prefer the idea of our heavenly Father guiding our occupations as Mother Ann taught us to believe."

"Is she still among you? Your Mother Ann. Would she allow her likeness drawn?"

"Nay, she only lives among us in spirit now, but perhaps you are capturing something of her likeness in the lines of our staircase."

"A Shaker sister might be a better avenue to capturing her spirit," Adam suggested. "Perhaps one who is young and fair of face? Too often I have seen Shakers portrayed in an unflattering light."

"That matters naught to us insofar as our outward looks are concerned. Beauty as the world judges it is not important to us. Only the inward peace and love that shines through from the windows to our souls." The elder pointed to his eyes. "That is the desire of a Believer."

Adam looked up from his sketch pad at the elder. While the man's face was deeply lined from years of living, his light brown eyes sparkled with the energy of a much younger man, and he seemed to radiate a calm acceptance of the world around him. "I do see peace in your eyes."

The elder stared back at him. "I fear I cannot say the same of your eyes, my brother."

"What do you see?" Adam asked with an amused smile.

"You ask that question in some jest, but I will answer with none." The elder looked at him with gentle kindness as he said, "I see someone forever seeking."

"Seeking what?" Adam's smile faded as he waited for the elder's answer. Somehow the conversation had been turned from him trying to understand the Shakers to trying to understand himself. When Elder Logan kept looking at him and didn't speak right away, Adam tried to rush his response. "Truth? Fame? Success? Love? What?"

The elder smiled now with a tinge of sad understanding as he finally answered, "That is a question only the seeker can answer. We here at Harmony Hill know the answers we seek, and we guide those who come into our village to live in such a way that true and worthy answers may be found for each of them."

"Do you try to convert all who come into your village?" Adam laughed to cover up his unease.

"Only those who might be seeking our answers."

"That's not me. I'm just here to do some illustrations of your buildings and perhaps some of your people if you agree to it. Maybe I could draw you." It was easier to think of lines on a paper than questions of the soul.

Before the elder could answer, a young Shaker sister came in the door. Even before she spoke, Adam was shaping the lines of her face. The cap hid most of her dark hair except for a few tendrils along the side of her face. Her skin was fair and her eyes even bluer than his brother Jake's. She wore nothing to enhance her beauty, but there was a pureness to her face that made jewels or lace unnecessary. She almost glowed with innocence. With little thought of what he was doing, he turned the page on his sketchpad and began capturing her face. She was the perfect Shaker sister he had asked to draw.

She turned her eyes downward at his blatant stare and spoke to Elder Logan. "Forgive me for interrupting. I seek Sister Altha. I thought she asked me to find her here, but I must be mistaken." She eased backward toward the door as she spoke.

"Nay, you are in the proper place, Sister Gemma. Sister Altha asked that you wait here for a moment while she spoke with Eldress Susan. And that is well, since our visitor was seeking one such as you to draw. Do you mind if he captures your image on his paper?"

"Nay, I do not mind," the young sister said with a quick smile toward Adam. "Not so long as such is not improper and I don't have to stand motionless overlong. A posture of silent stillness is not a gift I have attained as yet."

"I sketch very quickly," Adam assured her and was rewarded with another smile. He drew with fast strokes of his pencil. "What are your gifts then, Sister?"

She seemed disconcerted by his direct question and lowered her eyes to the floor again.

Elder Logan answered for her. "Sister Gemma is gifted with kindness and patience. She often guides our novitiate sisters in adjusting to their new life. She is working with a new sister now." Elder Logan turned toward the young sister. "How is Sister Charlotte doing? She seemed to have a conflicted spirit when last I saw her."

Adam's hand froze and his head came up at the name. But there were many Charlottes. The Charlotte he longed to see was in Virginia. He looked back down at his sketch and began shading in the girl's face as she answered the elder.

"She works hard to satisfy the duties required of her, but she has not yet left behind her worldly thinking. Sister Martha said she received a letter from the world yesterday, and she seems much subdued today." A fleeting look of concern chased across the young sister's face.

"Has she confessed her worry to you?" Elder Logan seemed to have no concern that Adam was listening to them talk of the new sister convert.

"Nay. She is to make confession to Sister Altha, not me."

"I see. Where is our new sister now?"

"In the ironing room at the Gathering Family House. I am not gifted with pressing. I always scorch something, but Sister Charlotte is in capable hands with Sister Dulcie helping her to learn the proper methods while I assist Sister Altha this week. Sister Altha has need to write to our sister societies and her arthritis makes such difficult."

Adam couldn't keep from smiling at the thought of the Charlotte he knew, the senator's daughter, trying to press anything other than perhaps a flower between the pages of a book. While she might not have been the usual Southern belle with her peculiar penchant for honesty, she certainly would have never picked up an iron. She had servants for that. He doubted she would even know what an iron looked like. He shook his head a little at the image that came to mind of Charlotte in Shaker dress, wielding an iron. That was too ridiculous to even consider. He would not find Charlotte Vance among the Shakers.

An older woman came in the door behind the young sister called Gemma. Her eyes narrowed and her mouth screwed up in a sour look when she saw Adam. It was the same old sister he'd seen on the path weeks before. The woman whose sketch had made Sam Johnson shudder. But Adam felt as if the spirits were smiling down on him as he began sketching her face in the corner above the young sister's. The contrast was remarkable.

"What goes on here?" she asked, turning her frown on Elder Logan. "I thought this man was to draw our stairways. If so, why does it appear Sister Gemma is the object of his eye?"

Elder Logan didn't seem upset by the old sister's cross tone. "He wanted to draw a young sister, and so when Sister Gemma came, I allowed him to sketch her face. I saw no harm in that."

"There's always harm when one of the world comes among us."

"Please, Sister Altha, we must be considerate of our guest."

"Yea, it is so." The old sister turned toward Adam and almost lost her frown. "I ask your forbearance and forgiveness. I spoke without kindness."

"Don't be concerned on my account. I'm grateful to be allowed to do the drawings. Especially of the stairways. My editor is very anxious to have that illustration for his newspaper." Adam gave her the smile that generally won him whatever he wanted from women, but it only brought a scowl back to her face as she ushered the younger sister down the hall and into one of the rooms out of sight. The door snapped shut behind them.

"I hope you spoke truth when you said you sketched quickly, for I have doubts that Sister Altha will allow Sister Gemma to return." Elder Logan smoothed his hand over his mouth as if to rub away a smile.

"She didn't seem too happy with the idea."

Adam turned his sketchbook back to the lines of stairs climbing the wall. "But worry not. I got enough. My mind captures the image of a face as I sketch, much the way those newfangled picture boxes do, and then I can recall that image and finish the details of the sketch even if the subject is no longer actually in front of my eyes. For some reason I have more difficulty with inanimate objects, when it would seem that those would be the easier to draw since they don't move."

"Take all the time you need to properly do your work. One of Mother Ann's basic teachings that all Believers must take to heart is to do our work as if we have a thousand years to live, and as if we might die tomorrow. Such advice would serve even an artist of the world well, I should think."

"I hope it doesn't take me a thousand years to get this right," Adam said as he rubbed away one of his lines. Simply getting the correct curvature of the handrail wasn't enough. He wanted to capture its innate grace.

Later, with three sketches of Sam's stairways safely tucked away, Adam wandered out of the building where those of the world were greeted and lodged. He would sleep in one of the upper rooms come nightfall. When he had followed Elder Logan up one of those beautiful stairways to the room he'd been assigned, Adam had been more than pleased with the light that had flooded the room. If he rose early enough in the morning, he should be able to complete the drawings to leave with Elder Logan, who had promised to post them to Sam come Monday morning. It was an added convenience that the Shakers operated a postal office right there in the village.

"We try to be self-sufficient inasmuch as we are able," Elder Logan had told him. "And then we market our excess to the world along with the many other items we produce with an eye on the needs of those with whom we trade. However, I must confess the current threat of conflict very much concerns us as it threatens to close our trade routes. You say you are recently from Washington. Were any there yet seeking a way to peace?"

"I wasn't privy to the circle of power, but the city is full of men responding to the President's call to arms. Peace did not seem likely."

The elder frowned and shook his head sadly. "I had feared it was such from the reports in the papers. Our traders who have come back from the states that have fallen away from the Union tell us the populace there also talk of nothing but the first battle to come. They are much more interested in buying guns than brooms and seed. As if there will no longer be need to continue sweeping or eating. And alas, that may become too true for many if bullets start flying."

"At least here in Kentucky I've heard the

government is voting to stay neutral." Adam tried to offer a cheerful word for the worried man.

The frown on Elder Logan's face grew darker. "I do not see how such a policy will be possible to enforce. Already we hear of enlistment camps being set up on the state's borders both to the north and to the south to gather men into their armies. Thankfully we gather only the fruits of peace here. If only those of the world desired to do the same."

Now with the sun sinking lower in the west, Adam studied the Shaker men and women he passed on Harmony Hill's pathways to see if they carried the same peace as Elder Logan so obviously did. It was hard to tell, for many of the people he met kept their heads bent with their eyes intent on the ground at their feet. Some who did glance up at him seemed to begrudge his presence on their pathways, as if simply being near one from the world might taint the peace they sought. A few turned and followed a different path that kept them from passing close to him.

A bell rang, perhaps to signal the end of the working day, because more men and women began filing out of the various buildings and walking toward the larger family houses. Adam moved off the pathway to keep from being an obstruction to their orderly flow. He leaned against a tree and wondered how it would be to live such a cloistered life.

He searched their faces as they passed by for some hint of why they might have withdrawn from the world. Were they simply seeking the perfect life of peace that Elder Logan seemed to have found? But many didn't carry the elder's peaceful expression. Some looked tired from their day's labor. Other faces were as devoid of expression as a smooth river stone. Their blank looks made Adam wonder what feelings they were taking such pains to conceal.

The men's faces were easier to see than the women's, whose features were shaded by their white bonnets. The few female faces he did glimpse brought to mind the old sister's suspicious look rather than young Gemma's easy smile. Perhaps because it was only the older sisters who dared look his way. The younger women kept their eyes so diligently on the path in front of them that Adam would not have been surprised to see one of them stoop down to retrieve a lost coin or some other bit of treasure.

The paths were emptying as the houses swallowed up the Shakers. Only a few stragglers remained, and those walked with quick steps to keep from being late for whatever was to happen next in the village. The evening meal perhaps. The sun had disappeared below the horizon and twilight was gathering. Adam felt the grumble of his own stomach as he pushed away from the tree to head back to his assigned room where

Elder Logan had said someone would bring his meal.

It seemed a strange life. Everything so ordered and serene. Elder Logan claimed all strife had been removed for those who dwelt there, but how could one live in a tranquil sea day in and day out? A man needed the water of his life stirred by breezes. Else he stayed in the doldrums and wasted away for lack of challenge. And yet here were all of these men and women seeking those doldrums. It was more than Adam could understand. And certainly nothing he could ever want.

He was so deep in thought that he didn't notice the two sisters coming toward him on the pathway until the older sister put out a hand to stop the other, a young black woman, from passing too closely to him. He moved off the path to give way to them. The older sister stepped faster to move between him and the younger sister. In the fading light it was difficult to see the young sister's black face under the white cap even though she didn't duck her head away from him. Instead her eyes widened in surprise as she peeked around the older sister at him.

He stepped forward to get a better look at her face. "Do I know you?" he asked.

She seemed to want to stop, but the older sister didn't allow it as she put an arm around the girl and hurried her past Adam. "Come, Sister Melana. It is not proper for us to speak with those of the world without first receiving permission from the elders and eldresses."

"But I only wanted to ask if he'd come for her."

"His business here is no concern of ours."

"But . . ." The girl tried to look back at him, but the other sister tugged her along.

Adam watched them until they disappeared into the brick family house. Melana. Not a familiar name, but even so, something about the woman's face tugged at his memory. If he could have gotten a better look at her, then he might place where he'd seen her. Perhaps she'd been a servant from one of the great houses he'd visited in Frankfort, and now she'd found freedom here with the Shakers.

But who in the world would she think he might have come for? He shook his head a little as he started back down the path. She must have mistaken him for someone else. He knew no one among the Shakers.

20

The day after Selena's letter came, Charlotte got up at the sound of the rising bell. She knelt in pretense of prayer. She put on the Shaker dress and cap and went into their biting room where she forced food into her stomach. She listened to

Dulcie's chatter in the pressing room as she pushed the iron across the fabric. And she was glad for the toil that brought sweat to her face and made her shoulders ache, because it took some of her mind off the ache in her heart.

She had lost her home. Her life. She had nothing. She who had always planned and arranged and made things happen as she wished. Now there were no wishes left. Grayson would never be hers. She had nothing left but this shell of Charlotte Mayda Vance that the ones around her called Sister Charlotte. Her father had cut her off. In spite of Selena's words to the contrary, Charlotte knew the woman would see that the wound never healed. She had outflanked Charlotte once more.

She couldn't blame it all on Selena. She was the one who had let foolish pride set her feet on this strange path. She should have stayed at Grayson and kept her place. They couldn't have forced her to go to Virginia. Her father wouldn't have pushed her out the door. But no, Charlotte had gone through that door herself. Had run out that door.

The thought tormented her as she pushed the heavy irons over the woven fabric of the sheets. She didn't want to think. She closed her mind to everything but the task at hand. Pick up one iron and move it back and forth until it cooled and then pick up another one to do the same.

Dulcie touched her shoulder when it was time for the evening meal and led her out of the pressing room to where Gemma waited. Gemma was smiling, talking about a man drawing a staircase. Charlotte paid scant attention as she let Gemma's words float on the surface of her mind like leaves on a still pond. If she started listening, really listening, her mind might awaken and she would have to think of losing Grayson again.

She sat at the evening meal and didn't dip any food onto her plate even when Gemma edged the bowls of potatoes and beans closer to her. Sister Altha frowned at her across the table but could say nothing because speaking wasn't allowed in the room where they ate. Each group of four Shakers had their own set of serving bowls in front of them so that no one had to ask for a bowl to be passed. The food was good and plentiful, but Gemma had greatly stressed that Charlotte must Shaker her plate, which meant she must eat every bite of whatever she might take from the bowls. Charlotte had forced down the morning meal and the meal at noon, but now she only stared at her empty plate and was glad no food was there. What was it Selena had written? That at least she would be well fed.

After the meal was over, they once again knelt in silent prayer before filing out of the biting room to retire to their rooms for a time of rest and meditation.

Sister Altha stopped Charlotte in the hallway. "Are you unwell, Sister Charlotte?" There was no hint of sympathy in her voice.

"Nay," Charlotte answered.

"You did not eat."

"I felt no appetite."

"A Believer must take care of her body in order to maintain proper health and strength for her duties."

"Yea, so you have told me. I will eat tomorrow." Charlotte said the words she thought Sister Altha wished to hear. She just wanted the woman to go away so she could return to her dark box and shut away all thought.

But Sister Altha was not satisfied with Charlotte's answer. "Is there some wrong you have need to confess? Sin can fester in one's soul and lead to blackness of the mind. But with proper confession, Mother Ann can bring your spirit back into harmony."

"Yea, so you have told me."

Sister Altha stood unmoving in front of her waiting for Charlotte to say more. When Charlotte didn't speak, Sister Altha's face tightened with disapproval before she said, "I fear, my sister, that you seek the blackness of sin and that your presence here is nothing but a farce."

"Nay, Sister Altha. I want to learn the Shaker way." What other choice did she have now? She had no place to go. She would become Sister

Charlotte. She would learn to dance in worship. She would work with her hands. She would never again stand and let a servant dress her in a ball gown she could not button or unbutton. That Charlotte was gone, lost to her own foolishness.

That didn't mean she would never see Grayson again. She would. Somehow. Some way. But until she figured out that new way, she'd bide her time here among these strange people where, as Selena had written, she would be safe and well fed. The war that was threatening the country seemed far removed from this place where peace was sought by all true Believers. And sometimes found. Edwin claimed to have found it. Gemma wore it like a crown of light. Eldress Sadie preached it. Sister Martha knew it. Sister Altha demanded it.

Peace. If it was all around her, then surely some of it would wear off on her no matter what else was happening at Grayson or in the country. She had told Adam Wade she was going to do the unexpected. But she had not expected the road she chose to be so full of crooks and turns that even she had not foreseen.

She remembered Mellie's words as they rode into the village a few weeks earlier. How she'd said they were being swallowed by a whale just as Jonah had been in the Bible story. The village seemed that different and strange. But the three days in the belly of Jonah's whale was long past, and here she remained with no hope of being spit out for a second chance for many more days.

All she could do was bend her spirit, wipe away her thoughts, and search for the right words to pray when she knelt in obedience to the Shaker rules. They did not order her to silently pray any special words. The prayer was to be from her heart. Perhaps she could discover the proper words to convince the Lord to let her be spit out of the belly of the whale the same as Jonah was once he prayed with a reformed heart.

Mellie. At least that was one thing that had gone right with her plan. Mellie was as safe and well fed as she was.

Charlotte was glad when Sister Altha ceased speaking and left her alone in the hallway. She was relieved when Gemma didn't think it necessary to accompany her to the outhouse. She welcomed the cool dark air that made her feel even more invisible. She wanted to walk into the shadows and dwell there for a while. Perhaps forever.

"Miss Lottie." The whisper came from the corner of the building. "Over here, Miss Lottie."

Charlotte moved toward the sound of Mellie's voice, but couldn't see her. A hand reached out and pulled her to the side of the building. Even with Mellie directly in front of her, Charlotte could barely make out her shape in the darkness.

Her cap was gone, along with the large white collar and apron from her dress, and her black face melted into the night.

Mellie snatched off Charlotte's cap and turned her toward the building. "Here," she said as she handed the cap to Charlotte. "We won't be as easy to spot with the white hidden."

"What are you doing, Mellie?"

"Same as you. I told them I had to relieve myself, and then I hid out here hopin' and prayin' you'd come along without your guard before they come huntin' for me. I prayed strong as I could, and praises be, he give me the answer I wanted. The one I had to have. Thank the good Lord above." She kept her voice low, just above a whisper. "That's one thing these Shaker folks has got right. All the prayin' time. But they done messed up on a bunch of other things."

Charlotte grabbed Mellie's shoulders. "Slow down and tell me what's going on."

"I guess I better. They liable to show up after us any minute and there is a lot to tell." She rushed out the words. "Has he come for you?"

"Who?" The black sadness filled her heart. "Not Father. He . . ." She hesitated and then pushed the words out around the lump that wanted to form in her throat. She hadn't cried when she read the letter or since, but now with Mellie there beside her, the tears wanted to break free. "He says I'm no longer his daughter."

"Who says? Massah Charles?" Mellie's voice carried disbelief. "That can't be right."

"I got a letter."

"Well, that woman must've made him write it. She got your daddy under some kind of devil spell."

"I've not only lost Father to her, Mellie. I've lost Grayson." Charlotte choked back a sob.

"You'll figure somethin' out, Miss Lottie. Don't you always." Mellie put her arms around her and pulled her close. "Didn't you figure out a way to keep that woman from sellin' me down the river? And that wasn't no easy thing."

"I'm glad I did that much right." This time Charlotte couldn't hold the sob in.

Mellie leaned back from her and shook her a little. "Now don't you go cryin' on me or I'll never get what needs sayin' said."

Charlotte swallowed hard and peered at Mellie's face, but her expression was hidden in the shadowy darkness. "All right. What needs saying?"

Mellie didn't speak right away, as if now that she had the chance to talk, she didn't know which words to say. Charlotte didn't think her heart could grow any heavier, but she was wrong. Even before Mellie spoke the words, Charlotte knew what they were going to be.

"I don't know if I ought to tell you this or not, but I's always trusted you, Miss Lottie. Nate's runnin' away. Goin' north." Again she hesitated before she pushed out the rest of her words. "I'm goin' with him, Miss Lottie."

"No, you can't do that. It won't be safe. He might get caught, and if he gets caught and you're with him, then no telling what might happen." Charlotte grabbed Mellie's arms and held onto her as though she'd never let go.

Mellie didn't try to pull away. "I has to, Miss Lottie. I love him." Her voice sounded sad, excited, and frightened all at the same time.

Charlotte loosened her hold and pulled in a deep breath. She didn't know what to say.

Mellie put her hands over Charlotte's and pulled them away from her arms. She held her hands softly as she went on. "I loves you too, Miss Lottie. You knows I do. And Mammy. Can't nobody love their mother more than I love Mammy, but we's already apart. Her there cookin' for Massah Charles 'til you figure out a way to get her free. And me here." She squeezed Charlotte's hands a little before she turned them loose. "I don't know as how I can explain, but this way I feel for Nate, it's different love. I has to go with him. Even if I die, I has to 'cause I'll die in my heart if I don't."

"Wait and get the Shakers to take you across the river. They take trips to their other villages in the north. Tell them you want to live at one of them." Charlotte's mind was racing, trying to think of a better way. "Then you can run away from there to meet up with Nate."

"You always has good plans, but I's already decided. The' ain't no turnin' back. I'm goin' tonight. Now. I got my papers." She touched her bosom and Charlotte heard a rustle of paper. "They give them to me to keep. So I'd feel free, they said. I want to feel free, Miss Lottie. Really free and not just stuck here with these folks who has a funny idea of free with all their rules and watchin' eyes. You don't really want to be here either, do you?"

"I don't know. I can't go home. So where else could I go?" Charlotte said.

"What about him? Has he come for you?"

"Has who come for me? What in the world are you talking about?" Charlotte frowned at her.

"That artist gentleman."

"Adam Wade?" Charlotte stared at Mellie with disbelief. She couldn't really be meaning that Adam was there at Harmony Hill.

"Right. The artist man. He was on the path when me and Sister Cora come back from the washhouse after our workin' time."

"Are you sure?" Charlotte asked with doubt in her voice even as she was remembering Gemma's chatter about somebody drawing the spiral staircases in the visitors' house. She hadn't paid attention to the words then. She was too busy shutting everything out, but now they echoed in her brain. She'd said the man from the world had even drawn her likeness.

"Sure as night follows day. We passed right by him. But Sister Cora, she wouldn't let me say nothin' to him. More of them rules."

"Did he know you?"

"He didn't act like it. It was goin' on dark and me with the Shaker garb on. Well, it ain't no wonder he didn't know me. He only talked to me that one time at the party anyhow. It was Mammy he drew the picture of. She liked that."

"He drew my picture too." Charlotte thought of the drawing hidden behind the drawer in the chest. But the face on that paper was the old Charlotte. The lost Charlotte. Not this woebegone Sister Charlotte who followed after the other sisters like a blind sheep and bent her will to theirs.

"He done more than that." Mellie leaned her head over very close to Charlotte's face until Charlotte could see her eyes gleaming in the early darkness. "Remember I saw you in the garden 'fore he left, and I already tol' you a man kisses a woman like that he aims to be back."

"He can't be here for me. How would he even know I'm here?" Charlotte tried to ignore the way hope fluttered awake in her heart just at Mellie's crazy imagining that Adam Wade had come for her.

"Somebody coulda tol' him. Maybe your papa."

"Father wouldn't tell him. He wouldn't tell anybody. Me being here is not only an embarrassment to him, the general knowledge of it might cost him votes. Think how the opposing party could use it against him. The senator's daughter running away from home. Dancing like a heathen in church."

"Not like heathens. Leastways most of the time. Most times they could be right at Grayson dancin' in the big room," Mellie said.

"But not for the same reason."

"For sure. It ain't to catch a man." Mellie blew a snort of air out her nose. Silence stretched between them for a moment before she went on. "You can go home, Miss Lottie. The Massah, he won't stay mad at you once he sees you face-to-face.

He'll be like that daddy in the Bible what runs to meet his wayward boy." Mellie's voice was soft, urging.

"There wasn't a stepmother in that story," Charlotte said.

"You's right there," Mellie agreed, but then her voice softened again. "But he's loved you longer than he has her."

Charlotte stared down at the ground as she said, "I can't go home. At least not yet. I'm not starving. There's no need for me to look at the pig food with hungry eyes like the prodigal son in that story. There's plenty of food here. I am safe and well fed." Charlotte's ending words were flat, without feeling.

"Then if you don't want to go home, go find that artist feller. He's got to be still here. It was nigh dark when I saw him."

"No." The word came out sharp and clipped.

"I's hearin' a lot in that no, Miss Lottie. I know you good as I knows myself. Maybe better. You in love with that man."

Charlotte didn't have to be able to see Mellie's face to know how she was staring at her with narrowed eyes, seeing straight through her even in the darkness. She didn't try to argue with Mellie. Not now. Not when her heart was already too bruised to think about love. Instead she grabbed Mellie's wrist. "You can't tell him I'm here."

"You's right there. I can't tell him nothin'. Remember. I'm leavin' with Nate. Soon's we get through huggin' and cryin' our goodbyes." Mellie put her other hand gently over Charlotte's. "You's the one that needs to tell him. You's the one he's come for."

"He's not here for me. He's here for his work. To draw the Shakers." She said the words as firmly as she could, not for Mellie, but to keep hope from spreading its wings and trying to take flight in her own heart. Adam Wade had no plans that included Charlotte. No one did. Not even Mellie.

"Then ask that sour old Sister Altha to let him draw you." There was a smile in Mellie's voice. "That ought to get things rollin' in the right direction."

"Oh, Mellie, I don't know what I'll do without you." Charlotte pulled her close and breathed in the familiar scent of her hair and skin. "I'm so afraid for you."

"Don't you be scared for me. You done give me a chance. You give me my papers. They say up north a black face don't have to be turned down to the ground all the time. That a person like me can be hired out and collect her own pay. Nate and me, we'll be all right. The Union army ain't signin' Negroes up to fight, but they's usin' them to build bridges and roads. He hears tell that them Yankees ain't all that worried about whether a man has papers. Not so long as he has a strong back."

"I'll pray for you," Charlotte said and she meant it. She'd have a purpose now when she knelt to pray as the Shakers demanded. She reluctantly stepped back from Mellie.

"And me for you." Then in the darkness Charlotte saw Mellie's teeth shine as her smile spread across her face. "That you and that artist gentlemen will meet up in some more gardens. Maybe he'll ask you home to walk in his garden."

"I don't think he even has a home."

"You don't have to have walls and a roof, Miss

Lottie. Where the most of your heart is, that's where home can be." Mellie touched Charlotte's cheek. "Mine's with Nate, but I'll be leavin' a chunk of it here with you." She pulled her hand away as she turned to go. She stopped before she went two steps and turned back. With tears in her voice, she said, "When you go home to Grayson and see Mammy agin, you tell her I'm takin' her love ever' bit with me."

And then she was gone. Melting away in the darkness. Charlotte stood very still staring after her. She could just make out Mellie, and then another figure rose up out of the grass and joined her before the two disappeared into the trees beyond the village houses. Charlotte watched the spot for a long time before she finally looked up at the dark sky and was glad for the clouds that covered the stars and moon. "Keep it dark, dear Lord, and lead her steps safely over the river."

No prayer had ever risen more sincerely from her heart. She stepped back up on the pathway and positioned her cap over her hair. She would not think about her father or Grayson. She would not think about Adam Wade somewhere in the village. He had not come to Harmony Hill seeking her. If he saw her in the Shaker dress, he would laugh at her foolishness. It was all a game with Adam. A game he had won with the kiss he had stolen from her before he left. He would have no interest in playing another round. She could not let him see her here.

She mashed her lips together tightly so that she wouldn't recall the softness of his lips on hers. She would not allow her mind to run after him. She would not allow her heart to yearn for his touch. Mellie was wrong. She wasn't in love with him. It had been a game to her too. A silly game she had no chance of winning any more than she'd had any chance of pulling Edwin away from the Shakers. She had gravely under-estimated Edwin's need for spiritual peace and order in his life.

And now she would continue down the path she had chosen perhaps without proper thought, but even so her feet were upon it. If she was going to forget about Charlotte Mayda Vance and become simply Sister Charlotte seeking the gifts of simplicity and peaceful harmony, then she would do it the best she could. She would dwell on obedience and prayer the way Sister Altha told her to. She would learn to work. She would let more sincere prayers rise from her soul. And she would be safe and well fed.

The next morning, she filed out of her room with all the other sisters when the village bell rang to summon them to meeting. She didn't sing loudly, but she did add her voice to the gathering song. She went into the meetinghouse determined to be a proper novitiate. She had not expected to see Adam Wade on a bench just inside the door. He had his sketchbook open, drawing feverishly. She turned her head away before he could look up and see her face.

The Shaker mother must have taken pity on her at that moment and moved Sister Martha up beside her instead of Sister Altha. She took hold of Sister Martha's arm and whispered, "I feel sick, Sister Martha. I fear I might lose my breakfast. Please may I return to my room?"

"My dear sister, you are pale as a sheet." Sister Martha's wrinkled face looked concerned. "Lean on me and I will take you across to the infirmary."

Charlotte peeked out of the corner of her eyes. Adam had raised his head and was looking her way. She couldn't let him recognize her. She couldn't. He would think she had lost her mind. And he wouldn't be too wrong. A tremble chased through her as she tugged her cap down to cover her face.

Sister Martha patted her arm. "There, there, child. Calm yourself. We will find some medicine to ease your stomach."

Charlotte attempted a weak smile toward the old woman as they caused a disruption in the orderly stream of sisters coming in the door and pushed past them out into the open air, but she doubted there was medicine for what ailed her.

Her heart was pounding at the thought of the artist in the room behind her. If only he had come for her.

As she let the old sister lead her across to the large stone building, Charlotte looked over her shoulder at the last of the sisters going in the meetinghouse. She tried to tell herself she was glad she'd escaped without Adam seeing her. She was. She couldn't have borne his laughter. Yet each step away from the meetinghouse took more effort as her heart yearned to once more stand in front of him, gaze into his blue gray eyes, and hear his voice in her ears.

With a start, Charlotte realized Mellie was right. Charlotte had allowed herself to fall in love with Adam Wade. Oh dear heavenly Father. She had done nothing right for weeks.

21

By the time the big bell sounded to summon the Shakers to worship, Elder Logan had already ushered Adam inside the meetinghouse and to a bench just inside the doors. Adam would have preferred the opposite side of the large open room to get a better view of the Shakers' faces as they came in, but he didn't complain as he settled on the bench with his sketchpad to wait. There would be plenty of faces and scenes to capture from any direction.

His fingers had been tingling with the anticipation of sketching something new and different ever since the elder had informed Adam after breakfast that he would be allowed to do illustrations of their worship experience.

"As long as you behave respectfully," the old man had added.

Adam didn't plan to be anything but respectful. At least outwardly. His inward thoughts were between him and the good Lord. Not that he expected the Lord to pay much attention to anything he thought. The Lord would be more than occupied with listening to the prayers his faithful worshipers all across the country would be sending up to him on this Sunday morning or maybe watching these Shakers dance their worship to him.

Adam hadn't expected the Shakers to start singing before they were inside the building, but minutes after the bell rang, one voice began and others joined in, the sound growing stronger by the minute. The Shakers' voices lifted into the air, alerting the Lord that they were coming. It was a sound of holiness. A sound of deep commitment. Something he'd never felt except to his art. But as he listened, chills walked up and down his spine.

Then as each Shaker stepped through the door

into the meetinghouse—the men through one door and the women through another—he or she fell silent. Inside there was only the sound of soft-soled shoes moving across the wooden floor to the benches while outside the song went on.

Adam searched through the faces. Not because he expected to know any of the Shakers, but because he wanted to understand these people as he sketched them. Why had they chosen to abstain from the normal impulses of life to dedicate themselves to worship and working in this cloistered community? He supposed he was dedicated to work. He'd given up most of the usual pursuits of a man his age and instead lived in pursuit of his next picture. But that work was for him. It wasn't worship, as Elder Logan claimed the Shakers' work to be.

So many people. Many more than he had expected. He'd seen them on the pathways, but it seemed different when they all filed into the building. He spotted Edwin Gilbey. So the man had done as he said and come to live in the village. He saw the young sister, Gemma, and mentally reviewed his sketch of her to be sure he'd done justice to her beautiful face. He let his eyes dwell extra long on the few black faces under the caps all the sisters wore, but he didn't see the black sister who'd tried to talk to him on the pathway the night before. Or perhaps he simply didn't recognize her in the light of the day.

But there was the older sister who had hurried the two of them past him. Her face, so stern and unyielding the night before, now looked troubled as she glanced to the left and right as though searching for someone. Perhaps the same sister his eyes were seeking. The one who thought he might be at Harmony Hill to carry someone away from the Shakers' paradise. When the woman caught him watching her, she glared at him without welcome before going on across the room to take her place on the benches.

Adam pushed aside the distraction of his curiosity about the missing black sister to start drawing the Shakers spilling into the meeting-house. A disturbance at the sisters' door pulled his attention away from his sketch as one of the sisters abruptly turned to go the opposite direction. Not a usual occurrence if the frowns that darkened the other sisters' faces were any indication as she pushed between them back toward the door. An ancient-looking Shaker sister took hold of the younger one's elbow and joined the rebel Shaker sister moving against the flow of women entering the meetinghouse.

He wondered at first if the younger one might be the Negro sister he had been watching for, but then she reached up to pull her cap down and her hand was white as a lily. Not the hand of a working woman, but the hand of a lady. He kept his eyes on the top of her cap as she and the old sister managed to make it past the line of inflowing sisters to the door. Something about her tickled his memory.

He stood up to follow her for a better look, but a Shaker brother stepped in front of him. "You must stay on the visitors' bench until all are inside and, then if you wish to leave our meeting you must do so quietly out the brothers' door, my friend." His voice was firm. He looked to be in his middle years with a barrel chest and muscular arms that stretched tight the sleeves of his dark coat. There was no way Adam could push him aside to go check out the departing sister if the man didn't give ground.

"Sorry." Adam stayed where he was. "I'm not accustomed to the separate doors for the sexes. I was simply concerned for the sister who was leaving. Do you think she was ill?"

"If so, Sister Martha will see to it that she has proper care." The man settled his eyes on Adam for a moment before he asked, "Did you know her in the world before she came here?"

"I'm not sure. I didn't get a good look at her, but something about her seemed familiar. Who is she?"

"She's new to our Society and her name escapes my memory. There are many sisters." The man looked over his shoulder toward the sisters' door now empty as the last of the Shakers had come into the building. "I can ask another if you have need to know, but our meeting is commencing and silence at the proper times is expected."

"Yes, of course. Forgive me. I promised Elder Logan I would abide by the rules and not disrupt your service in any way."

"That would be well."

It wasn't exactly a threat, but Adam noted that the man sat on a bench near him instead of crossing the room to join the other Shaker brethren as they sat ramrod straight on their rows of benches, facing the sisters perched primly on like benches across from them. For a brief moment, Adam considered breaking his promise and doing something outrageous like asking one of the sisters to dance, simply because he hated rules for rules' sake. He glanced over at the Shaker brother who continued to watch him warily. There was little doubt the man would escort Adam out of the building and perhaps the village if he had such a lapse of good sense. So he swallowed his penchant for rebellion, turned to a fresh sheet in his sketchpad, and settled down to work.

The first dances were sedate enough. The Shakers marched back and forth and then made circles within circles as the lines of men and women wove around each other in obviously practiced patterns of movement. Some of the faces were animated as they sang and danced. Others were stiff and without expression.

Occasionally on some signal that Adam never caught, the entire body would clap their hands or stomp their feet. There were no musical instruments other than the voices of the singers. The songs were simple and repetitious and the dances almost hypnotic as they shuffled back and forth in time to the voices.

Then just as Adam was wondering if all the reports of the Shakers' wild dancing had been nothing more than stories, the mood in the building changed. He could almost feel the charge in the air when the singers picked up the tempo and many of the dancers also started singing. The sound bounced off the walls and sent some of the dancers into a frenzy as the order of the dance completely broke down. A good number of the men and women began to throw their hands and feet out wildly as they leaped about in no particular fashion while shouts and screams against the devil took the place of the singing. Rules had obviously flown out the window, and those Shakers under the spirit were dancing and shouting in whatever way the spirit led them.

Adam stopped sketching and stared. He spotted Edwin Gilbey with his eyes closed and trembling violently before he collapsed to the floor. A couple of the brethren pulled him off to the side. He saw the stern sister who had worn such a dark frown as she had shooed the young

Sister Gemma from his sight the day before now wearing a peaceful, otherworldly look on her face as she spun in place with her hands lifted to heaven. A few of the younger-looking Shaker men were jumping into the air and making whooping noises with their hands clapping against their mouths as if they were children playing Indians.

A Shaker woman stopped her leaping directly in front of Adam to stare at his face as she shouted, "Away from me, Satan." She pushed the palms of her open hands toward him and began stomping, and the intensity of her feeling twisted her plain features into something fierce. Others caught the stomping fever from her until the building vibrated with the banging of feet against the floor. Some added to the noise by slapping their hands on the benches as if they were drums.

The man Adam had thought remained close by to guard the Shakers against his presence now moved in front of Adam to protect him from the fury that had overtaken so many of the Shakers but that seemed not to have affected him in any manner. Adam looked over the man's shoulder and caught sight of Elder Logan. He wasn't stomping or shouting, but was smiling serenely as he stood like an oasis of peace in the midst of the bedlam. Adam picked up his pencil and drew as quickly as he could. He wanted to capture that peace amid the fury.

Then as suddenly as it had started the furor died away, and those who had collapsed on the floor either crawled to the benches or were carried there by others while the remaining dancers began the orderly sedate marching back and forth. The singers' voices controlled the tempo of the meeting once more. Adam listened to the words of the song as his pen flew across the page almost without thought.

> O the simple gifts of God, they're
> flowing like an ocean,
> And I will strive with all my might to
> gather in my portion.
> I love, I love the gifts of God. I love
> to be partaker,
> And I will labor day and night to
> be an honest Shaker.

The singers repeated the song until all the Shakers had recovered from the fervor of their worship and began filing out of the building. Adam followed the last man out the proper men's door to watch the lines of Shakers walking back to their houses in disciplined columns of two. An odd people. He had thought to come among them, draw their faces, and be able to understand why they lived as they lived, but some things were beyond his understanding.

He didn't stay for the midday meal. Instead

he took the food Elder Logan had kindly asked the sisters to pack for Adam's journey and headed his horse toward Frankfort. Before he went back east, he wanted to check out how the state's legislature was doing at maintaining a neutral stance and staying out of the coming conflict. Adam aimed to maintain a neutral stance too, but he had no intention of missing the conflict while his competitors sent their illustrations of the action into the living rooms of the citizens. Most in Washington thought one battle would have the Confederate states begging for mercy, but nobody expected that attack to be launched for weeks, perhaps months, as the army was still gathering.

Plus, Adam no longer had an excuse to go to Virginia since Sam Johnson had telegraphed him not to worry about that illustration of General Lee in his Rebel uniform. It had been easy enough to take a picture already on file of the general in his Federal uniform and have someone redraw him in Confederate gray. Sam knew how to satisfy his readers, but he also knew how to save a dollar.

After a couple of hours, Adam spotted a creek along a deserted stretch of the road where he could let his horse drink. The creek, full from the spring rains, sparkled in the sun as it rushed along its rocky bed in a hurry to join up with a river somewhere downstream. The day was warm, and Adam slid out of the saddle to splash the cool water up on his face. He munched on the Shakers' meat and bread and watched his horse graze. The birds were in full song over his head, and off in the distance a dog barked like it might be trailing a rabbit. Here was real peace, Adam thought. Nature's peace. He'd met few travelers even on the more populated portions of the road.

On the Sabbath, the faithful rested. He imagined his own mother and grandfather sitting in their Boston parlor in their dark Sabbath clothes. His grandfather would be reading the Bible. His little brother Harry would be trying not to doze on the couch. And Jake, well, Jake was gone from the picture now the same as Adam was. Jake was in Washington learning to march and shoot a gun. Hardly a Sabbath day occupation.

Maybe Adam should have found a way to make Jake go home the way Phoebe wanted. But the boy was nineteen. A lot of the volunteers were even younger.

Adam's horse raised his head and pricked his ears forward, bringing Adam away from his thoughts. Something was running up the creek. Adam moved over to the horse and caught its reins before he reached into his saddlebag for the gun he carried there. He didn't often have occasion to pull it out, but in some of the places he'd been in the West, it was good to be prepared.

He checked the load and kept it pointed at the ground as the hairs on the back of his neck stood up. Trouble was coming. He didn't know how he knew, but he knew. The baying dog was still some distance away but getting closer. Perhaps it was on the trail of a fox or deer instead of a rabbit. His horse pranced sideways nervously, and Adam clucked his tongue to calm him as he climbed back into the saddle. It was probably just some locals out running their dog. Nothing that had to involve him in any way.

He was turning his horse away from the creek to head back to the road when he caught sight of a flash of blue through the trees that lined the creek. Adam's hands froze on the reins. It wasn't a deer the dog was trailing, but a person. He could hear the panting breaths of the runner along with the water splashing now. A runaway slave and absolutely nothing he could do to help the person as much as he might want to. It was against the law to interfere with those trying to capture a runaway. And in a godforsaken place like this, it wouldn't matter what was legal or what was not. He was liable to be shot for his trouble. Even so, he sat like a stone on his horse and waited for the poor man to come into sight.

It wasn't a man, but a woman grasping up her skirts and running through the knee-deep water. She stopped when she saw him, her eyes wide and frightened. Then she dropped her skirts down in the water and put her hands over her heart.

"Is you really there, Mr. Adam?" she gasped as she tried to catch her breath.

22

He recognized her at once. Not only as the black sister from the Shaker village, but now here with panic alive on her face, he knew why she had tried to speak to him. She was Charlotte's maid he'd met at Grayson. And it didn't matter what the law said anymore.

"How far behind you?" He got straight to the point.

"Don't know." She pushed the breathless words out as she stared back down the creek and shuddered with fear. "They wouldn't believe my papers. Tried to steal them from me."

"Grab that stick there in the water." He shoved his gun in the back of his waistband before he guided his horse down into the creek. When she obediently held up the stick, he said, "Now rip off a piece of your dress to tie to it."

She tried to do as he said, but the skirt's cloth was too tightly woven. "It won't tear."

He grasped the top of her sleeve and jerked the seam loose. She slipped it off her arm and with trembling hands managed to tie it to the stick. "What's this gonna help?"

He didn't take time to answer her as he reached for her to pull her up on his horse.

The creek water swirled around her skirt as she stared at him and didn't take his hand. "You best leave me be and ride on, Mr. Adam. They got guns. They'd a done shot me if I hadn't been worth more to them breathin'. But you, they might think it sport to shoot a Northerner like you."

"Take my hand, Mellie." He remembered the name Charlotte called her. "Hurry or my blood will be on your head."

She let him pull her up in front of him and awkwardly straddled the horse as she stuffed her full skirt under her legs. She grabbed hold of the horse's mane to steady her seat, then held up the stick with her other hand. "What am I supposed to do with this?"

"Hold on to it a minute." He walked his horse down the creek a little way until he found a spot where the bank was rocky. "Now drop it in." He watched the stick to be sure the current caught it and swept it downstream before he turned his horse to the bank. The dog was getting closer and now he heard a man shouting.

At the sound of the man's voice, Mellie began shaking so hard that Adam wrapped an arm around her waist to keep her from tumbling off the horse. She leaned back against him and whispered, "Lord a mercy, help us."

The words carried such raw feeling that even Adam hoped some higher power might be listening, but he wasn't ready to depend on that alone as he guided the horse through the trees. He wanted to kick his heels into the horse's flanks and push him to a full gallop, but it was wiser to go quietly like a fleeting shadow the chasers might not notice. Perhaps because of Mellie's simple prayer, a line of Scripture surfaced in his mind from all the passages his grandfather had forced him to memorize in his school. *Yea, though I walk through the valley of the shadow of death, I will fear no evil.*

As if Mellie had heard his thoughts, she whispered, "Puts your hand over top us, Lord, and bring us on out a this dark place."

Once back out on the road, the sun was too bright, pointing them out as something not right to anybody who might see them. A white stranger with a Negro woman in a bedraggled Shaker blue dress riding in front of him on his horse. That would be something a person would remember if the slave catchers talked to them. So maybe the darkness was more to be desired after all. Adam went off the road again at the next stand of trees. He needed to come up with a plan. He couldn't hear the dog or the men chasing Mellie anymore, so that was good. But they wouldn't give up. She must have looked like easy money to them. They'd keep looking.

When he was sure no one could see them from the road, he dismounted and helped Mellie down. Her legs almost gave way with her, and he had to hold her up until she was able to pull herself together and step away from him.

"You was an answer to prayer, Mr. Adam, but you's can go on and leaves me here now. I can make my way on to the freedom river from here."

"You're a long way from that river, Mellie. And even if you can get there, how do you plan to get across to the other side?" With the horse's reins in his hand, Adam leaned back against a tree and studied the problem in front of him. It wasn't like him to get pulled into this kind of mess. What was it Jake had said about him? That he was an observer. He didn't get involved. And now here he stood with a fugitive slave in the middle of nowhere with no idea of what to do next. "Everybody will know you're a runaway."

She lifted her chin. "I ain't no runaway. Leastwise no runaway slave like as how you're meaning. I did run away from them Shaker people, but they ain't likely to send nobody after me. They knowed I was free and could do what I wanted. Miss Lottie give me my papers." She touched her bosom. "That woman Massah Charles brung home was wantin' to sell me down the river, but Miss Lottie didn't let that happen. She took me to that Shakertown and told me to stay there where I'd be safe."

"But you didn't stay."

"I couldn't. Not after Nate come after me."

"Nate? Who's Nate?"

"He come from Grayson like me." She stared down at the ground, her defiance gone. "Only he don't have no papers. We was goin' north where that might not matter."

"Where is he? Did they catch him?"

"No, sir. Least not that I knows. I tol' him to go on. They hadn't seen him. I tol' him they couldn't take me since I had my papers." Mellie's lip trembled. "They said they didn't care about no papers. That paper burned right easy. And that good, healthy breeding stock brought top money where they was headed. I didn't wait to hear no more. I think they thought I was too scared to run, but I give them the slip and was makin' headway till they set their dog on me."

"So where's Nate now?"

She shook her head. "I ain't got no way of knowin'. I made him promise to go on. He didn't want to, but weren't no need in both of us gettin' caught. And I thought I'd be right behind him soon's as I showed them men my free papers."

"How were you supposed to find him?"

"He told me about this house up 'round the river. Some place called Maysville. Nate knew the way. He drew a map in the dirt. It just looked like chicken scratchin' to me, but I pretended I understood the way so he'd go on." She looked up at Adam. "You know where he was talkin' about?"

He met the woman's dark brown eyes. "I might be able to find out." What other choice did he have? He couldn't just leave her there. Not and ever look Charlotte in the eye again, and no matter how much he tried to deny it, he wanted to see Charlotte again. "If you do something for me first."

Fear flashed in her eyes, but then she squared her shoulders a bit and took a step toward him. "Whatever you want, I'll do."

He held his hand out to stop her when he realized what she was thinking. "Nothing like that, Mellie. I'm not a monster like those men you were running from. I just want to know where Charlotte is."

Her shoulders slumped and she mashed her mouth together. "I can't tell you that. She asked me not to and I ain't never broke my word to Miss Lottie."

"I know she's been sent to a school in Virginia. I just need to know what town."

Mellie frowned a little and opened her mouth to say something, but then shut it tight.

295

"It might not be safe for her in Virginia," he added.

Mellie looked almost sad as she said, "I'd help you, Mr. Adam, but I don't know nothin' about Virginia 'cept the Shakers say there's fixin' to be a war there. You needs to go ask Massah Charles about Miss Lottie. He can tell you where she's at."

"Why's it such a secret?"

"Miss Lottie, she sometimes gets overproud and then shamed if things don't go the way she thinks they should. What with Mr. Edwin turnin' her down and then that woman tearin' apart her home, things has gone bad lately." She looked straight at Adam's face again. "And she don't trust you, Mr. Adam. I'm thinkin' she's lovin' you, but she's not trustin' you. She thinks you's just playin' with her, that that kiss in the garden didn't mean nothin'. But I'm thinkin' she might be wrong from what I can see on your face."

"It won't matter if I can't find her."

"You two is suited. Neither one wants to admit you need any lovin', but I think Miss Lottie's findin' out different and maybe you will too."

When he just looked at her without saying anything, she sighed and went on. "I thank you for helpin' me out back there, Mr. Adam. I wouldn't have got away without you. But guess I'd better be movin' on north now." She looked around and then started off in the wrong direction.

Adam let her walk a ways before he called after her, "That's south."

She turned to look back at him. "You sure?"

"Surer than you are." He couldn't keep from laughing. "Come on back here. We need to come up with a plan."

"That's Miss Lottie too. Always with a plan. I'm hopin' yours has a better chance of workin' than that last one of hers."

"What plan was that?" Adam asked casually as if he didn't care what she answered.

"You ain't trickin' me into breakin' my word to Miss Lottie." She planted her feet on the ground and crossed her arms in front of her chest. "I done tol' you. You gonna have to ask Massah Charles. That's who."

"All right, Mellie. I know when I'm beat." He let out an exaggerated sigh as he beckoned her toward him. "No more questions about Charlotte. But we better put our heads together to figure out a way to this house in Maysville Nate told you about."

The plan was simple. They waited till almost dark and then rode in the gathering twilight to the nearest town. There at daylight, Adam bought train tickets to Maysville for him and the slave he was taking to his sister. Nobody thought a thing out of the way about it. Mellie rode in the baggage car with a few other slaves. One of them had heard about the house on the way to freedom, and he whispered what he knew to Mellie. A rusty roof with an edge of tin curled up on the left dormer, and if it was safe to come to the door, a white wooden flower box between the second and third posts on the porch.

It was late afternoon when they got off the train in Maysville and near dark before they found the house. Out of sight behind a nearby barn, Adam gave Mellie most of the money in his pockets and then smiled a little as he wrote out Phoebe's address again in case she made it all the way to Boston. Phoebe was going to have a houseful of servants before he was through, but it served her right. None of this would be happening if she hadn't insisted he do that wretched portrait of Selena Vance. But then he wouldn't have met Charlotte either, if not for Phoebe. Right now he wasn't sure if he should thank her for that or wish Charlotte from his thoughts forever. Love complicated things. Yet every time he remembered Mellie's words saying Charlotte loved him, his heart practically floated inside his chest.

He didn't go with Mellie to the house. He told her goodbye in the deepening shadows.

"The good Lord will bless you for your goodness, Mr. Adam."

"I didn't do this for the Lord," Adam said.

"I knows who you did it for. Miss Lottie." Mellie stared at him in the dim light. "If I ever sees her again, I'll tell her I ended up safe 'cause of you."

"But is she? Safe?"

"She's safe enough, but what good is it to be safe if a person don't never get the chance to know love?" She didn't expect him to give her an answer as she went on. "Me and Nate, at least we wasn't too scared to try."

"I hope you find him."

"I will. Either here or on the other side."

Adam knew she wasn't talking about the other side of the river. She brushed his hand shyly with her fingertips before she started toward the house. Then she turned back to him to say, "Ain't no need lookin' for her in Virginia."

"Did she go to the Shakers with you?" He frowned, hardly able to believe he gave that idea enough serious consideration to even speak the question aloud, but at the same time the memory of the lady's hand pulling down the Shaker cap to cover her hair popped into his mind.

Mellie stared back at him. "I just told you she wasn't in Virginia. You got to ask Massah Charles the rest of it."

And then she was slipping from shadow to shadow until she was on the porch. The door opened and hands pulled her inside. No one saw her. He'd done what he could. For Charlotte.

The next morning, he went to the train station

with no sure destination in mind. He could go to Frankfort and find Charles Vance. He could find out about Charlotte and about Kentucky's determined neutral stand. But he already knew about Charlotte. As hard as it was to believe, that had been her pushing her way out of the Shaker meetinghouse to escape his notice. He was sure of it. He was also sure if she hadn't wanted to see him two days ago, she wouldn't want to see him now.

And if she'd gone to the Shakers, it would have been to chase after Edwin Gilbey. Some plan she had, according to Mellie. A plan that hadn't worked out. But for certain a plan that included no thought of Adam.

What of his own plans? Was he going to just toss them aside because he'd kissed a pretty red-head? So what if he couldn't get her out of his thoughts. So what if every time he picked up a pen or pencil he wanted to draw her eyes. That didn't mean he had to rush back to the Shaker village to beg to see her and perhaps suffer the humiliation of being refused. It would be better to give it time, to see if his infatuation faded. Besides, the war drums were beating louder. He couldn't miss the battle chasing after a woman in Shaker blue.

He stepped up to the ticket window and said, "Next train to Washington, D.C."

He ignored the way his heart grew suddenly

heavier. It was the right decision. The only decision for him. He couldn't be tied down. Not by a woman. Even one as entrancing as Charlotte Vance. There'd be time for love later on. After the war. After he had the pictures he wanted.

She was safe at the Shaker village. He smiled a little at the thought of Charlotte living the Shaker life. It was almost more than he could imagine. A Southern belle in drab Shaker dress. Working with her hands. Dancing for the Lord instead of to capture a husband. No husband-capturing would be going on in the Shaker village. Not even if she was still trying to convince Edwin Gilbey to stand by his promise to her. That wasn't going to happen. Adam had seen Edwin's face during the Shaker worship. He would not give up his newfound passion with the Shaker way.

So it wasn't as if Adam had to worry about Charlotte marrying another before he returned. If he decided to return. Not as long as she was with the Shakers. While there was much he still didn't know about the Shakers, everybody knew the normal bonds of marriage were strictly taboo in their society. Charlotte would be safe both from the impending war and a hasty marriage.

Life matters shouldn't be decided in haste. If he truly loved Charlotte, if she truly loved him, a few months wouldn't make that much difference. Better to hesitate and be sure than to jump into a quagmire that might trap him forever. He believed that. He was sure of it, but even so his feet very reluctantly climbed the steps up onto the train. His mind was telling him one thing, but his heart wanted to run back in the other direction.

He found his seat and looked around to see if he could spot a likely subject for his pencil. But when he opened his sketchbook, he began drawing Charlotte's hand pulling the Shaker cap down to cover her red hair, running out the door away from him. What was it Mellie had said? That at least she and her man weren't too scared to try for freedom and love. And as he drew, he imagined a tremble in Charlotte's hand.

When he got to Washington, he sent a telegram to Senator Charles Vance. *Want to see Charlotte. Where is she?*

In spite of the drawing Adam had made on the train where every line he remembered of the Shaker sister running from the meetinghouse matched perfectly his memory of Charlotte, it seemed necessary to have absolute proof that it had really been her in that Shaker dress. Mellie had kept telling him to ask the senator.

He got a return message the next day. *In Virginia. Miss Josephine's School for Young Ladies. Tell her all well at Grayson.*

Adam read the telegram from the senator three times. Then he stared at the sketch he'd drawn on the train. And he wasn't sure which was the lie.

23

As the days passed and became weeks, Charlotte found a certain comfort in being relieved of the need to make decisions. No more plans to go awry. Instead she got up every morning at the sound of the rising bell and followed the path laid out for her. She didn't have to think. Just do.

She discovered her hands were strong and capable, work was not offensive, and a sincere prayer could take wing from her heart up toward heaven. Now when she knelt to silently pray at the appointed times, her mind didn't stay blank. At first her timidly offered prayers were for Mellie's safety and that only, but as the prayers piled up, other thoughts began to come to mind. Even when she stumbled around in her mind searching for proper words, she rose from her knees with a lighter spirit. In her heart the assurance grew that someday, somehow there would be answers. She prayed for Grayson and her father's forgiveness. She prayed for her countrymen both to the north and to the south as soldiers massed in the east for battle.

While the Shakers had withdrawn from worldly living, they did not avoid news of what was happening in the world outside their village. Instead the leaders read newspaper reports at meetings and expressed much concern over what war could mean to their Shaker communities here in the state and all across the northeast. It was feared that even if Kentucky did block the war from between her borders with a neutrality stance, the conflict between the states would greatly hinder their travel into the South where the Harmony Hill traders sold most of their products. The Shakers prayed often and with much conviction for the peaceful preservation of the Union and a just end to the abhorrent institution of slavery.

That was a prayer Charlotte echoed fervently in her heart. She knew her father claimed Grayson could not survive without slavery, but perhaps he was wrong. He was wrong about Selena. He could be wrong about much else.

Sister Martha claimed those of the world were often plagued by wrong thinking and that Charlotte's father demonstrated an obvious lack of understanding when he refused to accept the wisdom of Charlotte's desire to seek spiritual peace among the Believers. When the letter from Grayson and the departure of Mellie had threatened to plunge Charlotte into a dark state of melancholy, the elders had taken pity on her and replaced Sister Altha's stern guidance with Sister Martha's gentle encouragement. Sister Martha, while not straying from the uncompromising Shaker tenets, was gifted with patience as she listened to Charlotte's hesitant confessions of what the Shakers considered wrongs.

And unlike Sister Altha, she voiced no condemnation of Mellie for leaving the village. In those first days after Mellie ran away, Sister Altha had refused to even allow Charlotte to speak Mellie's name as she ranted about the worldly destruction that would surely swallow up their "former sister."

Thankfully Sister Martha had not shown the same indignation and encouraged Charlotte to speak to her of Mellie leaving the village. She had responded with sad kindness. "It is a sorrow to lose our sister, but each who comes among us must choose her own path. Our Sister Melana chose as many do. I regret to say it is not uncommon for those in the Gathering Family to cling to their worldly desires and slip away from our village."

Not long after Mellie left, Gemma began working with a new novitiate and Dulcie became Charlotte's instructor insofar as her work duties. They finished their stretch of ironing duty and then spent a few weeks in the kitchen peeling mounds of potatoes for the giant pots and kneading and shaping dozens of loaves of bread every morning. In spite of the mindnumbing sameness of the chores, Charlotte found the kitchen to be an amazing place where it seemed the Shakers had fashioned a new tool to make nearly every chore easier and quicker.

The cupboards were built into recesses in the wall to keep the floor uncluttered. The work area was open and full of light from the tall windows. Huge ovens accommodated the large multiple-loaf pans. The smell of the bread baking and the clang of spoons in the pans made Charlotte wish she could look up from her chores and see Aunt Tish standing in front of the stove instead of Sister Wilma who was in charge of this kitchen.

Dear Aunt Tish. She'd heard nothing from Grayson since Mellie had left the village in the middle of the night. No news at all. Sometimes Charlotte stood on the southwest side of the village and stared overland toward Grayson. She could not see even the first Grayson fence post, but her mind dwelt on the roll of the land and the graceful lift of the Grayson manor house dormers. She imagined standing in her mother's garden and sometimes, if she couldn't block the thought in time, Adam came from the shadows to enfold her in his arms. At those times she regretted running from his eyes. It had been the right thing to do. The only sensible thing to do. And yet, she wished now she had thrown caution to the wind and dared his scorn and laughter. At least then her heart wouldn't wonder.

Sister Martha said it was best to shut away such wondering. Not about Adam. Charlotte saw no need to confess her wayward thoughts about him. But she did sometimes speak of her wish to see Grayson again.

"It's best for our spirits to look forward rather than back," Sister Martha instructed her at those times. "We cannot change what has been done, although we can beg Mother Ann's forgiveness for our sins, but we can change how we live in the days ahead. Our minds must engage in proper thinking. Mother Ann teaches that our thoughts are character molds. They shape language and action. So with proper thoughts you can come to know peace here at Harmony Hill."

Charlotte pretended to believe her. Sometimes she even pretended to herself, and when she and Dulcie were assigned to the duty of gathering rose petals to make the Shakers' rose water to sell to those of the world, the pretense was not so hard. She liked being out in the sun among the roses that brought to mind memories of her mother, who had loved roses above all other flowers. Her mother was every inch a complete lady.

Charlotte smiled when she thought of how distressed her mother would surely be if she could see Charlotte in bonnet and apron, cutting the roses and then stripping the petals from the stem. She didn't know which would upset her mother the most—Charlotte working like a common servant or the destruction of the roses. The rose petals were to be stripped at once to keep the sisters from the temptation of keeping one of the roses intact to sinfully enjoy its beauty by placing it in a vase. To Charlotte it seemed more of a sin to deny themselves the beauty of the roses so freely given by the Lord. So now and again she stole a moment to admire a bloom she had plucked from the bushes before she tore off the soft petals and let them drift down into her basket.

When Dulcie noticed her lifting a pink rose close to her face to catch its sweet fragrance, she warned her. "We are not to smell the roses, Sister Charlotte. It slows the progress of filling our baskets."

"But the fragrance brings peace to my spirit, and aren't we all to seek such peace?"

"Sister Altha would tell you such peace is found through prayer and laboring of our songs in meeting. Not in shirking the proper performance of your duties."

"And what do you say, Sister Dulcie? Do you not want to bury your nose in one of the roses and let the fragrance fill your head?" Charlotte ran her finger across the velvety petals of the perfectly shaped rose she held.

Dulcie looked at the rose in her own hand, then laughed softly as she stripped off its petals before reaching for another bloom. "I have been with the Believers long enough to know that if I stuck my nose in one of the blooms to revel in its scent, an angry bee would be deep among the petals ready to sting me for my waywardness."

"Yea, Sister Dulcie, but would not the bee sting our fingers as well when we pull off the petals?" Charlotte asked with a smile.

"Better a stung finger than a stung nose."

"But we work with our fingers and not our noses."

Dulcie looked up from her work with a hint of exasperation on her face. "You are being purposely contrary this day, Sister Charlotte."

"Yea, you are right." Charlotte pulled the petals from the rose. "I will confess my contrariness to Sister Martha and beg your pardon."

"You know my pardon is always readily given." Dulcie seemed to struggle to keep her face solemn as the Shakers preferred while they were engaged in their work duties before she went on. "But what you have to remember is that I must confess my wrongs to Sister Altha. If you would like to trade confessors, your Sister Martha for mine, then I will sniff the roses and you can worry about the bee stinging your nose."

"I think that is a trade I'd best not make until I become a more dedicated sister."

Dulcie stood up. She glanced around quickly to see if anyone was nearby. Then she looked straight at Charlotte across the rosebush and asked, "And do you plan to become a dedicated sister?"

"I have stopped making plans." Charlotte turned her eyes away from Dulcie back to the roses. She picked off a bud just beginning to unfurl and stripped its petals without hesitation. Then she looked back at Dulcie, who was no longer watching her but staring away down the row of roses to where some of the little girls were gathering the baskets of petals. "And what of your plans, Sister Dulcie?"

She didn't answer Charlotte. Instead she said, "A wise decision, my sister. Many plans are better not made, for they do naught but tear holes in your heart."

"They will call you mother again," Charlotte offered softly.

Dulcie didn't acknowledge her words. Instead she said, "Work time is wasted in idle chatter, Sister Charlotte." She brushed the tears sliding down her cheeks away with an impatient hand as she bent her head back to her task. "There are many rose petals yet to gather."

Later that day, during their rest time after the evening meal, Charlotte did confess her contrariness to Sister Martha, but the old sister barely listened.

"As long as you realize you did wrong, my sister, and vow to do better on the morrow." She waved away Charlotte's words as if she thought her wrong was of such little consequence it was hardly worth notice.

"Yea, Sister. I vow to be kinder to my sisters tomorrow and more diligent in my duties."

"Such an attitude will serve you well," Sister Martha said by rote. Then she pulled a bulky envelope out from under her apron. "You have a letter." Her faded blue eyes sparkled as if she were presenting Charlotte with a prize.

Charlotte kept her hands in her lap. She had no desire to read more words of censure from her father. Nor did she want to allow hope that they might be happier words spring up in her heart only to have such hopes trampled by whatever words were on the paper Sister Martha was holding toward her. "Must I read it?" Charlotte asked.

Sister Martha's eyes softened in understanding. "This is not like the other letter." She reached to take one of Charlotte's hands and turn it over so she could place the envelope on it. Her eyes brightened again. "This is from that artist who put our stairways in *Harper's Weekly* as he promised he would. It was a very fine drawing and the illustration of our dance was done with respect instead of ridicule. So often that is not the case when those of the world report on our worship."

"Yea, I saw the newspaper." Charlotte stared at her name on the envelope.

"He claims he was acquainted with you in the world. Is that true? You didn't speak of it while he was here." Sister Martha was watching her very closely.

"I did not think it important." Charlotte tried to keep the tremble out of her voice. How could just looking at how Adam Wade's hand shaped the letters of her name make her heart want to jump out of her chest? She pulled in a steadying breath. "How did he know I was here?"

"That is an interesting question." Sister Martha's eyes were boring into Charlotte now, seeing more than Charlotte wished her to see. "Perhaps if you choose to look at what he sent you, then you will know the answer."

When Charlotte still made no move to pull the letter out of the envelope, Sister Martha went on in a kind voice. "The Ministry has already looked at it as they do all letters. He sent nothing evil."

"But shouldn't I shut it away as part of the world?" Charlotte said.

"If that is what you wish. I will take the letter away and the Ministry will decide if it should be returned to the one who sent it." Sister Martha reached toward the letter.

Charlotte pulled it back from her fingers. "Nay, it might be best if I read it rather than imagine what it might say."

"That could be wise." Sister Martha sat back and looked pleased. Whatever was in the envelope seemed to be of no mystery to her. "But you may be surprised."

"I am already surprised. Just holding it."

Charlotte pulled in a slow breath as she took

the paper from the envelope. It was thick, the same sort of paper as that with the sketch of her face, hidden in the bureau behind Sister Martha. Charlotte unfolded the paper. It was a sketch of her running out of the meetinghouse on the day Adam was in the village.

Sister Martha actually chuckled. "Now I understand your illness that morning, my sister."

"I did not wish him to see me." Charlotte stared at the drawing. Alone it revealed nothing of whether Adam knew whom he was sketching. Adam made many sketches. However, in an envelope bearing her name, it revealed a great deal.

"It appears that he did in spite of your hasty departure." Her smile disappeared. "How well are you and Mr. Wade acquainted?"

"Hardly at all. He was at Grayson for a week or so doing a portrait of my father's wife. He left when word came of the shelling of Fort Sumter. As an illustrator he was needed in Washington to report on the decisions being made there."

Sister Martha sighed as she shook her head. "And such sorrowful decisions for our country, I regret to say." Then she seemed to push aside worries of the impending war as she pointed toward the envelope. "There is more."

Charlotte pulled out a scrap of paper obviously torn from Adam's sketching pad and heard his voice in her ear as she read the words he'd written.

I can't believe this is you, Charlotte, but then when I look at it, I can't believe it is not. If it is and you're reading this, write to me and tell me the story behind the picture. It has me puzzled. On a side note, M is working for my sister in Boston. N is running errands for a captain in one of the Union regiments. Both are safe. The Potomac Army is equipping to march on Richmond. Some think that will squash the rebellion. I am not so hopeful. Relieved you are not in Virginia. M told me that and nothing more so she did not break her promise to you. It is only the picture that makes me imagine you in Shaker blue. Am I imagining right?

Adam

Charlotte read through the letter again, letting her eyes linger on the welcome news about Mellie. She had no idea how he knew about Mellie or how she had ended up in Boston with his sister, but she had no doubt that was who the M in his letter meant. It was an answer to prayer and worth any laughter she might imagine between the lines of his letter. She folded the drawing and the letter and placed them back in the envelope.

Sister Martha seemed to be waiting for her to

314

speak, but when she did not, the old sister asked, "Will you write to him to relieve his puzzlement?"

"Nay, I think not." He would expect answers from the Charlotte of Grayson, and that Charlotte was lost. Sister Martha watched her quietly for a long time. At last she said, "I fear your heart runs after him."

"Nay, such is not allowed." Charlotte said the expected words. A Shaker sister denied any such feelings of the heart.

"My dear child," Sister Martha said kindly as she reached over to lay her wrinkled hand on Charlotte's arm. "I have been a Shaker for over fifty years. I was one of the first to come together with this Society here at Harmony Hill, and I have seen many Shaker sisters come and many go. My own dear daughter of the world was one such who went. All because her heart chased after an outsider. I didn't understand it then, but the years have given me more wisdom. The Shaker way is a hard path for some to walk."

"Do you think I should step away from it?" Charlotte looked up to meet her eyes.

"I think that is something only you can decide."

"Sister Altha would warn me about eternal damnation."

"Such is a concern in any life," Sister Martha said so softly Charlotte could barely hear her words. "I worried for many years about such a fate for my daughter in the world, but one day the Lord delivered me from those worries. While Sister Altha often tells me I should be sterner with the young sisters in our Society, I have come to believe that each must find her own path to the Lord. Sometimes that path leads through our village just as yours has, and when that happens, then it is good to tarry here until you are sure of your true way."

"But I see no way." There was despair in Charlotte's voice.

"You will. There is a reason your feet have been set on our path. Perhaps you will decide our way is good. We feel much love one for another here in this place. The laboring of our songs brings joy down to us. We give our hands to work and our hearts to God. It is a good way. A way of much peace for those whose feet are firmly set upon our path."

"As yours are," Charlotte said.

"Yea, as mine are." Sister Martha smiled and patted Charlotte's arm before she stood up. "The Ministry would like you to correspond with Mr. Wade, for they feel he will send firsthand news of the conflict he warns is about to take place. The elders and eldresses are much interested in knowing the movement of the troops in case there is some way to buttress our villages from disasters that might come upon us due to the war. But if you choose not to, I can write in your stead and not reveal that you are among us."

Charlotte ran her fingers across the writing of her name on the envelope in her lap. "Nay, I will write."

"The Ministry will, of course, read whatever you write before it is posted," Sister Martha warned.

"That will cause no concern." Whatever words she decided to write would reveal nothing of her heart, even though Sister Martha did speak the truth when she said Charlotte's heart ran after him.

"Very good. You will be supplied with paper and ink." Sister Martha was obviously pleased with Charlotte's decision.

For two days, Charlotte mulled over what she might write to Adam. In the end, she kept her letter short and to the point.

Dear Adam,

Thank you for your letter. I have lost my place at Grayson, so I am here at Harmony Hill. The Believers have received me among them with great kindness. Mellie was here with me, but she had no desire to stay. I am much relieved to know she is safe although now I am the one puzzled as to how Mellie ended up in Boston with your sister.

It seems there are puzzles all around. Some more terrible than others like the prospect of sister states taking up arms against one another. Such a thought saddens me. Saddens all of us here at Harmony Hill and worries us as well. If you have the time or opportunity, we would count it a boon if you would share with us the progress of the war or the possibility of peace from your front row seat to the conflict.

My sisters and brothers send their kind regards and wish me to tell you their gratitude for your proper depiction of their village in Harper's Weekly. They have hopes your pictures might bring converts into the village.

Charlotte

Three days after the letter was posted, Sister Martha came to find her in the rose garden to tell her she had a visitor. In spite of Charlotte's best efforts, her heart bounded up in her throat at the thought that it might be Adam Wade. Come for her.

24

Of course it wasn't Adam. Her letter answering his would not even have reached him yet, much less given him time to make his way back to Harmony Hill. Besides, she had no reason to imagine him coming back to the Shaker village just because he knew she was there. The words in his letter had been curious. Nothing more. In answer she had been careful to allow no words to spill out of her pen onto the stationery that might encourage him to think she desired his return.

Nor was it her father come in answer to her prayers to mend the rift between them. Instead Perkins, Grayson's overseer, perched uncomfortably on the Shaker chair in the small, bare room in the Trustee's House, twisting his felt hat between his hands until it had little chance of ever regaining its original shape. She could not have been more surprised if President Lincoln had been sitting there waiting to speak to her.

The chair legs scraped against the wooden floor as Perkins jumped up when Sister Altha led Charlotte into the room. Sister Martha trailed behind them. Even though he had obviously come seeking Charlotte, he seemed just as shocked to see her as she was to see him.

He took in her Shaker dress and cap. "They

told me that letter you sent came from over here, but I thought they had to be wrong. Charles Vance's daughter a Shaker? I couldn't believe it."

Charlotte had no answer for that as she stared at Perkins and wondered why he was there. Unless it was to deliver a message from her father. She didn't know whether to hope for that or dread the words he might say. The way the man kept staring at her made her uneasy.

She'd rarely spoken to the man at Grayson. If some message needed to be relayed to him in her father's absence, Gibson took care of it. She had no real reason to avoid him. Perkins had never said the first wrong word to her. The corners of his thin lips always lifted in what passed for a smile any time he greeted her, but when she was a child, just the sight of him striding up the steps into the house to speak to her father was enough to send her running to hide her face in Aunt Tish's apron. Aunt Tish would stroke Charlotte's head and murmur that she had no reason to fear Perkins, but Charlotte had felt the tremble in Aunt Tish's hand when she spoke the overseer's name.

That tremble kept Charlotte's fear alive, and then when she grew old enough to know what Perkins did for her father at Grayson, her fear was replaced with uneasy revulsion. Someone had to see that the slaves worked, her father told her. He said slaves were like children who must be disciplined when they didn't do as they were told. Sometimes the punishments had to be harsh, but a young lady like Charlotte had no need to dwell upon those realities of plantation life. Such thinking could damage a young lady's delicate mind the same as too much education. So it was best for her to remember that some things were the bailiwick of men and that she should concentrate on thoughts and occupations more becoming a lady such as reading poetry or doing needlework.

Now Charlotte tried to push aside the familiar distaste of being near Perkins as she waited for him to tell her what he wanted. The man had aged in the months since she'd seen him. Deep lines creased his weather-beaten face, and unruly gray hairs sprang up from heavy eyebrows that almost met over his narrowed eyes as he frowned first at Charlotte and then the two Shaker sisters with her.

"Why are you here, Perkins?" Charlotte asked. She saw no reason for the niceties of a polite greeting.

"I could ask you the same." He kept eyeing her much too boldly.

"That's hardly your concern." She was surprised to hear a little of the old Grayson Charlotte's commanding tone. When Sister Martha touched her arm to remind her to be kind, Charlotte softened her voice before she went on. "But since you are here, I assume there is a reason you came to speak to me. Is something wrong with Father?"

"No, no, not so far as I know. He's still in Frankfort. Trying to legislate the war out of Kentucky."

"That's good to know," Charlotte said, then waited for him to explain why he was there, but he seemed dumbstruck by her Shaker dress.

Sister Altha lost patience. She leveled her severest look on him and spoke briskly. "You asked to see our sister, Mr. Perkins. A request we granted since you claimed it to be a matter of some importance. So come forth with whatever it is you want. We do not wish to be kept from our duties overlong."

Perkins glanced toward Sister Altha, but didn't answer her. Instead he looked back at Charlotte. "It'd be better if they weren't in here."

"Nay, it is necessary for us to be here," Sister Martha said quietly before Sister Altha or Charlotte could speak.

He shifted uneasily on his feet and twisted his hat again. "All right. I'll just be out with it. Though the mistress will fire me without thinking twice if she finds out I came here. But the wife said I had to. That I couldn't sell Tish down the river without trying to stop it."

Charlotte felt like she'd just been punched in

the stomach. She could barely get out the words. "Sell Aunt Tish? You can't do that."

"That's what I tried to tell your father's wife, but she's done hired this fancy cook from up north. She let Tish cook for the field hands for a while, but now she says that's a waste of resources since Tish can run a manor kitchen and would bring a fair price on the market. She says Tish has to go." He looked straight at Charlotte. "That's why I'm here. I mean I've sent plenty of slaves down the river, but it don't seem right to do that to Tish."

"Father won't let her."

"That's just it. She don't have to ask him. He wrote out a paper giving her permission to do whatever she wants, and she ordered me not to tell him." Perkins looked down at the floor as though suddenly ashamed to meet Charlotte's eyes. "I've been at Grayson for thirty years. I'm too old to find a new place."

Charlotte wasn't concerned about his problems. Only Aunt Tish. She couldn't let Selena sell her. She had to stop this insanity. "I'll buy her."

Relief flashed across Perkins's face as he looked up at her. "That's what I was hoping you'd say." He pulled a wad of bills from his pocket and held them out toward Charlotte. "I'm even willing to put in a hundred dollars out of my pocket, long as you don't tell Mrs. Vance."

Charlotte stared at the money between them as the realization of the truth of her actual poverty slammed her in the heart. She had no money. She had nothing. She'd left it all at Grayson.

Sister Altha drove that truth home as she said, "Do you have wealth we know nothing about, Sister Charlotte? If so, you were to have turned such over to the Ministry when you came among us. We have all property in common here."

Charlotte shut her eyes and saw Aunt Tish looking at her with belief when Charlotte had promised to someday free her. She felt near tears as she said, "Nay. I have no money."

"I thought not," Sister Altha said.

Perkins dropped the hand holding the bills back to his side. He looked beaten, but Charlotte couldn't accept that. She had to find a way to stop Selena. Paper money was not the only thing of value in the world.

She fastened her eyes on Sister Altha to make an appeal. "I brought a necklace and ring with me that I gave over to you. And a horse. They had some value. And I know where I can get another very fine gold necklace."

"You would not steal it from your father of the world, would you?" Sister Altha looked at her with a good bit of suspicion.

"Nay. It is buried beside my mother's tombstone. It was hers, but she would want me to use it to keep Aunt Tish from being sold." Charlotte looked at Sister Altha. "Please, I beg of you. I'll do anything you ask if you will help buy her for me."

"For you?" Sister Altha said.

"To free her," Charlotte amended.

"And will she run away as soon as she gets here to Harmony Hill as Sister Melana did?" Sister Altha narrowed her eyes on Charlotte as though it was her fault that Mellie had left.

"Sister Altha, we cannot hold Sister Charlotte to blame for our former sister's lack of commitment," Sister Martha said in a soft voice but one that carried a hint of censure.

Sister Altha looked over at Perkins who had not stuffed his money back in his pocket. "We are not heartless, Mr. Perkins, but we are unable to purchase every slave we see being maltreated. Oh, that we could."

"You wouldn't have to repay my money," Perkins said. When Sister Altha didn't say anything, he looked as if he were choosing his next words carefully. "You might want to remember that someday Miss Charlotte here may inherit the Grayson land. If she stays with you, she'd have to give it over to you, wouldn't she?"

"Our charity is not dependent on such concerns. And even if it were, it remains to be seen whether our sister will be able to pick up the cross of sacrifice and become one with us here at Harmony Hill." Sister Altha frowned as she sent a side glance toward Charlotte. "I have many doubts as to that ever happening."

"She's been with you a good many months now when she could have been dancing in parlors and sitting on garden benches twirling her parasol." Perkins kept his eyes on Sister Altha. As a man used to seizing the upper hand in any confrontation, he had recognized the person with power in front of him.

"He speaks true words, Sister Altha," Sister Martha agreed quietly as she motioned with a barely lifted finger for Charlotte's silence. "Sister Charlotte has been working diligently in our Society."

Sister Altha's eyes narrowed on Charlotte. "And what say you, Sister? Are you willing to make such a bargain?"

"I may never own the land now that my father has remarried." Charlotte didn't try to lie to Sister Altha. "So it may not be mine to give, but if I do receive some land as any inheritance, I will deed you one hundred acres. I'll put it in writing and that will be true whether I remain with you or not."

"But you say that may not happen."

"Yea, that is true." Charlotte stared at Sister Altha. "All I truly have is the labor of my hands. I promise it to you for a year if you will buy Aunt Tish." She didn't know if it would be enough, but it was all she had.

Sister Martha spoke up. "Our Society does not deal in human bondage."

"Do not be so quick to find fault with her plan, Sister Martha," Sister Altha said without looking over at the older sister. Instead she was smiling slightly at Charlotte. "We do not talk of bondage here. We speak only of commitment. Do we not each commit to working with our hands for the good of all? It would not be right of us to deny our sister the blessing of giving the gift of self for such an honorable reason. To do so might hinder the growth of her spirit."

"Your thinking is faulty, my sister," Sister Martha warned.

Charlotte put her hand on Sister Martha's arm. "Please, Sister Martha, let Sister Altha approach the Ministry with my request."

"It is not right," Sister Martha insisted.

"Yea, it is. Many years ago I promised Aunt Tish her freedom if ever I had the means to provide it. I beg you not to deny me this means." What was one short year of her life to live in bondage to a promise when Aunt Tish had lived so many years in bondage to chains?

"It is not a decision for me to make," Sister Martha said with a little sigh. "The Ministry will so decide. In the past they have chosen to purchase the freedom of some—not for the guarantee of a return but only out of kindness."

"You speak truth. And because of Sister

Charlotte's willingness to bend her spirit, I will speak in favor of the kindness of rescuing this poor woman from the evils of slavery." Sister Altha almost smiled as she looked at Charlotte. "You will need to fetch the necklace," she said as if the decision had already been made by the Ministry. She reached for the money in the overseer's hand. "What price has been set on this woman of whom we speak?"

Perkins surrendered the money willingly. "Eight hundred. She is an excellent cook and knows many domestic skills, but her age has lowered her price."

"Very well. Come with me and if the Ministry allows this purchase as I feel certain they will, we will arrange the funds while our sister fetches the necklace of which she speaks." Sister Altha was all business now.

Brother Willard, who was almost as old as Sister Martha, drove Charlotte and the old sister to Grayson that afternoon. At Charlotte's request, he pulled the Shakers' wagon in among some trees a little way from the house where they would be hidden from easy view. Charlotte had no wish to see Selena or for Selena to see her.

Of course Selena might not even be at Grayson. She might have gone to a summer home somewhere in the north. Or to Frankfort to be with Charlotte's father. That would give her the chance to attend all the fancy events that were held in the capital. Charlotte wondered if Selena was planning entertainments at Grayson. Perhaps not, since so many in the county were pro-Secessionist while Charlotte's father would be maintaining his unyielding support of the Union even as he roundly condemned the President's talk of abolishing slavery.

If she was at Grayson, Charlotte hoped Selena would be taking her afternoon rest on the front veranda, as was the usual custom for ladies in the summer months. Charlotte could almost see the tray of sweet iced tea and shortbread cookies covered by a white linen cloth on the glass table beside the wicker chair. There might even be a young slave girl stirring the air and keeping the flies away with a palm leaf fan if visitors had come to call.

The thought of whiling away a summer afternoon so lazily seemed almost foreign to Charlotte now as she made the short walk to the graveyard. The July sun was hot. So the moment she was out of sight of Sister Martha, Charlotte stripped off the Shaker cap to let the slight breeze ruffle her hair. It was good to feel Grayson land under her feet and have Grayson air filling her lungs. Every inch of her skin tingled with joy as she lightly ran her hands over the bark of the trees and wished her shoes gone so the grass could tickle her toes. She was home.

But not to stay, she reminded herself sternly.

Perhaps never again to stay. That was no reason she couldn't rejoice in this moment as she paused at the edge of the stand of trees and looked toward Grayson's manor house. The rear of the house was plain in comparison to the front. No dormer windows. No veranda spreading out with shady welcome. The porch on the back was a working porch where servants shelled beans and shucked corn. She looked for Aunt Tish, but could see no one moving about.

That was good. Charlotte slipped across the open field to the graveyard where once again she felt concealed by the trees shading the graves. She'd promised Sister Martha she wouldn't linger, but once at her mother's grave, she touched the headstone warm from the day's sun and remembered the last time she'd touched the stone. Adam Wade had backed her into it, expecting her to kiss him. She hadn't. She'd wanted to, but she hadn't.

Would she ever again have the chance to feel his lips on hers? He was following the army into battle. Not to fight, but to draw illustrations of the conflict. That didn't mean he might not be in harm's way. And she, what of her? She had promised her hands to the Shakers. It was better to push all thought of Adam Wade far from her mind. She had told Sister Altha she would pick up the cross of sacrifice and carry it without complaint. She was no longer the Charlotte who was born to the manor house and a lady's life of ease. She was Sister Charlotte with a duty to do. Retrieve the necklace for the Shakers to sell to help gather the money needed for Aunt Tish's freedom.

She knelt down to feel for the edge of the circle of grass she had lifted up to bury the necklace. "I know you won't mind, Mother," she said aloud as she pushed the trowel she'd brought with her into the ground.

"Are you Mayda?" a timid voice asked behind her.

Startled, Charlotte whirled around. The trowel banged against the tombstone and bounced out of her hand. A boy was watching her with large, frightened eyes.

"Mayda?" she asked when she found her voice.

"Come out of the grave to haunt my mother." The child pointed a finger at the tombstone. He was very slender and too pale either from the fright of staring at a haunt or perhaps a recent illness that had kept him in out of the sun for too many days. "Little Jim says I'd better watch out for Grayson ghosts trying to chase me and Mother away." He paused a minute as if getting up his nerve to say his next words. "Ghosts like you."

"Do I look like a ghost?" Charlotte asked with a little smile.

"Not the way I imagined, but Miss Pennebaker says I don't always imagine things right. Like being a whaleboat captain. She tells me that really wouldn't be so much fun, that I'd have to start out swabbing decks and eating fishhead stew." He came a couple of steps closer. "Have you ever eaten fish-head stew?"

"I don't think I have, but then ghosts don't have much need to eat."

"You're not a ghost," the little boy said.

"Oh? Then who am I?" Charlotte laughed before she turned away from him to pick up the trowel and shove it into the ground to find the box she'd planted there only a few months before.

"My sister."

Charlotte froze as chills ran up her back. Perhaps instead of her being the ghost, this child was. Her little brother grown older in some sort of spirit world and haunting the graveyard where his little body was buried. Charlotte shook her head at the foolishness of her thoughts. The child behind her wasn't a ghost any more than she was. She dug deeper in the hole until she felt the hard edges of the box. She lifted it out of the dirt before she turned back to the boy. "Why do you think I'm your sister?"

"You have red hair. Ghosts don't have red hair, but my sister does."

He had to be Selena's child, even if he had little resemblance to her. "All right. You've caught me. I'm not a ghost. But who told you I'm your sister?"

"Mother." The boy had lost his nervous fright at the thought of ghosts and now merely looked curious. "Is it a long walk from Virginia?"

"Virginia?"

"From your school there. I would have thought it would be a very long walk. I had to ride a train with Miss Pennebaker when we came here from Boston. I wanted to come on a ship, but Mother said I couldn't."

"Grayson doesn't sit on the ocean, and my school is not quite so far as Virginia," Charlotte said. "You must be Landon."

"You know me then," the child said as if it was a common thing for the people he met to know him without introductions.

"Your mother told me you were coming to Grayson."

"But you were already gone when I got here. Did Mother make you leave?"

"Why do you say that?" Charlotte sat back on her heels and studied the child's sincere face. Not only did he not look like his mother, he seemed to have little of her ways.

"I don't know." He looked down at his shoes as if worried he'd said something that was going to get him in trouble. "It's just that Mother's very good at making things happen as she wants. That's why Miss Pennebaker says I won't get to be a whaleboat captain. Mother would never allow it. She says I have to be a gentleman." The little boy peeked back up at Charlotte. "Do you know what gentlemen do? Besides not going barefoot and always being polite."

Charlotte looked at the child Selena was pushing forward to take Charlotte's rightful place at Grayson, and in spite of that, she laughed and took pity on this pale boy who was doomed to years of attempting to please Selena. "Gentlemen might not harpoon whales, but they ride horses and practice shooting."

"I know. That's so they can go to the army and be captains and generals and not have to march on the ground." Landon looked worried again. "But I don't want to shoot people. I'd rather harpoon whales."

"Then perhaps someday you will," Charlotte said as she stood up and brushed the dirt off her hands on her apron. "Sometimes a gentleman or a lady does the most unexpected things. Now I must go back to my unexpected path."

"Can I tell Mother I saw you?"

"Do you think she'll believe you? As you said, it is a very long walk from Virginia." Charlotte looked at him with raised eyebrows before prizing the top off the powder box. She lifted out the necklace and dropped it down into her pocket. Sister Martha would be getting worried.

"Perhaps I will keep it a secret. Brothers and sisters have secrets, don't they?"

"They do."

"I hope you come back," Landon told her. He looked sad to see her go.

"I might. Someday." Charlotte smiled at the boy. Selena must have stolen him from another mother. "Until then, I'll share a secret with you. Gentlemen can go barefoot as long as their mothers don't see and they don't complain if they happen to step on a bee."

She left him sitting on a stone unlacing his shoes. She forgot to put her cap back on. Sister Martha had to remind her to cover her hair before she climbed up in the wagon. Brother Willard kept his eyes averted until she had done so.

Sister Altha was waiting to take the necklace when they got back to Harmony Hill. She said an elder would see to the details of selling the necklace and dealing with Perkins.

Two weeks later, Sister Latisha was introduced at meeting. Aunt Tish stood at the edge of the dancers and raised her hands to the heavens as tears streamed down her face. For the first time Charlotte's feet weren't reluctant to join in the laboring of the Shaker songs.

25

It took weeks for Charlotte's letter to make its way to Adam where he was camped with the Potomac Army waiting for the generals to give the order to march south. He'd put *Harper's* address on the letter he'd sent to Harmony Hill since he had never been anywhere that Sam Johnson didn't eventually track him down.

Adam could have stayed in a hotel and only come out to the encampments during the day the way many of the reporters and illustrators did, but he wanted more in his pictures than what he saw on the outside as the men passed the time marching drills and playing baseball or mumblety-peg. In order to capture the mixture of eagerness and fear, boredom and excitement, loneliness and comradeship in their faces, Adam had to sit down among the men and become one of them, even if his weapon of choice was a pencil and not one of the Lincoln guns.

He got on well with the men. Few questioned his courage the way Jake had. They didn't need him fighting alongside them to win the day. They much preferred the thought of their coming moments of derring-do being captured by his pen. Most were full of bluster when it came to talk of putting down Johnny Reb. Theirs was the holy cause, the divine duty of preserving the Union.

The preachers who roamed about the camps told them so right before they offered what might be a last chance for salvation. Some of the men of God wore the uniforms of the various state regiments. Others came out of the city to preach to any who would turn his head to listen. None seemed to consider the prayers of the preachers in the Southern pulpits not so many miles away across the Virginia border calling down the Lord's blessings on their cause of freedom from the oppressive North.

So while the army paused on the brink of warfare, Adam filled up book after book of sketches. More than Sam Johnson and all the newspapers and magazines in the country could ever use, but he kept sketching, seeking that perfect scene to show people the gritty face of war.

At night he put his sketching tools aside and gathered with the men around campfires where the talk generally turned to home. Charlotte filled Adam's mind at those times. He started a dozen letters to her in the near darkness, but he always ended up feeding the scraps of papers to the fire.

He assured himself that it wasn't because some of the words he wanted to write frightened him. That wasn't it at all. He didn't have to write those words. He could write of simple things like the sound of a soldier strumming a guitar and singing a song about a girl back home or the way the sparks from the fire rose up toward the stars. No, he burned his words because there was no need writing to her at Harmony Hill if she wasn't there. He hadn't seen her face or one tendril of red hair. He could be mistaken. He wavered between being sure he was mistaken because he couldn't imagine Charlotte with the Shakers and being sure he wasn't mistaken because his fingers had formed with such ease the lines of the Shaker sister running from the meetinghouse.

Of course he drew her into many of his pictures when she was nowhere near. She was the young lady sitting in the shadows deep in her carriage while her servant unloaded baskets of food for the soldiers. She was the lady dipping her full skirts out of a soldier's way as she walked down the street. She was the girl peeking around the curtains in the townhouse on the square to watch the soldiers go through their drills. She was the face in his dreams.

That didn't mean he had to chase after her with letters that might not even find her. Or be welcome if they did. Mellie had claimed Charlotte loved him, but even if that was true, would that be enough to pull her away from her beloved Kentucky? He couldn't settle in one place. No matter how grand the house or how beautiful the woman. The desire to capture the truth in pictures burned too strongly inside him. He had to be where things were happening and not tied to hearth and home. So he told himself it was better if she didn't write. Better for him to burn his own words to her. He had to follow the army. He had no time for love. At least not now. Not until after the war was won.

Then Sam Johnson's messenger came to pick up Adam's sketches and brought his mail. He sifted through the pile. Copies of *Harper's Weekly* and other newspapers. Letters from his mother and Phoebe. He didn't have to open them to know they would be more of the same words they wrote every time, telling him to send Jake home. A waste of ink.

There was the usual hastily scrawled and barely legible letter from Sam asking for this or that illustration. Adam flipped through half a dozen envelopes from other editors with checks for illustrations he'd sent them. And there, mixed among those letters, was the small envelope with the handwriting he'd never seen but that his heart recognized at once. His name formed by Charlotte wearing Shaker blue.

He swept his eyes over the words of her letter, swallowing it whole, and then let his eyes go back to the top to read it again slowly, savoring each pen stroke. Her words revealed little. But she had written. She was at the Shaker village. She wanted him to write again. The letter said the Shaker elders wanted him to write of the war, but he wouldn't be addressing the letters to them. He'd be addressing the letters to Charlotte. And even if his words revealed no more than hers, they would still be read by her eyes. Her hand would write the response. And that seemed to be enough. For now. He wondered if she would think the same.

How could he know? He'd only talked to her those few times, and while he'd thought he was seeing the girl she was, he could not imagine that girl wearing Shaker dress by choice. And yet she was. The letter he held proved it. He read the words again. *I have lost my place at Grayson.* No explanation. Just a statement of fact. He saw Selena's hand in that. And Selena's only. The senator thought his daughter in Virginia.

Or did he? Perhaps he had lied because he feared his constituents knowing his daughter had gone to the Shakers. The Shakers' worship was considered at best odd and, at worst, heretical. Not something a politician with his eye on the governorship would want to be tied to in any way. The senator had enough problems already with the divided feelings over Union or Secessionist in his district.

Adam decided not to mention the senator or the school in Virginia in his return letter. Instead he would do as Charlotte asked and send news of the war. The answers to their personal puzzles would have to wait until they were once more face-to-face. He could get a train and be there in two days. He could run after her if she ran from him again.

But the war might not wait for his return. Rumor had the army moving south within the week to strike at the new Confederate capital at Richmond. One swift thrust and the rebellion would be ended. So he wrote of the soldiers and sent a sketch of President Lincoln reviewing the troops and another of a soldier polishing his rifle stock. Not a picture the peace-loving Shakers might want to see, but they'd asked for news of the war. War meant weapons. At the end of his letter, he wrote, *I remember the garden. No puzzles there. With fondest regards, Adam.*

The next day General McDowell sent down orders for the army to pack up their gear, load up the tents and camp stoves, hitch the horses to the artillery pieces, and head south to end the rebellion. Spirits ran high among the men. A few rounds of artillery and Johnny Reb would high-tail it for home before the soldiers much more than had time to ram in their second load. Then the Union would be restored, and they could march home to a hero's welcome. Thoughts of maybe falling in battle were pushed aside on that July day as they fell in line to begin the assault on Richmond.

Adam didn't dwell on what the next few days

might hold either. At least not unless he was talking to one of the Mexican War veterans. Then with their words of caution in his ears, he worried about Jake and all the eager volunteers who were marching toward the field of battle with only a few months of playing soldier on a practice field.

But he wasn't worried about his own danger. He wouldn't be engaging in battle. He'd be the observer Jake had accused him of being. Rightly enough. He'd be drawing the pictures to make the people who read the news hear the echo of the artillery fire in the safety of their parlors. He and others. Matthew Brady would be there with his photography equipment that captured the images on glass plates. Adam had seen the van that carried the immense amount of equipment the man needed for the magic of those pictures. Adam preferred his sketchpads. Much lighter traveling.

But Brady's van wasn't the only vehicle horses were pulling down the dusty roads behind the army. Not everybody was content to sit in their parlors and wait for the news to be delivered to their doorsteps. A glut of carriages choked the road. A few like Brady's van carried reporters, but more carried citizens tagging along to witness the spectacle of the Rebels' defeat. Congressmen and their wives. Foreign observers and diplomats. Ladies and gentlemen. Many of them had servants following along with hampers of food, as though marching off to battle was simply a good excuse for a pleasure jaunt and picnic.

Adam found the Massachusetts regiment and rode alongside Jake. The boy had at least relented enough to move from a foot soldier to the cavalry. That was the best Adam had been able to do for Phoebe and his mother. And he'd only been able to do that by convincing Jake he'd have more opportunity to engage the enemy on horseback. An infantryman might be limited to one charge at the enemy, but a man on horseback might charge and wheel about and charge again. Adam had no idea if that was really true, but it was surely safer to be on a horse than marching on foot across an open field in the face of artillery fire. He intended to do all he could to see that Jake survived the battle. Something Jake seemed to give no consideration to at all.

"You will remember not to do anything foolhardy," Adam said as they jogged their horses slowly alongside the marching men.

"You mean charge the ramparts to save the day?" Jake laughed. He was in such high spirits that he was almost floating above his saddle. "It'll be good to finally have some ramparts to charge."

"I've talked to some of the old soldiers who say the troops aren't battle ready," Adam warned.

Jake waved his hand in dismissal. "Those old geezers." He looked around to be sure none of the veteran soldiers were near enough to overhear him. "I mean we're glad they're along and all. They've been a great help getting us in shape. But I want you to tell me how a man can be battle-hardened the way they say we need to be without going into battle."

"I don't guess he can."

"So they were bound to be green at their first battle too. But green or not, we're going to chase those Johnny Rebs all the way back to Richmond and teach them a thing or two. We'll give you plenty of fodder for your pens."

"Just don't you be fodder for the Confederate cannons."

"I wager they won't even stand and fight. We're thirty-five thousand strong. Thirty-five thousand! Nothing can stand against a force that big."

"They've been amassing troops too." Adam looked over at Jake and saw a hint of worry under Jake's bravado. He looked so young, his blond whiskers scarcely thick enough to put a beard on his chin. Maybe Adam shouldn't be pushing reality at the boy. There was no turning back for any of the soldiers now. Not with honor.

"They don't have that many, do they?" Jake took off his hat and wiped the sweat off his forehead. The uniforms were hot in the July sun. "Somebody said only twenty thousand under

Beauregard, the scoundrel. We'll pay him back for Fort Sumter. In spades."

"What about Johnstone?" Adam couldn't seem to help himself. "Rumor has it he has upwards to ten thousand men or more."

"Out toward Shenandoah. Not where General McDowell has us heading. The general has it planned out. I've heard he sent some troops out that way to keep Johnstone's bunch occupied. We'll have Beauregard beat before he even knows to holler help. You just watch."

"That's what I do best."

"Every man has his duty," Jake said.

Adam heard the jibe in Jake's words, but he just kept his horse in a steady jog alongside his brother and pretended he didn't. He didn't want angry words between them on the eve of battle.

The next couple of days they heard reports of a few skirmishes, but nothing of importance as the army continued south. They came across places the Confederates or perhaps citizens with rebellious leanings had thrown trees across the roads to impede the movement of the Union artillery and slow the advance of the troops. The delays hindered General McDowell's battle plan, and discipline among the citizen soldiers was lax. Men wandered away from their ranks at will to fill their canteens or pick handfuls of blackberries. No voice of command rose above the melee of the army's advance to keep the volunteers in line.

Early Sunday, the Union army met their first real resistance at the Bull Run stream near Manassas. Men accustomed to sitting on church pews on Sunday mornings lined up for battle against brothers and friends. Even to Adam, who hadn't regularly attended Sunday services since his school days, it seemed wrong to fire the first volleys to tear apart the country on a Lord's Day.

But when he said as much to one of the reporters taking notes on the formation of the troops, the man snorted a laugh through his nose before he said, "Those boys down there will be doing more praying this day than they ever did in any church building. You can take my word on that. And the people back home are gonna want to read all about it. Unanswered prayers and all."

"What makes you say they'll be unanswered?" Adam asked.

Bud Keeling had been writing for the *New York Times* since before Adam was born. He had the reputation of going anywhere to chase a story. And it was rumored that sometimes he wrote the story and sent it in before the event even happened so the *Times* could beat all the other papers with the headline. He had once told Adam that being first with the news paid off better than accuracy and that things pretty much happened the same, time in and time out. Or at least the part people wanted to read about.

"You been getting religion, Wade?" he asked

now as he looked around at Adam with an indulgent half smile. "If so, maybe you should tell me why you think they'll be answered. And how you think the good Lord up above decides which prayer to answer when Billy Yank meets Johnny Reb after they fire their loads and fix their bayonets. Both good boys with mamas back home down on their knees in church praying their sons will come home in one piece."

"I don't know." Adam's eyes went to the Union soldiers firing at a badly outnumbered group of Confederates trying to stop their advance. General McDowell's feint had worked and the Rebels were caught almost totally by surprise except for a few Rebel companies left to guard the bridges over Bull Run. It seemed Jake might be right and they would have a clear road all the way to Richmond. The artillery guns flashed fire and the shells whistled as they passed over top the Confederate force to crash through the trees on the hill before plowing into the ground and throwing up plumes of dirt.

"Don't nobody know the answer to that one. Anybody tells you they do, you can know they're lying." Bud pushed his hat back on his head and spat on the ground. "Me and you, we just have to tell the story. Each in our own way."

Adam drew the lines of the artillery guns belching smoke. The Confederates weren't running. Instead they were lining up to march into the face of the Union guns. He wondered, if he was down there as a part of that line, would he be afraid? "You ever been scared, Bud?"

"What's the matter? You think I'm not human?" Bud didn't wait for Adam to answer. "You get around a man what claims to have never been afraid, you give him a wide berth. He'll get you killed. A good dose of caution can keep a man breathing."

Adam nodded toward the men running forward, loading and firing their guns at one another on the field below them. "No chance for caution on a battlefield."

"I don't know." Bud frowned into the bright sun as he stared down at the battle. "Look how the boys in blue are just flopping down on the ground while the gunners fire over their heads at the Johnny Rebs." Bud scribbled something down in his notebook before he went on. "Don't seem to be hitting much though. Firing high. Whoever's giving the orders better be telling them to mount a charge before the Rebs have time to bring up reinforcements."

Adam drew some quick lines to show the Union soldiers on the ground, waiting the order to charge. The midday sun beat down on them without mercy. Even so, the Union was winning the day in spite of what Bud thought of their methods. Adam felt a terrible sorrow for the Confederate soldiers lining up for a last-ditch effort to slow the Union's advance. Their line was thin. Adam couldn't see their faces, but he could see how they stood shoulder to shoulder ready to march into the jaws of death. Their bravery was almost visible in the air above their heads. All at once they began their charge with a terrible cry that seemed to come from deep within them. Terror and courage exploding in an eerie scream that echoed through the Rebel line. And the battle that should have been won already by the Union soldiers went on.

The smoke of the musket fire and artillery pieces settled around the soldiers until it was hard for Adam to see what was happening. He wanted to go find Jake, but instead, as the sun crawled across the sky, he divided himself from the reality of men screaming and dying below him and became nothing more than a vehicle for his pencils drawing the scenes of battle.

26

The Union took the bridge over the Bull Run stream and charged forward on the cusp of victory. People in the carriages cheered them on, and a few reporters moved closer to better see the action as the army advanced up the rise to finish off the Rebels. But they met surprising resistance. Soon news came winding around to where Adam and Bud Keeling were observing the battle that a new Southern brigade under General Jackson had formed a defensive line on Henry Hill. The Union generals had delayed long enough to allow the Confederates to get some artillery pieces in place, and exploding shells began to rain down on the charging troops.

The stolid resistance knocked the wind out of the Union charge, and the men began to fall back. A couple of regiments quit the field entirely while others regrouped for a second assault, but the officers seemed confused as to the battle plan. Without leadership, many of the troops moved about totally bewildered as to what to do next. To give cover, the artillery company was ordered forward, but no supporting company was assigned to protect the artillery's new exposed position.

In short order the gunners were overrun and the Union howitzers silenced. After that, the dying began in earnest.

Up beside Adam, Bud Keeling swore under his breath. "The right hand don't know what the left is doing down there." He shoved his notebook in his pocket and glanced over at Adam. "Tide's turning, Wade. Best pack up your stuff and find your horse. Unless you want to spend some time with the Rebels. Not something I'd recommend. I hear tell they aren't too hospitable to Yanks like us even when we aren't shooting at them."

The retreat began orderly enough as those soldiers still standing began to fall back. But then the Rebels charged down the hill toward them, and the boys in blue threw down their muskets and bayonets and abandoned their wounded to run for their lives. Here and there a captain or other officer called for the men to re-form a line, but their voices were swallowed up in the chaos. Horses reared and fought against their traces as the Confederate shells shrieked overhead and exploded around them. Some of the horses hitched to artillery pieces ran uncontrolled through the fleeing soldiers and added to the carnage of the day.

Other drivers kept their horses under control as they waited to cross the bridge back to the north, but then a shell hit a wagon on the bridge. A horse let out an unearthly scream and fell in its traces. The other three horses scrambled madly to keep pulling in spite of the dead horse, but the shell had also splintered the front wagon wheel. The heavily loaded wagon skewed to the side, totally blocking the bridge and the army's escape route.

Now all semblance of order disappeared as the retreat became a rout, and men unable to cross the bridge plunged into the Bull Run stream to fight their way to the north side. Soldiers who had escaped the shells and bullets of the battlefield were swept away in the swift current of the stream.

Adam sat on his horse, removed from the action, and watched. He didn't pull out his sketchpad. There was no need. The scene before him would be etched in his memory for life. The acrid smell of the battle smoke assaulted his nose as it gathered in thick clouds over the battle-field to mercifully obscure his view of the bodies of men who had fought their last battle. Dead horses lay among them, and Adam no longer had the sure feeling that a soldier was safer on horse-back than afoot.

He guided his own nervous horse down into the smoke-covered field, picking his way through smoldering shell fragments, splintered tree limbs and bodies. The corpses were already black with flies in the summer heat. Adam wanted to turn his eyes away, but he made himself look at the faces even as he dreaded seeing that of his brother.

A soldier struggled to his feet to plead for help as Adam passed by. He cradled what was left of his hand against his blood-soaked coat. His eyes staring out of a face blackened by gunpowder looked even younger than Jake's. Adam could have turned away from him and continued his search, but he didn't know if Jake was out there among the dead and the dying. He knew this boy in front of him needed a doctor to stop his bleeding. So he lifted the young soldier up on his horse and rode away from the battlefield. Only after he got across the stream and found the house the doctors had commandeered for a field hospital did he realize he'd plucked an Alabama Rebel from the field of battle. It didn't seem to matter.

The Confederates, satisfied with the spoils of victory left on the battlefield, didn't pursue the Northern army across Bull Run. The wounded Potomac Army limped back to the capital where the state regiments began to count up their losses. There were many.

The biggest to Adam's mind was their loss of confidence. They'd marched out of Washington sure they'd overwhelm the Rebels and end the war. Now they knew the Rebels weren't going to cave at the first show of force. Now they knew their leaders had failed to lead them effectively. Now they knew the war was not going to be ended on a picnic-filled day at the battlefield. The worst blow of all was the way many of the city's citizens openly celebrated the Confederate victory, some even being so bold as to fly Rebel flags on their porches.

Adam made a quick sketch of a Union soldier with one arm wrapped in a sling bandage tearing the Confederate colors off a porch post. It was the kind of conflict-laden illustration Sam Johnson liked best.

That night he finally found the Massachusetts 5th Regiment and Jake encamped not far from the White House where President Lincoln was reputed to be gathering with the Secretary of War and his top generals to figure out what had gone so wrong at Bull Run. Jake didn't want to talk about the failings of the army. He didn't seem to want to talk at all as Adam crouched down beside him where he was staring at the remnants of a cooking fire.

Adam's relief to see his brother uninjured was tempered by the boy's morose face. He wasn't the same cocky young soldier who had ridden away from the city, sure he was going to personally chase the Rebels all the way back to Richmond. While he had escaped the battlefield without any flesh-and-blood wounds, he hadn't escaped unscathed. Somewhere on the inside he was bleeding. At Adam's suggestion, they walked away from the other men to be alone in the silky black of the night. To the west the sky rumbled as lightning flickered on and off in a kind of warning signal.

As they moved through the camps without speaking, here and there raucous laughter made it evident some of the men had turned to alcohol in an attempt to wipe away the memory of battle. Jake didn't even turn his head toward the sound, so deep was he in his own gloom. Adam was determined not to speak first for fear he'd say the wrong words that might make whatever was spearing Jake's soul stab deeper. They stopped at the edge of a stand of trees and looked back at the camps spread across the opening. Here and there a campfire flickered, and the officers' white tents pulled light out of the night.

Once they stopped moving, the silence between them became almost suffocating. Adam finally broke his resolve to not speak first and asked, "You want to talk about it, Jake?"

Jake kept his eyes forward, and for a long minute Adam didn't think he was going to acknowledge his words, but then he muttered, "I ran away."

"The whole army ran away," Adam said.

"No," Jake said. "Not everybody."

The seconds ticked by as Adam waited for him to explain, each one seeming ten times as long as the last. Finally Jake said, "Not Bill Pickworth."

"Who's Bill Pickworth?"

"You met him. Black hair, skinny, not too tall, ears sticking out like some kind of monkey. Nobody paid him much mind. He was just there, you know. Never had much to say."

"Yeah, I remember him now." Adam thought of how the boy had looked as he sat on the fringes of the campfire before they marched to Bull Run. He couldn't have been more than sixteen, with wide brown eyes that seemed to be swallowing every sight whole. "What happened to him?"

"He didn't run. Not even when everybody else did. He stood there and loaded his gun and kept firing the way a soldier is supposed to. He didn't run." Jake looked over at Adam. "But I did."

Lightning flickered across the sky, but it wasn't enough for Adam to see Jake's face in the dark. He didn't really need to. He heard the sorrow in his voice, not as much for Bill as for the loss of who he'd thought he was himself. A soldier ready for battle.

"There are times when it's the better part of valor to quit the field," Adam said. "To live to fight another day."

"Tell that to Bill Pickworth," Jake said as he stared back down at his feet.

"Can I?"

"I don't know. I didn't see him fall, but he's not here. He must be dead or captured."

Adam didn't try to deny the truth of Jake's words. Instead he let the silence gather around them. It would just make Jake feel worse if he tried to coddle him.

After a minute, Jake went on. "He saw the elephant and didn't run."

"The elephant?" Adam frowned into the darkness.

"Yeah, that's what the old guys had been telling us. That a man can't measure his courage until he actually looks into the face of danger. Do you stand and turn the elephant back or do you run like a yellow-bellied coward?" Jake kept his eyes on the ground. "And now I know. I saw the elephant and ran like the coward I am."

"Do you want to go home, Jake?" Adam directed his words out into the night and didn't look at Jake as he waited for his answer.

It was slow in coming. "I can't go home. I enlisted for six months."

"Phoebe would pay someone to take your place."

"Do they let you do that?" There was a touch of hope in Jake's voice as his head jerked up to look toward Adam.

"I don't know. Maybe. Money can buy most anything."

"Not self-respect." Jake let out a long sigh.

"No, not that."

"I don't want to be a coward. I want to be able to look a man like Bill Pickworth in the eye and stand shoulder to shoulder with him in battle."

"The war is far from over, Jake. There will be other battles."

"But what if I see the elephant and run again?"

"You won't." Adam put his hand on Jake's shoulder and squeezed it a little.

"How do you know?" Jake sounded like he used to when he was a little boy in some kind of fix he hoped Adam could make right.

"I know you." He stared straight at Jake's face. In the darkness all he could see was the shine of his eyes. "You mess up, but you don't stay messed up."

Jake let out a huff of breath and moved out

from under Adam's hand as though he wasn't sure he could accept Adam's words. The storm had come close enough that the wind had picked up and carried with it the smell of rain, but it looked like it might go around them. Adam hoped so. The men were dispirited enough without thunder crashing down to remind them of the artillery fire they'd escaped but many of their comrades had not.

Jake was quiet a moment before he said, "Were you afraid, Adam?"

"I wasn't fighting."

"I know, but I saw where you were. It wasn't that far removed from the field. You could have been hit by a shell or even the musket fire. A lot of the bullets were going high."

"I didn't think about it, Jake. I only thought about what I was seeing. And you. I worried about you."

"Did you pray for me?" Jake didn't wait for Adam to answer as he looked up at the clouds rolling across the sky and went on. "I prayed. Like I never prayed before."

"To live?"

"No, to be able to look a man in the face and shoot him dead if I had to. I didn't know if I could." Again Jake's little-boy voice came out. "I shouldn't have prayed that, should I? To be able to shoot another man."

"You'd best ask somebody who knows God better than me for that answer."

"Or maybe just ask God."

"Yeah, or maybe that." Adam pushed away from the tree he'd been leaning against. Talking about God was making him uneasy. As they began walking back to Jake's camp, he thought of Charlotte and wondered what kind of answers she was finding among the Shakers. They believed some woman was the daughter of God. But at least they believed something.

As if Jake heard his thoughts, he asked, "Do you believe in God, Adam?"

"Well, sure. Everybody believes there's a God out there somewhere." Adam tried to wave off Jake's question as if it didn't bother him. "Only heathens say there's no God."

"But Mother always said it wasn't enough to believe in a God out there." Jake looked back up at the sky where fingers of lightning sliced through the darkness. "She said you had to believe in God in your heart. Inside you." Jake pounded his fist against his chest. "She said it was like love. That you could believe in love, but until you felt it in your heart, it didn't mean a thing."

Adam wanted to change the subject and talk about the storm, the war, anything but God. Or love. But he didn't. Instead he said, "I used to pray. I prayed for Daddy to come home. He didn't. I prayed when Grandfather said I should. He still beat me."

"So you stopped praying."

"I stopped."

"Completely? You didn't pray any when the shells were screaming over your head?"

Adam could feel Jake staring at him, but he didn't look over at his brother. He could have. It would have been too dark for Jake to see how unsure he felt. "I wanted to pray for you, Jake. I wanted the Lord to hold a hand over you and keep you safe. But I was like you and your prayer about shooting somebody. How could I pray just for you when there were so many dying? If the Lord held his hand over you, over me, over every man on the battlefield, then we'd be in a bowl with no way to wage war."

"But wouldn't that be good?"

"Perhaps." Adam looked at Jake then. "But what of the Union? What of freedom?"

"Some questions don't have answers, do they, Adam?"

"I don't know. Maybe our lot is to seek the answers."

Long after Adam left Jake to return to his hotel room, the questions with no answers whirled in his head. He tried to push them aside so he could concentrate on getting his sketches ready before Sam Johnson's man knocked on his door at first light. He didn't have to have answers, only illustrations. But as he flipped through his sketches, the sounds of exploding shells and men dying echoed in his ears, and he wanted to rip the drawings into a thousand pieces. He shoved aside the scenes of death and pulled a writing tablet toward him.

Dear Charlotte,

You won't mind if I don't call you Sister Charlotte, will you? Thinking of you as a Shaker sister will take some time. It appears that how that came to be will remain a puzzle at least for now. Tell me of your life there. It has to be very different from that of a Southern belle, but as I told you at Grayson, even then you were not like most young ladies I have had the pleasure of meeting in drawing rooms across the South.

I realize you have probably not had time to receive my earlier letter, but this night as I sit in the capital surrounded by a wounded army, I seem to need to put pen to paper again to you. To tell you of the first real battle of the war at a stream called Bull Run near the town of Manassas in Virginia. The Rebels won the day. It appears the Confederates aren't as ready to be beaten as the Union generals had hoped. I have a sketchbook full of the most horrible scenes of war. My pens seemed to be dripping blood on the paper. I will send you a couple of sketches, but you can see more in Harper's if the Shakers read such. And it sounded as if they do if they saw their stairways on those pages.

Here in Washington the generals will meet and the soldiers will be given new guns to replace those left behind on the field of battle. The armies will meet again and I must be there to draw more pictures. It is what I do.

It is good you are in a place where peace can bloom undisturbed like roses in a garden. Tell me of your garden and I will let my hand trace the flowers you see and hope that once the battle smoke clears there will still be flowers to pick in our own personal gardens.

Yours, Adam

He folded a picture of the army lining up for battle and then one of the carriages of onlookers, wagons, and soldiers all vying for a place on the road north as they retreated. Last he picked up a small book where he sometimes jotted bits of scenes to keep the sights fresh in his mind. He drew the bench under the dogwood tree beside Grayson's veranda. The one where he was sitting when he first saw Charlotte. She would know.

27

Charlotte settled into the routine at Harmony Hill. Up with the rising bell, work at whatever duty she and Dulcie were assigned, kneel in prayer, partake of the bountiful meals in silence, attend the meetings, and give ear to the teachings Sister Martha pushed at her. And each time Charlotte's eyes fell on Aunt Tish in her Shaker dress with a smile of freedom lighting up her face, she felt glad to turn her hand to whatever task the Shakers asked of her. She felt no trace of resentment in her heart when she looked ahead at the months she'd promised to Sister Altha.

Sister Martha told Charlotte she need give no thought to that promise. "The Ministry had no part in the words of Sister Altha speaking of your service in exchange for our Sister Latisha. That is not the Believers' way. We have ever believed in the freedom of choice. While it is our hope that those who come among us will choose the way of salvation, no one is forced to stay here against her will. Our sister erred in asking such from you and has confessed her wrong thinking."

Sister Altha might have confessed, but Charlotte saw in her eyes that she still considered Charlotte bound by her words. Charlotte didn't tell Sister Martha that. The deal was between Sister Altha and her—no one else. Sister Altha had gotten the Ministry to do what Charlotte asked. Charlotte could do no less than what she had promised in return.

She didn't think about what would happen if Adam Wade did actually come seeking her at Harmony Hill the way she often dreamed he might. At night when sleep was slow to come, she lay in her narrow Shaker bed and remembered Adam seeking her out in her mother's garden. That didn't mean he would ever really search for her again. Adam Wade was a man of the world who had enjoyed a pleasurable dalliance with a pretty girl. She had no reason to imagine anything more, but she did. And the imaginings were sweet.

The first letters and sketches came in August. Sister Martha carried them to Charlotte. The summer heat sapped Sister Martha's strength, and although climbing the stairs to Charlotte's room made her breath come hard, she brought the letters there to Charlotte during the time of rest after the evening meal.

It was a diversion, she said. "A gift to lighten the burden of my advanced years. You and the letters from the artist."

"But news of the war is distressing." Charlotte looked up from Adam's letter. She tried not to let Sister Martha note her eyes lingering on the sentences mentioning gardens even as her mind did welcome the thoughts he'd intended to spark with his words and the sketch of the garden bench. She thought of how she would write to him of the rose gardens at Harmony Hill. There would be no need to tell of stripping the blooms of their beauty.

"Yea, it is ever so with wars that men of the world seem prone to engage in. But here at Harmony Hill, we will continue to gather peace to our bosoms and pray to keep the war from our village."

But days later, the Kentucky State Guard under the lead of John Hunt Morgan held a muster on the road that ran directly through Harmony Hill. The Guard leaders deemed the Shaker village a good central spot for men from the surrounding towns to join forces on the way south. Only weeks before, both North and South had promised not to recruit inside Kentucky's borders, but the promise was ignored as the cocky young men noisily gathered to march to the aid of the Confederacy. Not so far away across the river bottoms, a man offered his farm as a place for Union recruits to be mustered into service. When word first came of that, a few young Shaker men had slipped away from the village to sign up to save the Union. The elders promptly went after them to fetch them back into the peaceful life at the village.

Charlotte pulled her bonnet forward and kept her face away from the young men in the street. She knew many of them from social gatherings and political functions, but she had no desire for them to recognize her in turn. As was their custom, the Shakers provided the men who asked with food and drink. The Believers never turned any wayfarer away hungry or in need.

"And these men are surely in need. If not of food then of spiritual rectitude," Sister Martha said with a sad shake of her head when she came to get Charlotte from the hat-making shop to help with the extra cooking. "It is as Elder Quinton says. Such a grievous sorrow to see fine young men, though of the world, so ready to learn the best way to let out the heart's blood of the ones they march against. You can see them out there practicing the thrust of their lances." Sister Martha glanced over at Charlotte to be sure she was paying attention. "All the while calling themselves Christians. It cannot be. Mother Ann teaches us that."

"Yea," Charlotte agreed. If she had learned nothing else while with the Shakers, she knew the value they put on peace. And yet at the same time, they seemed to hunger for news of the conflict as evidenced by their desire for her to carry on a correspondence with Adam.

Sister Martha went on with the rest of her little sermon. "Our testimony is for peace, now and always. No Christian can use carnal weapons or fight. Not and be true to the faith. We oppose wars of households, and wars of nations. All wars are the result of lusts for lands and for women. Those who marry will fight." She often repeated this teaching of Mother Ann along with other tenets as if by mere repetition she could plant the words in Charlotte's heart where they might become as deeply rooted there as they were in her own.

And so as the war clouds grew darker and Charlotte obediently walked the Shaker way, the letters back and forth marked the weeks and months that passed.

August 11, 1861
Dear Adam,
It is not necessary for you to call me sister if the word sits uncomfortably on your tongue or does not flow easily from your pen. It has come to sound familiar to my ear. Aunt Tish, Sister Latisha now, has joined with us here and rejoices in the freedoms of the Shaker way. If you have the opportunity, please pass that news on to Mellie at your sister's. Tell her she can write to us here if she wants. The Ministry allows letters as you surely

already know since your letters have been given to me.

Elder Quinton read portions of your letter at meeting. We had, of course, already heard news of the Battle at Bull Run, and were greatly disheartened by the Union defeat as it seems you were as well. The Believers seek peace in their villages and they can see that the country at war around them will greatly disturb that peace.

Roses of all colors bloom here in the Shaker gardens. My mother's garden bloomed with the same. I will hope the terrible smoke and fire of battle did not destroy every rose in the gardens you see.

As always, Charlotte

              CR Ω

September 15, 1861
Dear Charlotte,

Peace would be desired by many now, but it appears peace is far from reach. A new general has been put in command of the eastern army after the defeat at Bull Run. General McClellan is insisting on discipline among the troops even as more recruits are enrolled in the army every day. Discipline was greatly needed as many in our companies of soldiers were out of hand for some weeks after their return to Washington. It is rumored there won't be another major campaign before spring as the army licks its wounds and the leaders come to understand the need for intense training.

I hear that the peaceful neutrality Kentucky so desired has been shattered and a provisional Confederate government has been established in the southern part of your state. Is there not another Shaker village in that area?

The soldier in the sketch I enclose is my brother. He is nothing like me. I have also drawn your Shaker roses as I imagine them from your words. The gardens here bloom with the last roses of summer. But some roses never fade from a man's memory.

Your friend,
Adam.

∞ ∞

October 30, 1861
Dear Adam,

The Believers are very busy with harvest and I am going to the fields to help gather the seeds for their seed packets in the spring. The work dries my hands, but they have lotions that keep the skin from cracking. The elders worry their usual market routes to the south will be closed come spring unless the war ends very soon which as you indicate does not seem likely. We saw your sketches of the battle in Harper's Weekly. *The scenes of death caused much distress among us.*

We have heard little news of note except of course the conquest of the southern part of our state by the Confederates. My father must surely be beside himself. I think of him and Grayson often, but have no news from either since Sister Latisha came among us. They allow her to work in the kitchens almost exclusively since her rheumatism makes field work difficult. The Believers are kind to their elderly and infirm. Sister Latisha received a letter from Mellie, as did I. As you may know, she and Nate

370

are married and she is expecting a child. The Shakers believe both to be sin and so Mellie's news was no reason for rejoicing here, but I am thankful to know she is safe.

An older sister named Martha has been instructing me in the Shaker way with great kindness. She is very patient with me even though I am slow to learn some of their tenets. Edwin, on the other hand, has embraced the peace of the village, and it is plain he is not the same Edwin I grew up with and once unwisely considered marrying. Even as I am not the same Charlotte. The Believers consider the individual family unit as the reason for much of the trouble in the world. That is why they live as brothers and sisters only.

The sisters picked the last of the roses for the rosewater before the frost last week. Thank you for the sketch of the roses and your brother. His eyes are much like yours. Sister Martha kept the sketch of your brother for the journal she keeps of the news of the war. Though I wrongfully desired to do so, I could not keep the one of the roses for it served no purpose other than ornamentation which is not allowed here.

I miss the garden and all that was in it at Grayson.

As always,
Charlotte

CR SO

November 25, 1861
Dear Charlotte,
I can't imagine you working in the field as a common laborer. What would your father say if he knew you were doing so? Does he know?
Here in the capital the men are settling into their winter camps. Some have been given leave to go home for a few weeks and others haven't waited for leave, but have simply deserted their posts. I consider deserting mine. I am not enlisted in the army as the men are, but I am obligated to Mr. Johnson of Harper's Weekly *who wishes me to winter with the army and to stay abreast of the political maneuvering of the President and his Cabinet. I have gone to some of the parties and entertainments, but the gardens here are cold and without beauty.*
I send a sketch of the President. He looks very grave and ages by the week. I will

send you no more pictures of roses, but we both must remember the rose sleeps under the snow of winter and blooms again with new life in the spring.

Your servant,
Adam

∽ ∾

December 29, 1861
Dear Adam,
   My father has other problems on his mind with his support of the Union. There are many with Secesh sympathies in his district and I can only imagine the problems he may be having. It would be my mother who would be horrified by my day-to-day activities if she still lived.
   She would be surprised, as you may be as well, that I enjoy working with my hands at useful enterprise. While some of the duties are tedious and tiring, there is purpose in the performing of those duties. Unlike the tedious needlework pushed on a young lady as the proper way for her to idle away the time. Here there is no idle time and the needle is plied to make useful things such as dresses or shirts to wear or hats to sell. They let me try to spin

silk from the cocoons of their own silk-worms, but that is a skill that takes much practice. I am better suited to weaving baskets. Another thing that is hard on the hands, but there is no shortage of their medicinal lotions.

I do miss my books, but Sister Martha says it is best to read the books about Mother Ann's life and study her precepts and teachings. Even so I think of the garden of books in my father's library and cannot always keep from regretting that I can no longer pluck the flower of one of those stories to bring the beauty of its words to my heart. The Ministry might strike out these sentences for they believe the beauty of anything lies in its useful-ness and if the words only sing to one's heart and do not instruct in right living then such words are better left on the shelf.

It is good to think of the rose sleeping under the snow and to imagine it bloom-ing again when I am able to return to the garden.

As always,
Charlotte

CR SO

February 7, 1862
Dear Charlotte,

The New Year has commenced. Your letter was late making its way into my hands due to the heavy snow in the east. The messenger could not come to bring my mail for over two weeks. I felt fortunate to receive it before I left the winter camps around Washington, D.C.

Mr. Johnson asked me to go west to observe and illustrate the troops under the command of General Ulysses S. Grant who has undertaken the task of securing the Mississippi River for the Union and disrupting the Confederates' supply lines to Kentucky and Tennessee. Yesterday with the help of newly equipped ironclad ships, he surrounded Ft. Henry on the Tennessee River and easily defeated the Confederate forces there. When the fort's commanding officer asked for the best terms for capitulation, General Grant gave no ground and called for immediate and unconditional surrender.

With no chance for reinforcements, the Rebels had little choice but to lay down their weapons and be taken prisoners. Fifteen thousand of them. Some of the *prisoners are being sent north, but others were paroled with the provision they won't take up arms against the Union again. A condition there is no way to enforce, but there is also no way to handle such a large group of prisoners.*

The victory with so few losses is a good beginning for the Union forces in the west and may cheer the worried masses in the north. Bud Keeling, a reporter here, has sent in a report calling the taciturn Grant "Unconditional Surrender" Grant. He claims his story in the NY Times will make Grant an imme-diate hero. I doubt the General cares as he focuses on moving to his next objec-tive which some say may be Ft. Donelson on the Cumberland River. Keeling and I are on one of the ironclads, but if the river narrows, we will have to find horses or march with the men. I will send a sketch of the ironclad for your Sister Martha's journal whenever I am able to post this missive to you. Not an easy thing in the midst of war.

It is difficult for me to imagine the Southern belle I met at Grayson now stir-ring soup and spinning thread. Are you gathering eggs and milking cows, too? What an image that brings to mind. One

I am tempted to draw. But it's far nicer to imagine you walking the snow-covered paths in the garden as you wait for the return of the rose.

Ever your friend,
Adam

❧ ☙

April 20, 1862
Dear Adam,

It took your letter some time to reach Harmony Hill. We hope you are still in health although we have heard of the many dead at Shiloh. It seems wrong to have a battle where thousands died or were wounded named after a church on the battlefield. The Lord must shudder at such brazenness. Sister Martha says the Believers' Mother Ann would do worse than shudder at the total disregard of peace and love. The elders and eldresses have us laboring many dances for the swift arrival of peace. The whirling and dancing are the Shakers' way of reaching for the spirit. I have learned many of the dances and songs. It is very different from the church I attended in town, but I never have to worry about dozing off.

Meeting is too lively for that, but you know. You were here to witness their meeting one Sunday.

Sister Martha says to thank you for the picture of the ironclad and wonders if you might include a sketch of General Grant in your next letter even though it appears he has lost some of his hero appeal. The papers indicate some in the North are calling for his removal due to the losses the army suffered at Shiloh. Still the Union came away victorious in the way battles are counted. The Believers were glad to hear that news and also of the abolishment of slavery in our great capital. I can only hope that the same will soon be true in Kentucky even though my father would argue against such an idea. But daily I see Sister Latisha's face and I am glad.

Sister Martha also asks me to remind you there is need to watch your words in your letters. She and they, the Ministry, are anxious to hear from the war front, but they will not allow wrong words such as those when you wrote of sketches that have naught to do with the war.

Sister Martha understands that you are not that familiar with the Shaker way, but she wants you to know that she and the

Ministry would welcome your questions if you should seek to learn more of the truth of the Second Coming of Christ who was their Mother Ann. That is the actual name of the Shakers, you know. The Believers in the Second Coming of Christ. Shakers is the name attached to the Believers by those of the world, but the Believers often use it themselves now. Shaker seeds and brooms and chairs are much sought by those of the world or were before the war disrupted so many lives. And gardens.

Brother Edwin signed the Covenant a month ago and has given over Hastings Farm to the Believers. His people were freed. Two stayed here at Harmony Hill, but most went north to begin their new lives. It is too perilous for a freed slave here as they are seized for work on the roads or bridges without warning or recompense.

I will pray for your safety and watch for your illustrations in Harper's Weekly.

With prayerful concern,
Charlotte

᯾ ᯿

May 21, 1862
Dear Charlotte,

I am picturing the beauty of the gardens at Harmony Hill. While I am beginning to understand the Shakers don't cultivate their gardens with the beauty an eye might behold in mind, as an artist I can't imagine not noticing nature's handiwork. I have been privy to so much beauty in gardens, but such beauty can seem very remote when the battles are raging around me. At times the battlefield scenes keep playing through my mind long after the guns fall silent. Then it is good to have the memory of a beautiful garden to dwell on in order to shut out the visions of death.

I am back in the capital where a new offensive is being planned. The men look more like soldiers now but it remains to be seen how well they will fare when once more they are ordered to march against the Rebel army. I also hear reports of rumblings to the south, some near your state. Guerilla bands are destroying rail lines and bridges and raiding the countryside for supplies. The Shakers might do well to think of what means they might take to protect their property if those raids should come near Harmony Hill.

Here is Sister Martha's picture of General Grant. He doesn't look prepossessing but some think he is the best general for winning the day the Union has. At least he does not run from the fray.

Assure Sister Martha and the others that I had no intention of offending them with any of my words. I will consider my words more carefully before I pen them in future letters. As I consider the garden.

In appreciation of your concern,
Your friend, Adam

ॐ ॐ

June 15, 1862
Dear Adam,

Sister Martha thanks you for the picture of General Grant. She has not been well and often is unable to walk. The Shakers have put wheels on a chair for her and I push her to meals and meetings, but she must stay on the lower floors. She has no fear of dying but instead welcomes the thought of stepping across the divide into heaven. She thinks she must be over 90 years old but has forgotten the year of her birth. *She and a daughter came into the Shakers in 1806. The daughter left the village, but Sister Martha has faithfully followed the Shaker way in her many years here. She says I have been a gift to her, but even more she is a gift to me as I accustom myself to this new life after losing my place at Grayson.*

Sister Latisha has heard that many of our people there are gone, either sold to the south by Selena or they have run away to the north. I hope they all ran away. Father would not like to hear me say that, but he has been blinded by his obsession with Selena. Besides he hears me say nothing. I have not spoken to him since I came to Harmony Hill. I am beginning not to care so much. Although I do long to walk again in the garden as I did before I came here.

Mellie has sent word her baby boy is healthy and even more important, was born free. She says she named him Nathaniel Adam. A proper name for a free child. If I have done nothing else right in my life, I did right by stealing her out of Selena's hand. We heard of the battle at Fair Oaks. Another Union victory or so it seemed in the accounts the elder read to us. Were you there?

We pick the roses again for the Shaker rosewater.
As always,
Charlotte

CR ⬪ SO

July 7, 1862
Dear Charlotte,
   I was at Fair Oaks as you ask in your last letter. It seems I have been at every battle or so my brother, Jake, tells me. He is at turns envious and grateful to have not been in the midst of the battle more than he has. He was at Fair Oaks and survived to fight again. That is all any soldier can wish for in this war. To gain an honorable victory and leave the field of battle with all limbs intact. The scenes around the hospital tents and houses are more than I can bear to draw and more than the readers could bear to see. Severed arms and legs are thrown out in a pile like so much stove wood and the flies come in clouds. Forgive me for putting that picture in front of your eyes. I should mark out those words, but I will not. It is part of war and I know you are one to face the truth.
   It was strange to celebrate Indepen-

dence Day with our nation so disastrously divided, but I hear the Southern troops celebrated the day with as much enthusiasm as those in the North. It is a strange time when Americans are shooting at Americans. Brothers at brothers, friends at friends. Who is the enemy?

Here is a picture of a little drummer boy with an Indiana regiment. The boy can't be over ten. But he beats the drum in cadence as the regiment marches into battle. He brings to mind Selena's son whom I met the last time I was at Grayson. Have you met him? He wants to be a whaleboat captain. At least he is not marching out to war like this poor child.

We will both walk in the garden again. I am sure of it.

Your friend,
Adam

∞ ∞

July 17, 1862
Dear Adam,

We are unsettled here as word has come to our ears that General John Hunt Morgan and his cavalry men are invading the state. They are not an army such as led by General McClellan or General Lee in that they do not line up for battle against an opposing army, but rather raid the countryside and take whatever they want. The Believers are very concerned about losing their horses and wagons to such raiders. There is much talk of hiding the horses should General Morgan's troops come this far north and the news that comes in seems to indicate they are headed this way leaving a path of destruction behind them.

Your sketch of the young drummer boy brought tears to Sister Martha's eyes and to mine. Sister Martha still struggles to talk without getting out of breath, but at least she is no worse except when she thinks of the raiders disturbing the peace at Harmony Hill.

It seems strange to think of our gardens of peace being disturbed here, but the elders impress upon us it is a possibility and we should be on guard. I wonder at the condition of the gardens at Grayson. Sister Martha says it would be better if I forget Grayson, but there are some things that are hard to put out of my mind and the garden is one of them. So many things flowered in that garden.

As always,
Charlotte

And so the year passed as the battles grew fiercer and edged nearer to Harmony Hill. There was no peace in Adam's letters or in Charlotte's heart. Except in the memory of the garden.

28

As July thunderstorms gave way to August heat, the news of General Morgan and his band of guerillas storming northward through the state toward Harmony Hill stretched the peace in the Shaker village to the breaking point. Rumors of barns and houses burned to the ground and of confiscated horses swept through the countryside like the wind rushing in before a storm. A man-made storm that struck like lightning and left a path of destruction.

At every meeting an elder from the West Family House stood up and prophesied doom for the village at the hands of the guerilla raiders. The Shakers could not defend their property. They had no weapons or any intent to have weapons. Even so, they had no desire to lose their horses or see their crops ruined before harvest. They sent some of the brethren out for news and appealed to their Mother Ann and the Eternal Father to keep the raiders far from their village. But each report that came in indicated the guerillas coming straight toward them.

Charlotte felt the tension that swept through the village, but her worries were more for Grayson. She saw no reason for the raiders to bother the peaceful Shakers, but her father's house was different. His Union sympathies were no secret.

In spite of her concerns, she didn't try to contact her father to get news of Grayson. She had written him in June when she turned twenty-one, but had no response. Not even through Selena. Her pride kept her from writing again. Her year of self-imposed servitude in exchange for Aunt Tish had come to an end, but she saw little choice except to stay where she was at Harmony Hill. One day passed into another with little difference except on the rare days a letter came from Adam.

When her eyes feasted on the words he wrote to her, she couldn't keep from dreaming of one day seeing Adam again. She imagined him desiring her hand on his arm, her lips surrendering to his. The way he never failed to mention gardens in each letter seemed to hint at that, but she could hardly expect him to desert the battle-field to seek her in the Shaker gardens. And so she waited as the fearsome shadow of the war edged closer to Harmony Hill and Grayson and darkened her mind with worry. She waited and she prayed.

At Grayson, she'd taken little time for more than a token childish prayer whispered occasionally at bedtime, sort of the way one might wish upon a star. Not out of any real belief, but simply on the off chance it might help one's fortunes. Then she'd come to Harmony Hill and become Sister Charlotte who was required to kneel in silent prayer every morning and night and before and after every meal. At first she had merely assumed the posture of prayer while allowing her mind to meander wherever it willed, but then Charlotte had begged the Lord for Mellie's safety after she left the village.

Something about those prayers had awakened her spirit like spring showers sprouted the seeds in a freshly planted garden. Before she came to the Shakers, she had chased after her own answers as she tried to prove herself worthy. Now she felt the gentle hand of the Lord hovering over her, promising her answers, but even more, promising her love not because she was the senator's daughter or the heiress to Grayson or even Sister Charlotte, but because she was Charlotte. Simply Charlotte.

And she kept praying. For Aunt Tish. For Sister Martha. For peace. For the soldiers on both sides of the conflict. For Adam. Some of those prayers she let rise from her heart without words, for it was surely wrong to pray for love while she wore the Shaker dress and pretended to live a life where such feelings were deemed sin.

She didn't pretend so much as to sign the Shaker Covenant after she turned twenty-one in June, even though Sister Martha encouraged her daily to do so. Charlotte knew she stood outside the circle of full belief in their ways. Grayson called to her. Adam called to her. She did not want to stop dreaming of love.

Sister Martha sensed the reason for Charlotte's divided spirit, but she didn't condemn her nor try to push her out of the village. Sister Altha showed no such kindness. Even though she had asked for the promise of Charlotte's labor, she could not seem to accept Charlotte's service or humble behavior. Instead she kept looking at her with suspicious doubt.

"I don't know why the Ministry allows Sister Martha to waste her time with you," she told Charlotte late one afternoon in August when they crossed paths. "It is plain to see you will never walk the Shaker way with commitment. You are only biding your time here. For what purpose, I cannot discern."

"I perform the duties asked of me." Charlotte kept her voice quiet. There was naught to be gained by testing her will against that of Sister Altha's. Even so, she was unable to keep from reminding her of how she had kept her word. "I have done the year you asked for Sister Latisha."

Sister Altha waved her hand in dismissal. "That was of little worth. Where is the land you promised?"

"I will keep my promise. When and if it is mine to give." Charlotte kept her eyes on the path as she wondered if she dared edge over on the grass to pass around Sister Altha. She was on her way to her room and rest after pushing Sister Martha in her wheeled chair back to the Centre Family House. The humid heat sapped Sister Martha's energy and she could not walk over a dozen steps without losing her breath.

Charlotte started to step to the side, but Sister Altha shifted over in front of her. The woman glanced around to be sure no one was near enough to hear them before she said, "What of your promise to Mother Ann and the Eternal Father? Do you not want to sign the Covenant as Brother Edwin did? You passed your twenty-first birthday, did you not?"

"Sister Martha says it is best to feel sure in one's heart before such a decision is made." Charlotte answered carefully in the meekest voice she could summon. She had no wish to cross Sister Altha, who could see that she and Dulcie worked nowhere but in the laundry house all through the rest of the summer. That was Charlotte's most dreaded duty. That and ironing in the heat-filled upper room of the Gathering Family House.

"Your heart does not run after the truth of a Believer, but after Brother Edwin."

"Nay, that is not true. I have confessed my wrong motives when I followed Brother Edwin here. I have seen how he has embraced your teachings. At Union meeting last week he explained as much. But I yet have much to learn and it would not be right to sign the Covenant until I have a better understanding."

"Sister Martha fools herself thinking you desire such. Speak the truth. You want to run back to your easy life with servants to fan you and bring your food on silver platters." Sister Altha's voice was filled with scorn.

Rather than anger at Sister Altha's harsh words, Charlotte was surprised to feel a sudden compassion for the woman in front of her. She had rarely seen her with a look of peace or happiness. Instead she always seemed anxious to catch someone doing wrong and had no eye for the good even among these people who professed to seek the good gifts of the spirit each and every day.

For a brief moment, Charlotte thought to reach out and touch Sister Altha's arm, but she stayed her hand as she answered calmly, "Nay. While it is true I miss many things about my home before I came to Harmony Hill, I count it a blessing to learn the simple gift of laboring with my hands. There is satisfaction in doing a task well. However menial that task might be."

"I don't believe you." Sister Altha narrowed her eyes on Charlotte.

"Why not?" Charlotte sincerely wanted to know as she met the woman's sour look.

"You have a wrong spirit. That's easy enough to see."

"And what of your spirit, Sister Altha?" Charlotte still felt no anger as she kept her voice as gentle and kind as possible. "In all the years you have been here at Harmony Hill, haven't you ever wanted to seek a gift of kindness instead of one of faultfinding?"

For a moment Charlotte thought Sister Altha might strike her as the sister's face flushed beet red under her white cap. She seemed at a loss for words at Charlotte's effrontery.

Charlotte spoke again. "I beg your forgiveness if my words were ill spoken. Or untrue." She made the last two words a bit of a question.

"You dare to try to give me spiritual lessons. You who cling to your wrong spirit. My spirit is true." Underneath the fire flashing in the woman's eyes, Charlotte thought she glimpsed a hint of doubt.

"As you say, Sister Altha. I am surely wrong." And just as surely to be doing laundry duty for weeks, she thought with an inward groan. She would have to beg Dulcie's forgiveness for not bridling her tongue.

"Be about your duties and stop wagging your tongue about things of which you know nothing." Sister Altha pushed past Charlotte and hurried up the path as if she were late for her own duties.

Charlotte watched her for a moment before sighing and going on toward her sleeping room. She would have to confess her unrestrained words to Sister Martha on the morrow.

But the next day, unkind words were the least of the Believers' concerns after news came that General Morgan's raiders were in the next county and headed their way. Some of the brethren hurried the best horses into the woods to be hidden out of sight. Others hid away some of their stores while the rest of the Shakers prayed their diligent prayers and went about their assigned duties even as they kept an anxious eye to the south.

Charlotte kept her eye a bit to the southeast as she and Dulcie picked beans in the garden. By the middle of the morning, smoke was rising on the distant southern horizon. Too far for Grayson, Charlotte assured herself. Even so, she wanted to set down her picking bucket and run to Grayson to be sure it and her father were safe, but a year of obedience to the Shaker way kept her pulling the beans from the vines as was her duty. Besides, her father would not want to see her.

By the time the bells called them to their mid-day meal, new plumes of smoke in the sky showed the advance of the raiders. Charlotte found it almost impossible to sit and silently eat her food in the biting room while the feeling of foreboding grew stronger inside her by the minute. The squeak of the benches as the sisters on one side and the brothers on the far side of the room shifted in their seats indicated she wasn't the only one feeling uneasy. When she knelt for her moment of prayer after the meal, she prayed for Grayson even as she wondered if the others prayed for Harmony Hill or perhaps some other worry of their worldly homes as she did.

A few hours later, General Morgan and his soldiers rode into the village carrying the smell of smoke with them, but they held no lit torches. The Shaker elders were quick to offer food for the soldiers and water and grain for their horses with the unspoken hope that with their bellies full they might ride on without doing damage to the village. Even more the Believers never turned away the hungry. It was their duty to be generous and share the bounty of their labor as Mother Ann's teachings demanded, but they'd never had the hungry show up on their doorsteps in such number.

Charlotte and Dulcie were summoned to the kitchen to help prepare the food for the tables the brethren set up out in the open for the soldiers. Charlotte was slicing bread when Edwin appeared at the kitchen door. She knew as soon as she heard him speak her name that he brought bad news.

"Sister Charlotte. Elder Logan has given me permission to speak to you."

Charlotte looked over at Sister Altha who was overseeing the food preparation in the Gathering Family kitchen. It mattered not whether she received permission. She would still go hear what Edwin had come to tell her, but out of habit, she sought consent. Sister Altha nodded her head once.

Aunt Tish paused in rolling out pie crusts at the work table to reach out to squeeze Charlotte's arm with a flour-covered hand as though to give her courage. Charlotte carefully placed the bread knife on the cutting board before she turned toward the door. She moved across the floor as though pushing her feet through a fast-moving stream.

Once she was face-to-face with Edwin, he hesitated and Charlotte wanted to grab him as she had many times when they were children to shake the words out of him. Instead she moistened her lips and said, "Say what you have come to say."

He pushed the words out all in a rush. "Grayson's burning. Harlan Fulton told me. He says they just came from there. That it is as much as your father deserves for speaking against the Confederate States."

Charlotte remembered Harlan Fulton. He was the hothead nephew of one of her father's fiercest opponents in the county. She'd seen him get into fisticuffs over something no more serious than a spilled glass of lemonade. "Can you believe him?" she asked now.

"Yea," Edwin said. "The smoke rises from the right direction."

Charlotte stepped out of the kitchen but the building blocked her view to the southeast. Even so, smoke hung in the air. It seemed impossible to think that smoke might be from her burning home. Her beloved Grayson. She stared back at Edwin. "And Father? Was he there?"

"He was." Again Edwin looked reluctant to speak. "You might want to go to him. Harlan says he's in a bad way."

"Did they shoot him?" She was surprised at how calmly she asked the words, as if she were doing no more than inquiring after a horse with a broken leg. She wasn't letting herself feel.

"Nay. Harlan claims some among them wanted to, but it turned out there was no need. The senator climbed out a window onto the roof to hide from the raiders but they saw him. He was coming back inside at gunpoint when Harlan says he must have suffered a heart attack."

"Is he dead?" Again the icy calmness in her voice.

"Nay. Not when they rode away. That is why I came to tell you. So you can go to him. To tell him goodbye if you so desire."

"Selena is with him."

"Nay. Harlan says she hardly looked toward him when they carried him out of the house. He said she seemed more worried about what yet remained within the house."

"Perhaps her son," Charlotte said.

"Perhaps." Edwin shrugged as if it was of no matter and of truth it was not. "Elder Logan let me bring you a horse."

"I thought they were all hidden."

Edwin looked quickly over his shoulder to be sure none of the soldiers were near enough to hear her words. "Not all," he whispered.

Charlotte looked up at Sister Altha, who had come to the kitchen door. Her face was set in harsh lines, but it had been so ever since they had begun to prepare the food for the guerilla raiders. It did not change as she said, "It might not be safe for a sister alone among these . . ." She waved her hand as if unable to come up with a proper word of disdain before she finished. "These ruffians who claim to be soldiers but merely loot and burn."

"Please, I beg you not to speak so plainly, Sister Altha." Edwin looked over his shoulder again. "We hope to placate them with food and not anger them with words."

"Yea, you are right, Brother Edwin." Sister Altha lowered her voice.

"Please." The icy calmness deserted Charlotte as her chest began to feel tight. Tight like her father's. "My father may be dying. Please, I must go."

"You need not my permission if Elder Logan has supplied you with a horse."

Charlotte waited for no more words. She was already halfway across the yard to the back fence where she saw the horse tied.

Edwin ran after her. "Wait, Charlotte. Elder Logan requested Harlan's captain get a guard together to ride with you and ensure your safety."

But Charlotte didn't wait. She loosed the reins and, putting one foot in the stirrup, easily swung up into the saddle. She had not been on a horse since she had come to the Shakers, but she hadn't forgotten how to ride. She yanked the full Shaker skirt down to cover her legs with one hand before leaning close to the horse's neck as she urged him forward. She saw no reason to delay her leaving to wait for a guard of the very men who had put a torch to her home and perhaps killed her father. Panic rose in her that she wouldn't be in time, and she dug her heels into the horse's flanks. She hardly noticed when her cap flew off behind her.

29

By the time she cut across the front field to the house, the roof had already surrendered to the flames and caved in. The fire was like a live thing, slamming her in the face with its heat and roaring its victory as it raced up the walls and shot flames out the shattered windows. Her home, everything she treasured, going up in smoke.

Furniture littered the lawn. The hall tree. A rocking chair. The wicker pieces from the veranda. Lamps and other small items were pitched about as though spewed from the windows. Down the way, Perkins was yelling at some men as they pulled the carriages out of the carriage house before its roof caught a stray cinder. The rest of the slaves stood in a tight cluster, staring at the burning house as though spellbound by the flames. Only a few of the faces looked familiar. Twilight was giving way to night, but the fire pushed back the darkness and danced an eerie light on the scene.

Charlotte searched through the other people scattered about the lawn. She recognized some neighbors who must have been attracted by the smoke. Others she didn't know.

The child, Landon, leaned against a tall angular woman in a dress not unlike her own without the collar and apron. Perhaps his governess. The boy's face gleamed in the light of the fire, but Charlotte couldn't tell whether he was enjoying the spectacle or mourning his loss.

When he heard the horse, he turned, and there was no doubt that he was glad to see her. He tried to pull away from the woman, but her long fingers dug into his shoulders to hold him there against her as she leaned down to speak fiercely in his right ear. She was so focused on keeping the child under control that she didn't give Charlotte a second glance.

Charlotte didn't see her father. Or Selena. Perhaps her father had been carried somewhere away from the fire. Or hurried off in a carriage to town to find a doctor. Or had a blanket pulled over his body. She shook away that thought. She couldn't be too late.

She tried to guide her horse across the lawn toward Perkins. He would know about her father. But the horse already spooked by the flames neighed in panic as something exploded in the fire with a loud pop. The horse skittered sideways and tried to rear up.

Willis appeared out of the shadows by the horse's head to grab its bridle and throw a bandanna over the horse's eyes. "Your horse won't be wantin' to get any nearer the fire, Miss Lottie. I'd better hold him here for you."

It might have been any day she'd come in from

riding. He was that calm. Even with the house burning and her riding up in Shaker garb after being gone more than a year.

"Where's Father? Am I too late?" Charlotte slid off the horse to the ground.

"The Massah's bad, Miss Lottie, but he was still breathin' last I was over there."

"Where?"

"He's out in Miss Mayda's garden or what's left of it. We pulled your momma's faintin' couch out for him to lay on after those sons of the devil set the house on fire." Willis pointed toward the side of the house. "We tried to move him back a ways from the flames before he threatened to shoot us all. Says he has to stay in the garden. You try to talk him back some, Miss Lottie. Where it's not so hot."

"Where's Selena?"

"I ain't knowin' that, Miss." The black man's face went stiff as he turned away from her back to the horse.

It didn't matter. Selena couldn't keep her away from her father now. Nothing could. Nothing but death.

She lifted her skirts and ran across the yard. A few of the neighbors called out to her, but she acted as if she didn't hear them as she hurried on toward the garden and her father. She was almost to the corner of what used to be the veranda when Landon jerked free from the woman holding him and ran to grab Charlotte's skirt. She had to stop.

"I knew you would come, Charlotte. I told Miss Pennebaker you would. She says I don't have a sister. Not really. That you were just part of a game my mother was playing, but she's wrong." Tears glistened on his cheeks in the light of the fire. "Isn't she?"

They were too near the flames. Charlotte gasped to get her breath as she stepped back from the heat, yanking the child with her. He seemed unaware of their danger as his eyes never left her face. He needed her to say yes. So she did. "I am your sister. Come." Wasn't she being sister to a few hundred at Harmony Hill? What difference could one more little brother make? She took his hand. "Let's go find our father."

He wasn't on the couch that stood a little distance from the fire. Instead he sat slumped on a bench much too close to the flames as his long-time valet stood over him stoically fanning air toward his face with a spray of leaves. The heat was overpowering. Selena was nowhere to be seen.

"Father, we have to move back from the fire," Charlotte cried.

He looked up at the sound of her voice, but his eyes showed no recognition.

Ruben spoke up. "Massah Charles won't leave the tree he planted for Miss Mayda."

That tree was the only thing left from the

garden Charlotte had known. Her mother's rose-bushes and lilacs were gone, replaced by evergreen shrubs and ironwork benches. Selena had wiped away the touch of Charlotte's mother from the garden. Except for the dogwood tree, and now its leaves were scorched and shriveling in the heat of the fire.

"He can't stay here. We can't stay here." Charlotte pulled one of her father's limp arms across her shoulders. Even through her skirt, the bench felt hot against her leg.

Ruben hesitated. "I've always done what the Massah tol' me to do. He tol' me not to let nobody move him."

"I'm not nobody." Charlotte tugged on her father's arm, but there was no way she could move him by herself. "Help me get him back from the fire. Now."

She put authority in the word, but Ruben stared down at the ground and mumbled, "I can't, Miss Lottie. He tol' me."

Charlotte stared at Ruben, nonplussed by his refusal to do as she said. She'd almost forgotten Landon when he slipped around her to push his face right up in front of her father's. "Papa," he said with no hint of panic in his voice. "I'm thirsty. Can we go find a drink?"

Her father put his hand on the boy's head and actually smiled. "Landon, my boy. Where's your mother?"

"I don't know, Papa. But Charlotte's here."

"Charlotte!" And now his smile included her. "When did you get here from Virginia?"

"Virginia?" Charlotte stared at her father, not sure she'd heard him right. But then she remembered Landon asking her the same thing in the graveyard. Could her father have really thought she was in Virginia? "I haven't been in Virginia."

He didn't seem to comprehend her words as he reached a trembling hand toward her. "I've been so worried about you with all the news of battles in the East, but Selena assured me you were safer there than trying to come home." His lips stuck together and made each word a struggle.

"I'm home now," she said as she took his hand. There was so much to say, so much to try to understand, but not here with the fire nearly singeing their hair. "But remember, we've got to get Landon something to drink."

"Yes, yes. Landon." He looked up at Ruben. "Ruben, bring some drinks."

"Yassir. I has them ready down at the end of the garden."

"Please, Papa. It's too hot for me here," Landon said.

Her father looked past them then at the fire before he turned his eyes back to Charlotte. "Grayson's burning, you know," he said as though announcing a rainstorm to her after her head was already soaked. His voice quivered as he went on. "Your mother's crying out to me from the flames. She loved this place. More than she ever did me."

"Nay." Charlotte shook her head a little as if to clear away the Shaker talk before she went on. "That's not true. She loved nothing more than you." She and Ruben pulled him to his feet to begin inching him away from the fire. "A house can be rebuilt."

"Not by me, I fear." He looked down. "I can't feel my feet. Selena won't like that. She does love to dance." His eyes fell on Landon again as they lowered him to the fainting couch. The heat of the flames was not as intense there. "Did you tell me where your mother is?"

"No sir. I don't know where she is."

"She's not in the fire, is she?" He didn't sound worried so much as curious. Then he remembered Landon again. "Of course she's not, lad. I wouldn't want you to think that. I'm sure she's around somewhere."

Ruben had run off toward the slave quarters as soon as they got her father down on the couch, and now he came back with a mason jar of water. Charlotte's father took the jar, but his hand shook so that a good bit of the water spilled out on his pants.

Charlotte eased the jar out of his hand and held it to his lips. "Drink, Father."

He gulped the water greedily before he put his hand over hers on the jar. His hand was still shaking. "I'm so relieved you're safe, Charley. I could have never forgiven myself if something had happened to you in Virginia. Selena shouldn't have let you go after they seceded, but she said you insisted on leaving. That you were angry with me for trying to replace your mother by marrying her. And then when you kept sending my letters back unopened, I knew she must be right." He squeezed her hand. "I'm glad you came home."

Charlotte looked at him and tried to take in what he was saying. Unopened letters? There had been no letters. Her hand started trembling like his as she realized what Selena had done. When water sloshed out of the jar, Ruben lifted it from her hand.

"But, Father," Charlotte said. "I never—"

"Shh, Charley. None of that matters now." He touched her lips with his fingertips to stop her words, then took her hand and squeezed it. "I'm just glad you came home."

"So am I, Father." Charlotte blinked back tears as she tightly held his hand, so familiar, so loved. Selena had lied to them both. She fumbled about in her head for the right words, the gentlest words, to explain how they'd been fooled.

Those words were forgotten when her father

gasped and started jerking on his shirt front. "Why is this shirt so tight? It's binding me."

Charlotte pulled free his buttons, but he still clutched at his chest. He sounded out of breath as he went on. "They thought I was a coward, but it was her. She was the one who made me climb out on the roof. She thought she could sweet-talk them into going away if I wasn't there. But they saw me and accused me of cowardice. I would have rather they shot me clean and true through the heart. It would have been an easier way to pass."

"No, Papa," Landon cried out and laid his head on her father's chest.

"Now, don't take on so, Son." He stroked Landon's head a few times before he looked back up at Charlotte. "You're going to like Landon. He's a fine boy. Wants to be a whale-boat captain when he grows up."

"So I've heard," Charlotte said.

Her father looked back toward the fire. "Might be a good place to be right now. Floating on the open sea. The salt air in your face. Searching for that one whale that might take you on the ride of your life."

"You can sail with me, Papa," Landon said.

"You just think about me when you stand in the helm. That will be my ride, Landon." He smiled weakly down at the boy. Sweat beads popped out all over his face. He reached for

Charlotte's hand again. "Do you forgive me, Charley? After you left, I wanted to follow you to Virginia to talk to you, but everybody said it was too dangerous, and now look at me. Grayson conquered by the Rebels."

"Not conquered. Never conquered," Charlotte said. "Under us is still Grayson land. Our land." She wanted to take off her shoes and stockings and feel the grass and dirt between her toes.

"Grayson land, yes. But not my land. Your grandfather just endured my presence here. I was the necessary evil to see that the Grayson blood continued even if the name did not." He looked around. "Yours now, Charley. Or what's left of it."

"What of Selena?" Charlotte wanted to sling the woman's deceit in his face, but he looked so sad that she didn't have the heart to add to his sorrow.

"Ah, Selena. I fancied I loved her. You can forgive me for that, can't you, Charley? I tried to explain in my letters. An old man's last folly." He made a sound that started out a laugh and changed to another gasp of pain as he grabbed his chest. "Too tight."

"Hold on, Father. We'll get a doctor." Charlotte pushed her words at him, willing him to listen and keep breathing, but his eyes glazed over as his head slumped down on his chest. She grabbed him and tried to shake life back into him. "Wait, Father! Wait."

Ruben bent down in front of her with tears streaming down his cheeks. "Ain't no use, Miss Lottie. He's done gone on."

Beside her, Landon let out a pitiful whimper.

Charlotte blinked her eyes and let Ruben gently ease her father away from her hands. "I didn't get to tell him I forgave him. That I never saw his letters," she said softly more to herself than to Ruben or Landon. "I wanted to tell him."

"He knows now," Landon said.

Charlotte looked at the child. "But he died before he heard me."

"The Lord will tell him," Landon assured her with true faith. "The Lord will want him to be happy in heaven, so he'll tell him. My first papa told me that before he died. He was real sick, but he told me everybody's happy in heaven. That all the tears stay down here."

"Listen to the child. He knows what he's talkin' 'bout. Things is always good up in paradise even if there is plenty of tears falling down here," Ruben said as he laid her father back on the couch with great care. He pushed her father's eyelids down over his eyes and folded his arms across his chest. "I'll get a blanket out of the carriage house."

Charlotte stared at her father's body and desperately wished he would even yet gasp and rise up off the couch to talk to her again. But of course he didn't.

Landon edged closer to Charlotte and spoke in a small voice. "I wish I could go hide. It's easier when you can hide."

Charlotte put her arm around him. "Does it frighten you to look at him?"

"No. It only frightens me that he's gone. I liked my second papa. I might not like my third. Or he might not like me."

"Will there be a third?"

"Oh yes. I think Mother already has him picked out. She doesn't like to leave things to chance. She says it's best to always have a plan."

"I used to think that," Charlotte said. She tightened her arm around the boy and felt the trembles shaking him. She turned him toward her. "Here, Landon, hide against me."

He buried his face in her dress. His voice was muffled as he asked, "Can I cry? Mother says young gentlemen don't cry, but I don't think I can keep from it."

"Everybody cries sometimes," Charlotte whispered as tears rolled down her cheek and fell on Landon's messed curls. "Even whaleboat captains."

And behind them Grayson burned.

30

August 22, 1862
Dear Adam,

My father was buried last Thursday. Elder Logan, Sister Martha, and Dulcie came to be with me as the preacher from town spoke words over his grave. I'm sure my father's political friends and our neighbors were shocked to see me in Shaker dress with a cap covering my hair. What a change for them to witness, but then the whole nation is in a constant state of flux with the way the current conflict is tearing us apart.

There is much sorrow. Neighbors down the way, the Jacksons, just got word their son was killed at White Oak Swamp. Other neighbors, the Andersons, lost their son at Bull Run a year ago. One fought for the Confederates and the other for the Union, but at my father's funeral, Mr. Jackson and Mr. Anderson stood shoulder to shoulder and grieved with me and with each other. Death is the great equalizer.

Behind us as we stood around my father's grave, smoke still rose from the skeletal remains of my Grayson home.

General Morgan's raiders set it afire when they came through here. They did not shoot my father, but the result was the same. His heart could not bear the destruction of his home and his life.

Selena disappeared the night of the fire and was not at the graveside to be a grieving widow. Landon, her young son, is in the charge of his governess and they are at a hotel in town waiting for her to return. The governess says Selena has left him in her charge for extended periods before and that she is confident Selena will return for him. As a mother should. Landon was very sad the day we laid Father to rest. He and Father had established a family bond. So much so that he considers me his rightful sister. I don't mind. He is a charming child. So charming I wonder if Selena can really be his natural mother. I, of course, would not suggest such a thing to him.

The Rebel raiders did no harm to Harmony Hill. The Shakers fed them gladly as they do all who come hungry to their doorsteps and in gratitude the men went on their way without stealing so much as one horse. The elders and eldresses were much relieved. But there is great consternation that General Morgan's raid is only a beginning. A Union cavalry troop camped out in the Shaker pastures not four days after Morgan passed through here. It is unthinkable what would have been the result if they had met in our village.

I remain with the Believers. Sister Martha still instructs me in their ways and says I will surely someday know the peace she carries in her heart if I open my ears to her words. Aunt Tish, Sister Latisha, has embraced the life. In one way she was sorry to hear Grayson was ashes for she knew how it wounded me, but I think she cared not a whit for herself. Grayson wasn't her home. It was her prison.

Every day I recall a new thing to mourn. My mother's portrait. The book of children's poems my grandfather often read to me before he died. The silver bell my mother gave me when I was four so that I could call for help if I was afraid in the night. But they are only things. As Sister Martha says, it is better to give up ownership of all things and to gather only spiritual gifts.

My mother's garden is gone, destroyed by Selena long before the fire completed *her work. We will never again walk among the roses at Grayson.*

Sadly,
Charlotte

She was becoming one of the Shakers, Adam thought as he looked up from reading through the letter for a second time. Charlotte a Shaker with no will or spirit of her own. It was almost more than he could imagine, but the proof was there in the words in front of his eyes. He scanned through them again. *Our village. Remain with the Believers. Someday know the peace. Spiritual gifts.*

He shut his eyes and pulled her image into his mind. He longed to look into her green eyes and perhaps take the pins from her beautiful red hair. At times in the last year, Charlotte's letters were all that had kept him sane as he followed first Grant's army in the west before Sam urged him back to the east to be on hand for McClellan's great victory as the general launched his Peninsular Campaign.

The Yankee army marched to within six miles of Richmond, but the Confederates didn't give ground. McClellan was forced to fall into retreat before he was ordered to load his army on boats to join General Pope in northern Virginia where once more the armies were fated to meet at

Bull Run Creek. The Union army attacked, this time sent into battle by General Pope in a rash bid to conquer the Southern forces before all of McClellan's men had time to reach the field of battle. But Robert E. Lee, now in command of the Southern army, turned the tables on Pope's forces and launched a surprise counterattack. In a tragic repeat of the first battle at Bull Run, the Union troops once more retreated back to Washington. Yet again there was no great victory to encourage the Northern people.

On the march away from the Bull Run battleground, Adam gave up his horse to a wounded soldier and trudged along the muddy roads with Jake's Massachusetts regiment. Since he often bivouacked with the men, they had become his company. He knew each of them by name and had done sketches of many of the men to send to their wives and mothers. And now those sketches would be all that ever returned home of some of the men who had fought their last battle.

Jake no longer worried aloud to Adam about what he would do when he saw the elephant. He knew, for he had charged forward in the face of deadly fire time and again. He had loaded and fired his gun at the men in gray and seen them thrown backward when the bullets found their target. He had heard bullets sing past his head and watched the men beside him fall. His horse had died under him, but he had stood and not run. He had survived to fight again.

But though he came through the battle unwounded, he'd been weakened by a bout with dysentery the week before and began coughing as they marched away from Bull Run back toward Washington in defeat yet again. A defeat made even more disheartening by the heavy rain beating down on their heads.

The rain made talk impossible, but there was nothing to say anyway. Nothing to be done except plod on through the mud. To move one foot in front of the other and try not to remember the sight of too many young soldiers sprawled in death, too many exploding shells, too many wounds from minié balls that tore muscles asunder and made amputation the only treatment.

Adam wanted to shut from his ears the sounds of horses dying, artillery shells screaming over-head, wounded men crying for help. He wanted to get on a train and ride away from it all. Maybe go west again and be in the wide open spaces where he could sketch the faces of the pioneers pushing the nation westward. In the last year, his pen had drawn too many scenes of battle, sent back too many sketches of Union defeats. Gone were the early dreams of a quick victory and a fast return to peace. At times peace no longer seemed possible. And now it seemed that even the peace he'd always imagined at Harmony Hill was being disturbed by the war.

He looked up from Charlotte's letter as Jake stirred on the narrow bed in front of him. What the enemy hadn't been able to do on the battlefield, the miserable weather and wretched conditions in the camps were doing to his once strong young brother. Jake tried to lift his head up off the pillow, but he was too weak as he was wracked with coughs that tore at his lungs but gave him no relief. Adam stuffed the letter inside his shirt and moved to hold Jake's head. When his coughing was spent, Adam gently wiped the flecks of blood from his brother's lips and held the draught of medicine the doctor had prepared for him to his mouth. He got him to swallow a bit.

Jake's captain had moved him into the makeshift hospital the night before when he'd begun to burn with fever. Adam hadn't been at the camp. He'd gone to the hotel to put the finishing touches on his sketches of the battle. If he'd been there when his brother most needed him, Adam would have never let him be brought to this long, narrow building that had been turned into a hospital for soldiers like Jake who had survived the battle only to be felled by disease. Cots were set up so close together that the men could have reached out and held hands all the way down the line if most of them hadn't been too sick to even realize there was a man in the next bed.

Nurses wearing long white aprons and caps

that made him think of Charlotte in her Shaker dress moved among the men to comfort them with a gentle word or, if they were very bad, a dose of laudanum. Most of the women had no training, but simply showed up at the hospital to care for the men. A couple of doctors made the rounds. Twice while Adam watched, the doctors stood up after examining one of the men and let the nurse with him pull the sheet up over the soldier's face. And though he hated himself for it, Adam knew that when he next took out his sketchbook, he would draw that picture.

As the hours dragged by, Adam began to fear the face his pencil might draw under the sheet would be Jake's. Adam had come to sit with Jake as soon as he received word he'd been brought to the hospital, but he should have never left Jake to go to the hotel. He knew his brother was getting sick as they marched back to Washington. He'd heard his cough. He should have stayed in the camp to take care of him.

If he'd been there when Jake first began to burn with fever, he could have loaded him on a train and taken him to their mother and Phoebe. Even now he wanted to pick him up in his arms and carry him home. There Jake might fight off the pneumonia, but the doctor claimed moving him would surely kill him. That his only chance was to ride out the fever. To fight off the pneumonia. He was a young man. He had a chance.

The second morning, Jake seemed improved. The sheen of fever still sat on his face and the coughing continued to bring up blood, but at least there was recognition in his eyes when he looked at Adam.

"What are you doing here?" Jake's voice was little more than a hoarse whisper.

"What do you think?" Adam helped Jake sit up a little as he put a glass of water to Jake's lips. The nurse had promised to bring broth when she saw Jake was awake.

Jake turned his head and looked around. The water had moistened his mouth and made his voice stronger. "I don't know. For sure, there's nothing to draw here that any of the people back home will want to see."

"You've got that right," Adam agreed in a voice that he knew at once was too hearty.

Jake eyed him for a moment before he said, "I must be fearful sick." He made a sound that might have been an attempt at a laugh, but it triggered his coughing.

Adam held Jake's shoulders while the coughs tore at his lungs. In the last few weeks, Jake had lost so much weight while he battled dysentery and now the pneumonia that his bones almost protruded from his skin.

When at last the coughs eased, Jake wiped his mouth and looked at the blood on the rag. He stared at it a long time before he whispered, "I am fearful sick." He looked up at Adam as if hoping he might deny it.

Adam didn't. Jake needed the truth. "You are. Pneumonia, the doctor says."

"Giles Whited died of pneumonia in May. Homer Martin went down to it in June. Or was it typhoid that got Homer?" He frowned a minute before he shook his head a little. "Doesn't matter. Either way it seemed a wrong way to die in a war." He stared across the room. "Funny, you think about somebody shooting you or maybe getting torn apart by a shell, but you don't think about your body letting you down by getting sick. Not my body anyway. I never got sick back home."

"When you feel a little better, I'll take you home. Once there, Phoebe will see to it that you get well."

Jake smiled. "She would, wouldn't she? This wouldn't be in her plan for me."

"Did she have a plan for you?"

"Oh yeah. Marry well and have handsome children and become a gentleman with the means to do good. Said it would make Mother happy."

"Not a bad plan," Adam said as he pushed another drink on Jake. "Till the war got in the way."

"That did disrupt her plans. Or at least me joining up did. How about you? Did she have a plan for you too?"

"Probably, but if she did, she gave up on it some time back. For one, she had to accept that I'd never settle for hearth and home over art."

"Couldn't you do both?" Jake asked.

"I never thought so. Maybe because I never met the woman that made me want to try." At least until now, Adam added silently as he felt Charlotte's letter touching his skin inside his shirt.

Again Jake looked away from Adam to stare across the room. He turned the rag and spat in it before he muffled a few coughs and wiped his mouth again. His face was very pale as he closed his eyes and sank back on the pillow Adam had propped behind him.

Adam pulled the chair a nurse had found for him up closer to the bed so that he could steady Jake if his head fell to the side in his sleep. But Jake wasn't through talking. He kept his eyes closed as he said, "I was in love once."

"Were you?" Adam said.

"Oona was beautiful. And fun. Her father sold fruits and vegetables to us. He and her mother came over from Ireland. She claimed they had a big farm there. Were richer than we ever thought of being before the potato blight. Her mother hated America, wished for Ireland from the time she got up in the morning until she went to bed at night, but her father refused to speak of

Ireland at all. He said there was no purpose to looking back. He had such an accent I could barely understand him when he brought the produce for Mother's kitchen."

"What happened?" Adam asked. Of course, he knew the story. Jake's youth, barely seventeen at the time. The inappropriate girl. Phoebe taking charge and nipping the romance in the bud.

Jake looked at Adam. "You know what happened." A touch of anger sparked in his eyes.

"Phoebe."

"And you helped her." Jake was hit by another spasm of coughing.

Adam waited until the coughing subsided and Jake was once more lying back on the pillow before he said, "I didn't help her, Jake, but neither did I try to dissuade her. You were too young to think of marriage."

"That didn't mean I couldn't be in love." Jake shut his eyes as if he didn't have the energy to hold his eyelids open. It was a long time before he went on, but Adam knew he wasn't sleeping. At last he said, "Phoebe told me it couldn't be real love, as if she could know. Not married to that old stick she latched on to for his money. If it wasn't your money she used to pay Oona's father to send Oona away, then it must have been his."

"I don't know," Adam answered honestly.

"I should have gone after her, hunted until I

found her. I should have, but instead I listened to Phoebe saying what was best for the family. As if that was best for me." Jake blew out a breath that made him cough again. "And now look at me. About to die with nothing to leave behind to ever show I walked this green earth. At least it used to be green before we started blowing up the pastures."

"You're not going to die."

"We all die," Jake said. "Every last one of us." Jake opened his eyes and stared straight at Adam. "Have you ever been in love?"

"I think so," Adam said, shifting in his chair. Why couldn't he just admit to his brother that he loved Charlotte? Perhaps because he hadn't fully admitted it to his own heart yet.

"If you ever are, you won't have to think so. You'll know. I'm glad I at least felt the feeling. You think people will fall in love in heaven?"

"If it makes them happy." But again he was thinking of the Shaker community that was turning Charlotte into one of them. They claimed to be making a paradise on earth, but there was no love between man and woman there.

"Love takes you past mere happiness. At least until you lose it." Jake coughed again and shut his eyes before he went on. "But you never have to wonder with love. If you love somebody, you know. Just like with Jesus. You know."

"What do you know?" Adam leaned forward in

his chair to be sure he didn't miss what Jake might say next.

But Jake didn't answer. He had finally fallen to sleep or slipped off into unconsciousness again. Adam stared at his brother's pale face and wished he did know whatever it was Jake knew about the Lord so that he could pray for him. Instead he pulled out Charlotte's letter and read her words again. He wondered if she prayed. It sounded like she might. If only he could rush a letter to her and ask her to pray for Jake. But a letter would take weeks. Jake might not have weeks.

Adam laid his hand gently on his brother's arm. His fingers were trembling and his heart began to pound as he whispered the words, "Please, Lord."

31

September 18, 1862
Dear Charlotte,
    Please forgive me for not writing sooner to convey my sympathy for the loss of your father, but it has been a time of sadness here as well. My brother, Jake, the one in the sketch I sent you some months back, succumbed to pneumonia on September 10 after the Union army's retreat

from *Bull Run* once again. You would have liked Jake. He embraced life and ran after adventure. He was only twenty and had escaped death on the battlefield several times, but what the enemy couldn't do, sickness did. Snuffed out his young life in less than a fortnight.

Phoebe, my sister, holds me directly responsible for Jake's death. I don't disagree with her. He was not much more than a boy and not ready for the army. But he showed staunch courage and acquitted himself well in battle. In spite of what Phoebe believes, I don't think I could have convinced him to quit his company. That said, I could have been with him when he fell so ill. Then I might have been able to see he got better treatment. The army doctors try, but there are so many succumbing to illness in the camps. Pneumonia isn't even the biggest killer. Dysentery is rampant and typhoid and measles have felled many more than bullets thus far. Although too many have died on the battlefield as well.

We are receiving news of the battle at Antietam and are told it is one of the most tragic yet with reports of thousands dead or wounded on both sides. Some other artist did the illustrations you will see in Harper's. I had to take Jake's body back to Boston and have continued here with my mother for a few days. In truth, I am glad I wasn't there to draw the scenes. I am weary of death.

How many men can we keep losing? Why don't sensible heads find a way to peace? Bud Keeling, the reporter I may have told you about, says things have gone too far to achieve any peace now except that wrested from the enemy on the battlefield. He claims that with the Union finally claiming a victory here in the east at Antietam, there are reliable reports Mr. Lincoln will issue some sort of emancipation proclamation. Few here harbor the least doubt any longer that the President plans to put an end to slavery. The South will not accept that and so the fight will continue until the Union finally overcomes. I cannot imagine our nation divided into two countries if the Union falls. The President must find the generals to win the war.

Forgive me for continuing on and on about the war. I would like to retreat from the conflict. Perhaps go to California far from the sound of cannons. But that is not to be. It is my job to draw the scenes even if they are scenes no one, including *myself, wants to see. The people deserve to know what is happening, and at times a picture can tell more than a page of words.*

I hear Lexington has been occupied by the Confederates. I hope that has not caused the Shakers at Harmony Hill undue trouble. I don't know where Sam will send me next, but wherever it is, I will take the memory of your mother's roses with me and think upon the beauty in her garden when I am most filled with despair. Keep in mind, as I think I told you once before, that gardens lay dormant every winter and grow afresh each spring.

If you have a moment or your Sister Martha has a moment, your prayers for my mother who mourns her son would be most appreciated.

Faithfully yours,
Adam

"Such sorrow in the world," Sister Martha said when Charlotte looked up from Adam's letter with tears in her eyes. "If only all could see the truth of the Believers' way. The truth Mother Ann taught us."

Charlotte wiped away her tears with the corner of her apron as Sister Martha continued her little sermon. "Our testimony is for peace, now and always. Mother Ann taught us to oppose wars of households, and wars of nations, and if we follow her teachings, we will know the peace that is promised the obedient follower."

"But how can we keep wars away? How can we not mourn our loved ones?"

Sister Martha kept her voice gentle even though there was a hint of reproof in her words. "We can love as we should love. As brothers and sisters love. With the proper peace in our hearts, we don't have to worry about wars or the hereafter. We only have to live our lives and do our work as though this could be the last day of our life or as if we might live a thousand years. We seek perfection in all."

"But this mother grieves the loss of her son." Charlotte looked down at the letter she still held. She ran her fingers across Adam's writing. "This brother grieves the loss of his brother."

"Yea, it is so. They know not the peace we have here. They are of the world. I can see that as yet your own mind continues to stray toward worldly thinking. Even after more than a year among us." Sister Martha mashed her lips together and studied Charlotte's face a moment before she heaved a sigh. "It could be I let my desire for news of the war front cloud my judgment and I was wrong to persuade the Ministry to allow you to receive these letters. I fear his words have encouraged you to keep one foot in the world."

"It is true that I have not been able to put my feet solidly on the Shaker pathway," Charlotte admitted. "My spirit seems to seek something more."

"As does our artist friend." Sister Martha pointed to the letter and then looked straight at Charlotte. "He seeks affection from you and not that of the brotherly sort."

Charlotte looked down quickly to hide the color burning her cheeks as her heart leaped with joy at the thought. If only it could be true. But such a response could not be condoned by the Shakers, even one as kind as Sister Martha.

Again Sister Martha sighed. She leaned nearer Charlotte and laid her dry, wrinkled hand on her arm. "I do not condemn you for allowing the temptations of the world to follow you here. You came into our village unsure of your direction, and since that time, you have stepped forward in your spiritual quest. I see that. But you carry with you the threads of your worldly life. Not only your feelings for this man, but also the attachment to your land and home that you now mourn as this man mourns his brother. You cannot cling forever to both sides. You must decide for the world or for the truth of a Believer."

"What would you have me choose?" Charlotte asked softly without looking up at Sister Martha.

She didn't think she would see disapproval on the woman's face, but because of her fondness for the old sister, she feared seeing disappointment there.

"Salvation seems the only choice to me, but many have chosen otherwise."

"Cannot those of the world find salvation without living the Shaker way?" She studied the letter she held in her lap. She did not want to make a choice between salvation and love. She could not believe the Lord required that of her.

"Not true salvation."

"What of your daughter? You told me once that she chose a different way." Charlotte peeked up at Sister Martha to be sure her question wasn't too bold. "Did that condemn her in your eyes?"

"You ask a difficult question. One that I should perhaps not answer, but the two of us, we have naught but truth between us. I know you haven't told me everything that is in your heart, but I also know that what you have told me has been truthful. I can do no less than the same for you."

Sister Martha turned her eyes away from Charlotte's face to stare toward the window. They were alone in the room on the first floor of the Centre Family House that Sister Martha rarely left anymore. Charlotte carried her meals to her every day. The summer had been especially hot and dry, and the heat had continued into September. Sister Martha could no longer summon the strength to go about the village. Instead she kept busy corresponding with other Shaker villages.

Now as Charlotte waited quietly for Sister Martha to start speaking again, she could faintly hear the bang of pans in the kitchen deep in the building where the sisters were cooking for the hungry soldiers who passed through the village like unending clouds of locusts sucking up water and food. Charlotte thought sometimes it was only the Shakers' prayers that kept the wells from running dry.

Finally Sister Martha looked back at Charlotte. "Often our eyes do not want to behold the truth. Just like with this war. We here at Harmony Hill would like to believe we can keep its conflict from our village, but we cannot. We are in its path and we will suffer some consequences of the worldly struggle. Just as Elder Homer did when the two soldiers held the gun to his head and demanded the horses last week. We would have surrendered a dozen horses to them before we would have chanced harm to Elder Homer, but he refused to give in to their violent demands. In the end his gentle spirit overpowered their evil intents and they went on their way empty-handed."

When Charlotte frowned a little, Sister Martha smiled and held up a hand to keep Charlotte from speaking as she continued. "I see your confusion. You wonder why I speak of the war and Elder Homer when you asked of my daughter of the world. Perhaps because I have no ready answer. I think I once told you of my despair when she first left the village years ago. She was the same as lost to me then. Dead to our Society here."

Sister Martha reached up and absently tucked a strand of gray hair back under her cap before she pulled it down tighter on her head. She patted her feet lightly on the floor as if that might help her come up with the best words to explain. "Of course you have to understand I had already given her up as a daughter. That was required as soon as we joined with the Believers. We were sisters just as you and I are sisters. I embraced the ways of the Society and I thought she did as well. There were those among the Ministry who thought Gabrielle would become a leader here. She had amazing gifts of the spirit. Many more than I. But then the stranger came into our midst and held out his hand to her and she went with him."

"Did you ever see her again?"

"Once. She came with her firstborn. A girl she called Martha. Named after me. I stood in the visitors' room and told her not to come again. I think I feared losing my own way as I believed she had lost hers." Sister Martha hesitated a moment as if her next words were too hard to speak. "For the little child—she couldn't have been over two—pulled at my heartstrings. I wanted to pick her up and feel her sweet breath against my cheek. But I couldn't deny the way I had chosen any more than my daughter who went to the world could deny her own path. It was how it had to be."

Sister Martha leaned forward until she was looking directly into Charlotte's eyes. "And that is how your path must be, my child. If the seeker comes for you, then perhaps the good Lord will put the right answer in your heart and you will see the proper path before you. You must pray so."

"Yea," Charlotte said. She didn't add that her prayers had seemed empty since the loss of her father. She worried that would make Sister Martha feel the need for more words to buoy Charlotte's spirit when it was obvious her many words had already drained the old sister of strength as she sat back and panted a little to gather her breath.

"We shall pray this nation will find the right answers as well. That the two sides will find a way to cease their hostilities." Again she breathed in and out before she said, "You must get back to your duties. Those in the kitchen at the Gathering House will need your hands."

Charlotte carefully folded Adam's letter and

slid it back in the envelope. She wanted to let her eyes dwell on his words again, on his promise of the garden coming back to life after the winter. Perhaps that was what she was feeling, a winter of the soul that had nothing to do with the date on the calendar.

As she hurried back to the Gathering Family House where there would be a new sack of potatoes or perhaps a basket of apples waiting for her paring knife, she thought the whole country seemed to be deep in a winter of sorrow with so many fields turning to battlegrounds. Sister Martha had been right that no matter how much the Believers desired peace, there was none to be had in Harmony Hill with the Confederate soldiers passing through the village on a daily basis now. Not three nights before, a company had camped in the middle of their village and posted sentries all around. They had been enveloped by the Rebel army. The hungry Rebel army.

Elder Quinton said that the Southern army must have invaded Kentucky simply because there was no food to be had in the South. In truth many of the barefoot Rebel soldiers were ragged and dirty. They were surely out of place at Harmony Hill where, in obedience to Mother Ann's teachings, dirt was chased from every crack and crevice, but there had been little rain for weeks and no way for the men to present a better appearance.

As the dry, hot days of September passed, all attempts to maintain the regular industry of the village had been suspended. Instead the Shakers hurried to pick their corn and fruit to secrete some of it for the winter and keep it from all being devoured by the soldiers passing through the village. There was no time for making brooms or hats and no market for them if they had been made. The war controlled everything now. Even Harmony Hill—where it began to feel as if every soldier in the Confederate army sought food in their village.

They had little choice but to prepare the meals and feed the men who came to their doors famished for food and drink. It was no less than their Christian duty and what Mother Ann would require them do, Sister Altha told Charlotte and Dulcie as they worked side by side in the Gathering Family kitchen.

"She would have us do good in every way we can." Sister Altha frowned, yet it was not crossly but more from sadness. "These poor men need some goodness in their lives."

"Or at least some bread," Dulcie said.

"Yea, at the very least some bread," Sister Altha agreed.

Sister Altha had tempered her attitude toward Charlotte since Grayson had burned. Charlotte wasn't sure if that was because she felt sympathy for Charlotte or because she thought that now

435

the hundred acres promised might become a thousand if Charlotte inherited the land as it seemed she would. A letter had come to Harmony Hill from her father's lawyer indicating that under the terms of her Grandfather Grayson's will the land was only given over to her father for use in his lifetime. Upon his death Grayson was to pass directly to Charlotte.

Selena would have no claim upon the land if she returned. The letter stated in clear terms that the deceased's widow was entitled to a portion of the personal property of the deceased. But the household goods were now ashes, most of the able-bodied slaves of any worth had slipped away to the North after the fire, and the Confederates had made off with the horses. With Grayson in ruins, Selena had little reason to return except to claim her son. It was rumored she had ridden south with one of the Confederate officers, but that was all it was. Rumors and gossip.

Charlotte didn't care. She'd put Selena from her mind as soon as she returned to Harmony Hill after the funeral. She had too much to worry about in determining her own path to waste time wondering about Selena's. She did worry about Landon, but there was nothing she could do for him except pray that perhaps father number three would be as kind to him as her own father had obviously been.

Until Charlotte was called from the kitchen to the visitors' room, she had assumed Selena had come for Landon weeks before. But when Sister Altha ushered her into the room, he jumped up off the hard bench and ran to bury his face against her and hide among her skirts as he had at the fire. The smoke no longer circled about them nor did the flames reach for them as they had that night, but even so in some ways the fire would always bind them together.

"Miss Pennebaker says you have to tell them you're my sister the way you said you were." He spoke the first words into her skirt before he peered up at Charlotte with a fierce look that demanded she say the words he wanted to hear, but down under the fierceness in his brown eyes was such a deep well of sadness, it made Charlotte's heart hurt.

He didn't give her time to speak before he said, "Remember?" His voice cracked on the word.

Charlotte tightened her arms around him and pulled him close. She could feel him almost melting against her as the tension drained from him. She forgot about Sister Altha frowning beside her and Miss Pennebaker staring down her long, thin nose at them from where she stood in front of the bench against the wall.

Nobody else in the room mattered as she gently pushed Landon back from her to kneel down and stare straight into his face with eyes every bit as fierce as his own. "I am your sister."

"Thank you," he whispered. His hands gripped the sleeves of her dress so tightly she thought he might never turn her loose. "I've always wanted a sister."

32

"Don't let the child cling to you," Sister Altha said. "Such unrestrained demonstrations of affection are not seemly."

Charlotte squeezed Landon's hands as she pulled free from him to stand up. With her back to Sister Altha, she winked at Landon and smiled even as she kept her voice meek. "Yea, Sister Altha. He has no knowledge of the Shaker way."

"But it is assumed you do, Sister Charlotte."

"Yea." Charlotte smiled at Landon again before she turned toward Sister Altha and bent her head with a show of shame for her improper behavior. "You are right, Sister Altha."

Sister Altha must have seen the dregs of Charlotte's smile, for she blew out a burst of air in exasperation. "Sister Charlotte, explain yourself. Did you not tell us you had no brothers in the world?"

"Landon's mother was married to my father. He is my stepbrother."

"I see. That does not explain why he is here. What of his mother?"

"If you will allow me," Miss Pennebaker spoke up and advanced on them from the bench. Landon dropped his eyes to the floor as the thin, angular woman went on in a stilted voice. "His mother left the boy in my care. We have been at the hotel in town awaiting her return, but it appears that she has been detained. The hotel owner is naturally demanding the money due him and the funds Mrs. Vance left with me are long gone. It is only through the charity of some of Mr. Vance's friends that we have not gone hungry, but charity becomes a burden after a time."

"Yea, so it seems in the world," Sister Altha said with a slight nod toward the governess.

"I would not desert the child, you understand. He has been in my care for well over a year now, and though he is somewhat willful and a reluctant learner, he has a good heart."

She spoke about Landon as if he weren't in the room. He edged a step closer to Charlotte, who let her hand drift over to touch his arm as she said, "A good heart can cover many faults."

"Yes, well." The governess hesitated as if searching for the proper words. "In town it is said that you Shakers practice kindness for the unfortunate."

"We help those who come to our door," Sister Altha said.

"That is what I hoped to hear. Especially since I knew the one he keeps speaking of as his sister resides here with you. Which is the subject of much conjecture in the town, I can assure you." Miss Pennebaker raised her eyebrows at Charlotte before she looked back at Sister Altha.

"Our sister searches for the way to salvation here among us," Sister Altha said mildly.

"Yes, well, I suppose that is a worthy endeavor." Miss Pennebaker looked as if she doubted her own words before she cleared her throat and went on. "Be that as it may, what with the Rebel vagabond army in the area, conditions have become entirely too perilous for me to remain any longer. I have been fortunate enough to obtain a new position with a family in Chicago and have a ticket on a train tomorrow. But quite naturally there is no way I can take the boy with me."

"That is understandable," Sister Altha said. "What is it you ask of us?"

"To see to the boy until his mother returns. It should be the duty of his sister." The woman's eyes settled on Charlotte. "If she really considers herself thus."

"Yea, not only a duty but a desire," Charlotte said. She turned to Sister Altha. "I will do what-ever is needed to make a place for him here if

440

that is what he wants." Charlotte leaned over to ask him, "Is that what you want, Landon?"

"I want to stay with you." His brown eyes searched hers.

"It won't be exactly with me. We won't stay in the same houses, but we will be in the same village. We will see one another at times, and you will come to know other boys who can help you learn what is expected of you. They will teach you to work with your hands as do I."

"And you'll always be my sister?" He clutched her apron.

Charlotte touched his cheek and smiled. "I will always be your sister. That will never change. But at Harmony Hill all are sisters and brothers, so you will have many new sisters and brothers."

"I only want you as a sister." He looked worried.

"Here we must follow the rules of the Society," Charlotte said. "But such will be good discipline for a seafaring captain."

"Seafaring?" Sister Altha said behind her. "Of what do you speak, Sister Charlotte?"

The governess answered, "The child goes on and on about going to sea. It is no more than a foolish child's playmaking."

Charlotte didn't look at her, but she had no problem hearing the scorn in the woman's voice.

Landon paid their words no mind as he kept his eyes pinned on Charlotte's face. "You won't leave me like my mother did, will you?"

"She may return yet for you," Charlotte said.

"No. I have ever been a burden to her. Will I be a burden to you? Will you desert me here?"

"Nay." Charlotte leaned close to whisper for his ears only. "I never will."

"Whatever you speak, speak for all to hear, Sister Charlotte."

"Yea, I beg your forgiveness, Sister Altha. I was merely assuring Brother Landon he would not be a burden here." Charlotte stood up and turned toward Sister Altha. She met her eyes. "If I must promise a price, I will."

"Nay," Sister Altha said quickly with a wave of her hand. Charlotte was shocked to see a blush crawl up into her cheeks. "Our charity cannot be bought. You surely have learned that while with us, my sister. We take in many children in need."

"Yea," Charlotte said. There was no need to speak of the promise she'd made and kept for Aunt Tish. It lay in the air between them. But now it seemed to be a matter Sister Altha preferred not to recall.

"Come, we will take the little brother to the Children's House." Sister Altha held out her hand to him with as much of a smile as ever crossed her face before she gave the governess an unsmiling look of dismissal. "Good day, Miss Pennebaker."

Miss Pennebaker fiddled uneasily with the clasp on her receptacle and didn't move toward the door. "There is the small matter of the money due me if Miss Vance would be so generous."

In spite of the woman's stiff manner, Charlotte felt some sympathy for her. She had done her duty by Landon even if she didn't show any fondness for him. "I am sorry, but I have no money to pay you," she said with regret.

The woman's eyes widened in disbelief. "You own Grayson. Over a thousand acres of land and the slaves to work it. You can't stand there and say you have no money. You're rich, Miss Vance. Rich!"

Charlotte stared at Miss Pennebaker, and for the first time since her father's death realized that what the woman said was true. Charlotte was rich in land. She thought of the rolling hills she'd loved to gaze upon from Grayson's veranda. She thought of the stands of trees and the green pastures. She thought of the men working the fields and her fond memories halted. She would not be rich in people. As soon as allowed she would sign papers of manumission for any remaining servants. And land without workers filled no coffers.

"Here at Harmony Hill, we have all things in

common," she said after a moment. She still had her hand on Landon's shoulder.

"You have given them Grayson?" Miss Pennebaker sounded shocked.

"Nay. I am yet a novitiate and not a full member of the Society. But even though as you say I may be wealthy in land, I have no cash. Whatever might have been in the house was lost in the fire and all in the bank—if there is any and I do not know for I didn't know my father's business—"

Miss Pennebaker interrupted her. "Mrs. Vance did."

"Yea, but she is not here to reveal what she may have known," Charlotte said with as much patience as she could muster. Her sympathy for the governess was wearing thin. "Be that as it may, any money in my father's name is in his lawyer's hands until the estate is settled. So I do regret that I have naught to give you. Perhaps you can make a claim with the lawyer, Mr. Granville, in the town."

"How much do you want?" Sister Altha asked suddenly.

"Fifty dollars," Miss Pennebaker answered without hesitation.

"The Ministry will give you twenty. And at that you may be overpaid. Come with me." Sister Altha turned on her heel to lead the way out of the room.

In the hall she looked back at Charlotte who was following along behind Miss Pennebaker with Landon. She didn't smile, but Charlotte understood her look. Paying the governess was Sister Altha's way of making amends for the bargain she'd pushed on Charlotte the year before. Charlotte accepted her look with a slight bend of her head. And she knew that when the day came that she left the Shakers—and she suddenly knew without a doubt that day would come—she would deed two hundred acres of her beloved Grayson to them. Not because she owed it, but because here she had found love. From Sister Martha. From Dulcie and Gemma. And now if not love, then acceptance from Sister Altha.

Sister Altha lifted her chin a bit in acknowledgment of Charlotte's nod. "You may take the child to the Children's House, Sister Charlotte. Brother Ballard will help him settle in. He has a joyful way like our Sister Gemma."

Landon hung back and grabbed hold of Charlotte's apron when Brother Ballard reached for his hand. "Why can't I stay with you? You said you are my sister."

"Yea. And I am." She gave Brother Ballard a beseeching look as she pulled Landon a little apart to speak with him. With a kind smile, Brother Ballard stepped back to give her the moment she needed. She turned her full attention on Landon as she tried to explain. "But the Shakers have many rules, and while we are here we must abide by them. It was difficult for me too at first, but bending my will to their ways has taught me much about the strength of my spirit and helped me develop patience. It will do the same for you in the time you're here before your mother comes for you."

"She won't come. Not unless she has need of a son again as she did with my second papa. She knew he wanted a son."

"You're right. He did. As much as I tried, I could not fill that spot in his heart that desired a son," Charlotte admitted as sadness welled up in her.

"He loved you," Landon said simply. "He was always telling me about my sister, Charley, and how good it would be when you came home."

"But then I didn't." The sadness grew and sat like a heavy stone inside her chest.

"You came home when he needed you. To say goodbye." The little boy had his fierce look on again. "I didn't say goodbye to my first papa. He loved me like our papa loved you. He told me he was going to heaven, but I didn't know he meant that night. I wish I had hugged him longer. I wish I had said goodbye."

A tear slid out of the corner of his eye and trailed down his cheek. It loosed something inside Charlotte and released the tears that

446

she had been carrying around in a tight knot inside her. She knelt down and pulled the little boy close to let their tears mix. After a while, when she could find her voice, she said, "He knew. Just like you said my father knew." Charlotte rubbed the tears off his cheeks with her apron and then dried her own. "The Lord told him."

He watched her and then glanced back at Brother Ballard, waiting patiently a little ways behind them. "Did the Lord tell you to come here?"

"I don't think so, but sometimes our feet walk strange paths to get where we need to be."

"And where is that?" He frowned as he waited for her answer.

"I don't know, Landon, but wherever it is, I promise to let you walk the path with me if you want. But for a while we need to stay here and do as they ask us. Do you think you can put your seafaring spirit aside for a few weeks and listen to Brother Ballard? It is not a bad thing to learn to work."

"As long as you stay my sister."

"Forever I will be your sister." She did not allow herself to think of Adam and what her promise might mean if he did come back for her. He had told her he could not be tied down. But the promise had been made. Whatever the cost, she would keep it.

• • •

In October the news came to Harmony Hill that General Bragg's army was marching up from the south to join with the Confederate troops already deeply entrenched in the central and southern parts of the state in order to push the Union army out of Kentucky. With Kentucky in Southern hands, there would be a clear road to the north and new supplies of horses and food for the Rebel army.

Only a day after the news of troop movements reached them, General Kirby-Smith's army rode into Harmony Hill in search of food. The soldiers they'd fed prior to this had been hungry, but they had been respectful as the Shakers brought out meals for them. These soldiers were too tired, too hungry, too thirsty to worry about proper behavior. Brother Quinton said they rushed the pumps like herds of buffalo at a salt lick and cared not who they might trample in the stampede. Then with their thirst slaked, they flocked around the kitchen doors and windows like hungry wolves ready to devour every morsel thrown out to them. Some even leveled their guns at their fellow soldiers when it was concluded the cakes or pies were not divided equally.

The sisters and brethren worked from before daylight until midnight preparing hundreds of meals, and still it was not enough.

33

Adam got off the train in Louisville and headed toward where a man at the station said General Buell's army was mustering in new troops. He could have hired a buggy. Sam wouldn't complain about the expense since he'd sent Adam to Kentucky. Several hansom cabs waited at the station with horses hitched and ready, but Adam wanted a horse, not a cab. Usually at least one buggy horse demonstrated some spirit, and Adam could make a deal with the driver, but today he didn't see a decent-looking animal in the whole row of conveyances for hire.

When he asked one of the drivers about it, the heavily bearded man looked at Adam as though he might have just fallen out of the sky. His answer was a terse two words. "The war."

The war. The war was the reason for everything. Men, who a year before were friends and even brothers, now lined up on opposite sides of the battlefields and fired their muskets at one another. Men not much more than boys died before they even got a good sip of life. Horses were confiscated. Houses burned and gardens left in ruins.

He stopped walking and looked at the sky to get his directions. Then he turned to stare to the southeast. Charlotte was there. Not that far on the train. In her Shaker dress. Or perhaps she had left Harmony Hill to go back to rebuild Grayson. He didn't know. If she had written again, no letter had caught up with him.

After Jake's funeral, he'd gone from Boston to Washington, D.C., to hear the President's speech declaring that unless the rebelling states returned to the Union by January first, he would issue a proclamation freeing their slaves. Then Adam had ridden to where the Potomac Army was once more resting and waiting. It seemed even after the victory at Antietam, the Northern generals had seemed content to sit on their hands and once more do absolutely nothing to achieve an end to the conflict. Rumors were swirling that Mr. Lincoln was ready to replace General McClellan.

When Adam found the encampment of Jake's Massachusetts Company, many unfamiliar faces occupied the spots around the campfires with new recruits filling the ranks decimated by the last battle at Bull Run. An old sergeant by the name of Hoffman stood up from the camp stool in front of his tent when he saw Adam and came over to offer his sympathies.

"It was a bad one down there and a worse one after we got back. Lost five to typhoid, three to dysentery, and Jake to the lung rot. And that was just out of our company." The sergeant shook his head. "I never thought Jake would go down that way. Strong as an ox when he joined up. A good boy. Brave to a fault."

"Yes." A knot formed in Adam's throat and kept him from saying more.

Sergeant Hoffman turned his eyes away from Adam back toward the men spread out around them to give him time to bring his emotions under control. After a minute or two, the sergeant said, "Plenty more gonna be following him over to the other side. May the good Lord have mercy on us all."

Now as Adam stood staring in the direction of Harmony Hill, he wondered if Charlotte or her Sister Martha was praying for his mother the way he'd asked in his last letter. He had almost written the words to ask them to pray for him too, but he had no right to ask for such prayers. Not after years of pushing the Lord aside as though he were no more important than an old pair of shoes Adam had outgrown.

Yet as he'd sat by Jake through his brother's last hard hours, the need to pray burned within him as he leaned his head over on Jake's bed and wanted to put his own breath inside his brother's lungs to ease his labored breathing. In his anguish he knew no formal words of prayer other than those he'd been taught as a child. *Our Father who art in heaven . . . Now I lay me down to sleep . . . Thank you for the blessing of our food.*

Please don't let my brother die. That should have been easy to pray. The chaplain who came to pray over Jake the morning before he died said things about how the Lord heard and answered even unuttered prayers, but that the answer was not always healing. He said a child of God had to accept the Lord's will.

Adam had wanted to ask him if he thought the war was the Lord's will, but he had bit his lip and stayed silent. It didn't seem wise to challenge a man of God at the same time he was seeking prayers for his brother. Then before night fell, Jake let out one last shuddering breath and did not pull in another. The chaplain's prayers had not protected Jake. But even worse, Adam had not protected his little brother. Adam had stayed on the sidelines and watched while his little brother ran into battle. Always the watcher and not the doer, and now he'd watched his brother die.

The war. The reason for much death. Adam shook away thoughts of Jake. He had to think about drawing the scenes of war. That was his job. He couldn't think about how close he was to Harmony Hill and Charlotte. Not yet. There would come another day in a garden, but first the war.

And it looked as if Sam was right to send him to Kentucky. The man had a nose for where the next battle was going to be. Louisville was overrun with Union troops as General Buell's forces had just made a fast march from Tennessee to Louisville to stop the advance of the Confederate General Bragg and his troops who were trying to drive the Union out of Kentucky. Lexington had fallen to the Confederates and news was coming in that Bragg had left his main army in Bardstown to go to Frankfort for the purpose of installing a Confederate governor.

By the time Adam got to the Union's camp, the soldiers were packing up to move out of Louisville. Reinforced with the twenty-five thousand fresh troops that had been waiting in Louisville, Buell's army of almost sixty thousand marched toward Bardstown to crush the Rebel advance. The Union could ill afford to lose Kentucky.

As they moved swiftly southeast across the state, Adam noted with each mile he was getting closer to Harmony Hill. When the Confederates fell back from Bardstown, it began to look like the armies might meet in Harrodsburg, practically in the Shakers' backyard. That would be sure to disturb the peace they constantly sought.

Adam couldn't keep from wondering if Charlotte was seeking that spiritual peace now. Would she welcome him when his feet finally found his way back to her? This near, he would not leave the area without seeing her. It mattered not that every garden he passed was parched from lack of rain and picked clean of even the smallest corn nubbin by the throngs of soldiers passing through. It mattered not that the gardens at Grayson were shriveled and blackened by the fire. The garden he sought to walk with Charlotte was a garden of the heart. But if she had turned to the Shaker way as her last letter seemed to indicate, her feet would not want to walk in such a garden.

He pushed it from his mind. First the war. First he would draw more illustrations of soldiers and death for Sam to print in his newspaper. Adam had stayed purposely aloof from the soldiers marching in the ranks. He did not want to know their names. He did not want to hear their talk about the sons and daughters waiting for them to save the Union and march home heroes. It was better to just see eyes and noses and mouths with nothing behind them. Not as good for his art, but easier on his heart.

The sun beat down on their heads and dust rose in clouds around them as they marched in the unusual October heat. The countryside hadn't seen rain for weeks, and the creeks where the men might have slaked their thirst were bone dry. The few ponds they came across that still held water were little more than pig wallows, but the men drank anyway, sometimes chasing out the hogs in order to fill their cups or canteens.

The sight turned Adam's stomach, and he took tiny sips from his own canteen to make his water last as long as possible.

They didn't make it to Harrodsburg. Instead the Confederates had halted their march by a river that yet held water near a little town called Perryville. With the soldiers and horses so in need of water to drink, the river was more than enough reason for the lines of battle to be formed.

At daylight, Adam found a spot on a knoll with a good view of the rolling countryside. To one side a big field of drying cornstalks stood in rows waiting to be shocked. Stone fences snaked across the fields giving the possibility of cover to the soldiers. But that would be little help against the artillery the gunners were moving into place.

Adam had seen it all before. The men lining up, advancing into the musket fire. The smoke rising and settling around the artillery guns. The storm of shell, grape, canister, and minié balls. The terrible sounds of the shells screaming overhead. He could have drawn it from memory before the first shell was fired. Even so, it was his job to see it all again and he wondered uneasily if he'd chosen the best viewpoint to watch and record. He wished Bud Keeling was there, because somehow the reporter always knew where and when the action would happen first.

Bud had stayed in the East. Where he said Adam should stay. "I'm not saying Kentucky's not important to the Union," Bud had said when Adam told him he was going west. "But nothing that happens there is gonna compare to what might happen here. Here's where General Lee is. That's who we gotta beat. And if the President ever finds a general who might make that happen, it'll be here in the East. Here's where the big battles are gonna happen. Not out there in Kentucky."

But Adam had come to Kentucky anyway, and now he sat with his sketchpad waiting for another battle. The day had dawned clear, with the rising sun revealing the fall colors in the trees along the little river. On the far side of the river, the Rebels were forming lines, pulling artillery into place, but neither side seemed to be in a hurry to get the battle underway.

The morning hours crept by with only a spatter of gunfire now and again to indicate a few skirmishes. The previous day the information had come down to the reporters that the attack was to commence at dawn before the day's heat drained the men of fighting energy, but then General Buell had been thrown by his horse and injured his back. So instead of riding out to direct the troops, he'd set up headquarters in a house a few miles away from where Adam now sat atop his knoll. Couriers were carrying his orders to the field, so that could be why the troops were slow to move into place.

A young reporter, who had latched on to Adam as a battle-savvy veteran and was dogging his steps, watched the scene below for a few minutes before he yawned and lay back in the dry grass. "Ain't it just like the army. Chase the enemy clear across to tomorrow, and then nobody wants to fire the first salvo." He plopped his hat over his face. "Wake me when they're ready."

For lack of anything better to do Adam drew his picture. The kid was covering his first battle. That was why he could sleep. He had no idea of what was coming the way Adam did. Adam didn't want to think about it as the minutes ticked by. Eventually the artillery would begin firing and the battle would be engaged, but now peace still reigned in the scene spread out below them. Crows cawed as they flew in and out of the cornfield. The soft coo of a mourning dove was almost drowned out by the chirr of grasshoppers in the parched pastures around the cornfield. Adam didn't see the first cow. No doubt the farmers had hidden their stock when they heard the armies were coming to keep the soldiers from having chunks of beef roasting on spits over their fires.

As the sun rose higher in the sky, the reporter continued to snooze while Adam felt the tension growing inside him. He wished he were anywhere other than on that knoll waiting for another battle to begin. He calculated the miles to Harmony Hill and how long it would take him to ride there. He sketched a garden full of roses and then drew Charlotte in the midst of it.

He stared at the sketch a long time and wondered why he hadn't left room for himself beside her. He had never put his image in any of the many sketches he'd done of Charlotte. Was that because he knew in his heart that his dream of holding her in his arms again was just that—a dream that would never come true? Perhaps he was only in love with a woman his imagination had created to be drawn by his pen. Perhaps she was nothing as he remembered and it was only the drums of war that made him wish for love just as Jake had wished for his lost love before he died. To leave something of himself behind even if it was only his memory in the heart of someone who had loved him no matter how briefly.

Maybe the best thing to do instead of calculating the miles to Harmony Hill would be to forget the kisses in the garden. To leave her in the peace of the Shakers or perhaps rebuilding her Grayson. But then he touched his pocket where he carried the last letter he had received from her, the one he'd read while Jake was in the hospital. It held no words of love.

He knew enough about the Shakers to know such would not be allowed by them, but yet she always mentioned the garden. In those words he sought the flowering of love even as his love for her had grown in his heart. He would not forget. He could not forget.

The Rebels fired their first artillery piece when the sun was directly overhead. The young reporter sat up, startled by the noise. But then eagerness lit up his face as he jumped to his feet to get a better view.

"It's started," he said.

"It has," Adam agreed as he turned his sketchbook back to the peaceful pasture scene to begin drawing in the scenes of death.

"How come there aren't any soldiers charging across the field?" the reporter asked.

"They will. The artillery always gets things under way."

Adam tried to recall what the kid had said his name was. Max, maybe. Or Mike. That was it. Mike Putnam. Adam had told him to write his name on a piece of paper and put it in his pocket. A lot of the soldiers had started doing that so their remains could be identified even if they got hit by a shell that blew away their faces. Adam had his name in his pocket on Charlotte's letter. Not that he was worried about his remains. He wasn't one of the green troops about to be ordered to take up positions on the field. He was safe on his knoll.

Mike was on his feet, standing on his tiptoes as if that extra inch would show him even more. "Maybe we should move closer to the action."

"We're close enough." Adam kept his eyes on his sketch.

"But we can't see much from here. How are we going to know who's winning?"

"We'll get the word eventually. Especially if you see the men retreating. Besides, if you think you can't tell much about what's happening up here, believe me, it's ten times worse down there."

"Worse? How could it be worse? That's where it's happening."

"Down there each soldier is standing in one little pocket of what's happening. At least that's what the men I've talked to tell me. Down there in the heat of battle you're as likely to get shot by your own side as the other side if you're in the wrong spot. Better to be up here out of range."

"But . . ." The kid let the word hang in the air between them.

Adam sighed. The last thing he wanted to do was babysit a green newsman. But when he looked up at the kid, Adam saw Jake as he'd been the year before when they marched out to that first battle at Bull Run. Eagerness and fear mixed. At least this kid wouldn't have to run into a barrage of bullets. He could be an observer like Adam.

But the kid couldn't settle down. He kept hopping up at every boom of artillery and then when at last the sound of musket fire signaled the battle had commenced, he couldn't stand it. He looked at Adam and said, "I've got to be down there. I've got to know what it feels like to write about it, don't I?"

"Don't be stupid, Mike. You're not a soldier. You don't even have a gun," Adam said.

"I'm not planning to shoot anybody, just report on what it's like."

Short of tackling him and tying him to a tree, there was no way Adam could keep him up on the knoll out of artillery range. He watched the kid pick his way down the hill toward the cornfield where most of the action seemed to be going on. Cornstalks were flying up in the air as artillery shells dug deep furrows in the ground. Trees on both ends of the cornfield were exploding in splinters from the hits. And the shells kept screaming through the air, killing without partiality.

He saw the kid fall backward when the bullet hit him. Adam wanted to turn his eyes away, wash his hands of the crazy kid, but he couldn't. He saw him turn and begin to crawl. He'd seen dozens of men fall and not ventured into the battle to pull any of them to safety, but he couldn't leave the boy there. It would be like leaving Jake to die again.

Adam closed his sketchpad and looked over his shoulder toward his horse still tied to a tree. The horse had his head up and nostrils flared at the noise of battle, but he was there. If Adam could get the kid back up to the top of the knoll, then he could load him on the horse to take him to a field hospital at the back of the lines.

Adam moved as quickly as he could. There was no need trying to dodge the gunfire because there was no way to know where the next bullet might be. Adam cringed when a bullet whistled past his head, but then he remembered an old soldier telling him once that hearing the bullet was good. That meant the bullet had missed and was seeking out another target. But the one chasing it might be trouble.

The kid had taken a hit to the leg, the minié ball had torn half his calf away, and blood was soaking his britches. Adam put his arm around him to lift him up off the ground as he said, "You're going to have to help."

The kid looked dazed, but he nodded and leaned on Adam as they made their slow progress away from the field of battle. Exploding shells rocked the ground like a volcano about to break through the crust of the earth to add to the destruction. Adam shut his mind to the bullets. He didn't think about the artillery shells. He just thought about putting one foot in front of the other and getting the young reporter to safety. He hadn't been able to save his brother, but he could save this kid. *Please, Lord.*

The prayer rose unbidden in his thoughts almost at the same instant the shell exploded overhead. Fragments rained down to their left, but missed them. They were making it, moving out of range. A few more steps. Adam could hear the horse whinnying. He didn't know how with the crash of the guns all around, but he did. *Please, Lord.* A few more steps.

He didn't hear the bullet that hit the arm he had wrapped around the kid's waist. He just felt the thud as it knocked both of them forward. The kid cried out, but he didn't stop breathing, so Adam kept moving. He didn't even look at his arm until he was up on the horse with the boy in front of him. Blood was streaming down his hand. His right hand. His drawing hand.

He stared at the wound. The bullet had glanced off the bone of his forearm above the wrist. It was a good ten seconds before he had the nerve to try to move his fingers. The first two moved; the last two didn't. He fished a handkerchief out of his pocket and wrapped it tightly around his arm. A big chunk of his skin was gone, but he could live with that. As long as some of his fingers moved. As long as he could still hold a pen or a brush.

The kid in front of him on the horse groaned

and fell forward. Adam caught him and turned the horse away from the battle. He left the boy, still breathing, at a house the surgeons had turned into a field hospital. He didn't let the doctor look at his arm. Waved it off as nothing serious, even though his blood had soaked the handkerchief and his shirt. He couldn't take the chance of losing consciousness and waking up without his hand. The army surgeons were too quick with the knife and saw. He'd chance death before he chanced that.

Please, Lord.

34

On October 8 the day once more dawned hot and clear at Harmony Hill. The pastures and late gardens desperately needed rain, but the air carried so little moisture that the night no longer even licked the grass with dew.

That morning as the sisters left the Gathering Family House to go to their duties, Sister Altha paused to gaze up at the cloudless sky. After a moment she sighed and shook her head. "Not the least sign of rain. It must be the good Lord has turned his face from our village because he can't bear to look down on the misguided soldiers passing along our road on their way to slaughter one another. How sad the sinful hearts of the world."

"Yea." The sisters following her down the steps and out into the village echoed her words with obedient agreement. Charlotte spoke the word without thought.

Sister Altha lowered her eyes from the clear sky to the women behind her. "Never fear, my sisters. In time Mother Ann will convince the Eternal Father to turn his face back to us. When we can shed this odious burden of cooking for the Southern army and can once more go forth in exercising the worship due our Mother and the Lord, laboring songs and attending to proper industry, then the gift of refreshing rain will fall upon our ground again."

Indeed the whole village looked trampled and weary after the onslaught of Confederate soldiers passing through in such desperate need of food and water. But on this Wednesday morning with the road mercifully empty of soldiers, the Shakers set about taking stock of the damages done to their fences and gardens by the pillaging troops.

Charlotte hoped the Confederate soldiers would continue south and leave Kentucky behind forever. Many of the Shakers expressed that same hope as the morning passed quietly. And yet the workers seemed to be continually looking over their shoulders down the road as if fearful the peace of the day wouldn't last.

When Charlotte carried Sister Martha's midday meal to her, the old sister said a messenger had come in with the report of a large army of Union troops chasing after the Confederates.

"I hope the Rebels keep retreating to the south without stopping to engage the Northern army." Concern wrinkled Sister Martha's gentle face. "For if the armies meet, the encounter will surely result in a dreadful battle such as those in the East. Those illustrated in *Harper's* by our artist friend. Another time of death."

Charlotte did pray as she walked back to the Gathering House to partake in her own midday meal. Not just that there would be no battle, although she did fervently pray that. But she also prayed for rain and that Sister Martha would have enough appetite to eat the food she'd taken her. She prayed Adam would be kept from harm wherever he was. She prayed for a clear path, to know where she needed to be.

She wasn't sure why she lingered with the Shakers except that she seemed reluctant to step away from the safe haven of being Sister Charlotte. And didn't she need to stay to see to Sister Martha? And what of Aunt Tish? It was easier to simply be Sister Charlotte, one of many sisters instead of someone who had to make decisions about sifting through the ashes of Grayson and finding a way to keep her promise to Landon.

Then there was Adam. Charlotte dreamed of looking up and seeing him at the Shaker village again as she had last summer. This time she wouldn't run away from him. But even as she was sure of that, she wasn't sure what she would do. Or what he would want her to do. While he had often referred to the garden in his letters, their meetings there had been fleeting. Perhaps she was imagining things to think love could have taken seed in those brief moments together. At least in his heart. She could not deny that it had flowered in her own.

Each of his letters had been like rain and sunshine to cause her feelings for him to grow. But though she treasured every pen stroke, no one could imagine them love letters. The Shakers would have never allowed any improper words of sinful worldly love to be delivered to her eyes. Yet Sister Martha thought Adam did seek her affections. Affections that were already his if he would only come back to claim them. Then her way would be clear of doubts just as the sky had been clear of clouds for days.

She was hurrying up the steps to keep from being late for the midday meal when a boom that sounded much like thunder rumbled in the distance. Even though she chanced being late and missing her meal, she paused to look up at the sky. The sun was shining as brightly as ever. No storm clouds gathered on the horizon.

467

Another boom followed the first and then another. Charlotte shut her eyes and shuddered as she suddenly realized that instead of the welcome thunder of nature's rain clouds, these booms were the unnatural thunder of cannon fire. Even as she stood there and listened, men were dying. Men who perhaps only the day before had eaten food she set on a table for them. Men who had smiled and laughed before they marched away to die on this day. She felt so heartsick that she no longer cared about the meal she was missing.

As the afternoon passed, there was nothing to do but shut her ears to the distant booming reports of the cannons and try to close her mind to the image of bleeding and dying men as she worked in the garden alongside Dulcie, gathering the last of the dried bean pods from the vines. But each boom rattled her soul and made her want to put her hands over her ears. Dulcie seemed to feel the same as they picked the beans and filled their baskets without talking, each tensed waiting for the next sound of death in the air.

As the sun began to sink toward the western horizon, the booming continued unabated. When they came out of the garden, Landon broke away from a group of boys trailing after Brother Ballard to run and wrap his arms around Charlotte's waist.

"Is the world coming to an end, Sister

Charlotte?" he asked in a voice that trembled.

The child looked so woebegone in his Shaker clothes and hat that Charlotte wanted to hold him tight against her, but instead she pushed him away before Brother Ballard could reprimand him. She leaned down to look directly in his face as she answered. "Nay. Has not Brother Ballard told you the sounds are from cannons?"

"Like on pirate ships?" he asked.

"Yea, much like that described in storybooks."

"But this isn't in a storybook." Landon looked toward the horizon.

"Nay."

"Brother Landon," Brother Ballard called to him with firm expectation in his voice. "Come back. It is not permissible to run away from the group."

Charlotte gave him a little push toward where Brother Ballard waited for him. "It might be easier if you pay attention to Brother Ballard's rules," she told him.

"I do most of the time. But it's a bad rule if it keeps me from talking to my sister." He turned back to her to ask one last question as he did every time he saw her. "You won't forget your promise?"

"Never, my little brother," she whispered. Only Dulcie was near enough to hear their words, and Dulcie was not a faultfinder. Besides, her mother's heart would understand.

After he hurried back to be the obedient Shaker boy again, Dulcie fell in beside her on the path. "Will you take him with you when you leave?"

Charlotte quickly looked at Dulcie. She didn't say if. She said when. "Leave?" Charlotte said. "What makes you ask that?"

"And what keeps you from answering it?" Dulcie lowered her voice even though there was no one near them on the walkway. "Haven't we ever spoken frankly with each other when we worked as long as we didn't have to worry about spying eyes or listening ears?"

"Yea, forgive me, Sister Dulcie. It is my confusion of spirit that makes the answer difficult. Not your question. But I have promised to be his sister. So either I must stay here or take him if I go."

"I would that I had such a choice." Dulcie sighed.

"Perhaps someday you will." Charlotte's mind raced as she wondered how she could help Dulcie. "If I—"

With the ghost of a smile, Dulcie touched Charlotte's arm to stop her words. "You can't fix everything for everyone, Sister Charlotte. Even as much as you want to. You must leave some things to the Lord above."

"But I want you to be happy, Sister Dulcie."

"There are many ups and downs to happiness. I think contentedness might be a better blessing."

"Are you content?" Charlotte looked over at Dulcie walking beside her.

Dulcie kept her eyes on the pathway in front of them as they moved on toward the Gathering Family house. "In time I will be. My spirit no longer struggles so actively against the boundaries here. It is not a bad place."

"Nay," Charlotte agreed. "I have learned much about my own spirit here among the Believers."

Dulcie went on as if Charlotte hadn't spoken. "I think seeing the soldiers in the last few weeks has helped me appreciate the peace to be had here at Harmony Hill. I may not be able to hold my children to my bosom, but they are in the bosom of peace. I am thankful for that. If someday the Lord makes a new path for me to walk, then I will step out on it, but now I am not so reluctant to walk the Shaker way as I was." Dulcie turned to look directly at Charlotte's face. "But you don't have to settle for contentment. You can chase happiness. You should chase happiness."

"Yea," Charlotte said as she met Dulcie's honest brown eyes. "My spirit does seek such. If love can bring happiness."

Dulcie lowered her voice even more. "Perhaps not always happiness, but there will be joy." She reached over and squeezed Charlotte's arm. "If your pathway leads there, run along it."

Charlotte's heart leaped at the thought, but she had already spoken too plainly if other ears than

Dulcie's happened to hear. Besides, it surely was wrong for her to be contemplating happiness or joy even as the cannonade to the south continued to pound against her ears.

As the evening deepened into night, the thunder of the cannons thankfully ceased. A deep silence fell over the village, but there was little peace in it. It was too easy to imagine the scenes of death and destruction that might lay in the moonlit fields to the south.

Charlotte was awake the next morning before the rising bell. She stared out the open window in the sleeping room to watch the first fingers of dawn creep up into the sky and cringed as she waited for the cannons to start again with the light of day. But no booms came. All was quiet except for the call of a mourning dove and the crickets no night had yet been cold enough to silence. But it appeared the night had silenced the artillery. Perhaps the battle was over.

That proved to be the case as battle-weary soldiers began to straggle back through Harmony Hill. The beginning trickle became a streaming flood by the third day as once again soldiers clustered around the kitchen doors in search of food. As before, the Shaker sisters abandoned all other industry to prepare meals for the hungry troops. The brethren set up a long table on trestles in the yard of the Trustee's Offices next to the road. It not only seemed more efficient to lay the food out in the open in easy reach of the men as they passed through the village, it also kept men with the stain of death on them from too familiar contact with the sisters.

Once again it was the Confederates who came through Harmony Hill, and with them they brought news of the battle. The armies had met near Perryville where the Rebels claimed to outfight the Yankees in spite of being greatly outnumbered. It was only the sheer number of the Union army that had sent the Confederates into retreat back along the main route to the south.

Many had died. Many more had been wounded. When reports came in that churches and houses in the town had been converted into makeshift infirmaries, the Shakers loaded wagons with food and other necessary supplies for the wounded.

"We cannot grow weary of doing good," Sister Altha said as she directed Charlotte and Dulcie in helping gather the supplies to load on the wagons. "Mother Ann instructs us to share of our bounty. In her writings we read of the necessity to do all the good we can, in all the ways we can, as often as we can to all the people we can. That surely includes these hapless and misguided men."

When they had the wagons loaded, Sister Altha looked at Charlotte with a bit of challenge in her eyes. "We have been told there is also need for some to help nurse the wounded. Since you seem to want to keep one foot in the world, Sister Charlotte, and not make a full commitment to our way, I thought you might suit that duty better than a fully committed sister who would surely shudder at the thought of going into the world."

"I will go." Charlotte didn't refute Sister Altha's words. There was nothing to refute, for what she said was true.

35

Some noise pulled Adam back to consciousness. He lay on a narrow cot in a room surrounded by moaning men on other cots. Just like Jake. Except here the heat gathered and pressed down on Adam until it was hard to keep breathing in and out. As he had done every time he regained consciousness since he first awoke in this oven of misery, he shut his eyes and then lifted up his wounded arm where he could see the bandage covering it.

Please, God. The words ran through his mind before he forced open his eyes to see if his hand was still there. A rush of relief swept through him when he saw the bandage had not been shortened while he slept his fevered sleep.

He didn't know how he ended up on the cot in

the dim church building surrounded by wounded Confederate soldiers. He knew it was a church because he could see the altar at the front of the room. He remembered going down into the field of battle to help the reckless young reporter. He remembered that the man was still alive when he left him at the house the army surgeons had commandeered. He remembered riding away from there. He remembered how he could think of nothing but Harmony Hill so near. They had a doctor. They had medicine. They had Charlotte.

He remembered turning his horse's head that way, but he remembered nothing else until he woke up on this cot and little since except looking at his arm each time he woke to be sure his hand was still there. He'd seen enough wounded soldiers with empty shirtsleeves and pant legs to know that often as not a raging fever was reason enough for the doctors to get out their knives and saws. But he could not lose his hand. Not his right hand. His drawing hand. It would be more merciful for the doctors to cut out his heart.

If only he'd made it to Harmony Hill. Then at least if the fever conquered him as it had Jake, perhaps before that happened he would have seen Charlotte. Her touch would have been on his brow, her voice in his ear, and her beauty in his eyes before death took him.

Plus he was confident the Shakers wouldn't amputate his arm. They believed a man should use his hands to work for God. He did not think they would rob him of that ability. But the surgeons who moved between the cots here to check on the wounded were different. They might cut first and ask questions later.

So far they had left him alone except for a few draughts of a vile-tasting medicine that did nothing. But then he was still breathing. He did still have his hand. And the fever came and went. He just needed to get strong enough to get off the cot and walk away from this sick room.

He tried to lift his head up off the pillow, but everything started spinning. He felt so odd that he wondered if he was actually awake. Perhaps he was in a feverish dream. Perhaps he was already dead and it was his eternal punishment to forever dread the loss of his hand.

Please, God. He couldn't seem to pray further than that, even though the Lord would surely expect more words of pleading from someone who had ignored him for so many years. Was it even right to try to jump back into the Lord's camp simply because he needed help so desperately? All the men around Adam needed help every bit as much. And all those who had died. What made him think the Lord would favor him more than them? He had no right to pray, but yet the words welled up inside his mind again. *Please, God.*

His grandfather would say he was getting no

less than he deserved. He'd tell Adam that a man couldn't step away from God and then expect mercy just for the asking. Just by saying "please, God." Surely he would have to earn it with righteous living the way his grandfather had.

The old man had given Adam a curt nod when they'd come face-to-face after Jake's funeral. When Adam asked if he'd seen his illustrations of the war in *Harper's Weekly*, his grandfather's eyebrows had almost met over his eyes in a frown as he fondled the round knob top of his cane. He refused to acknowledge Adam's success as an artist. Instead he said, "But what have you done as a man? All I can see is that you've brought your brother home a corpse."

Adam had brushed off the question then as the sour words of an old man who had never liked him. But now lying there on the cot soaked with his own sweat the question came back to poke at him. What had he done as a man? Why should the Lord listen when he sent up his plea for mercy? The Lord gave him his hand. The Lord gave him his talent. He could take it away.

Please, God. A man somewhere in the room cried out in pain. Adam wondered if he had cried out when he was unconscious with no control of his mouth. The pain was like a live thing devouring him. He thought about how he might draw it. A monster from the deep with pointed teeth and long sharp talons on a dozen arms clawing at Adam. But he could bear the pain. He could overcome the pain. As long as he could stay awake and keep the surgeon's knife from his arm.

The man continued to scream and Adam raised his head enough to see the doctor and a nurse standing over him. He wondered if the man was screaming because of what they were doing to him. Adam let his head fall back down on the sodden pillow while the man in the bed next to him began to loudly recite the twenty-third Psalm.

"The Lord is my Shepherd," the man said.

Adam could have said the Psalm with him, but he didn't. Instead he tried to remember other Scripture just to shut out the man's screams. He thought about the stories of healings, of the blind man, of the lepers, of the demon-possessed man in the tombs. And then the story of the Prodigal Son popped into his mind. He had not earned his father's forgiveness with righteous living. He had lived riotously instead. And yet the father had welcomed the contrite son home with joy.

"Yea, though I walk through the valley of the shadow of death, I shall fear no evil: for thou art with me." The man beside him repeated that line three times until his voice lost its tremble and grew stronger as he continued. "Thy rod and thy staff they comfort me."

Please, God, forgive me.

"Thou preparest a table before me in the presence of mine enemies: thou anointest my head with oil; my cup runneth over."

As Adam listened to the man, a peaceful feeling came over him. It didn't take away the pain or even the fear of losing his hand, but it was there like bedrock under a flooding stream. It would not be washed away. It did not have to be earned. It was just there. His because the Lord heard his prayer. *Please, God.*

As the man went on with the last of the Psalm, Adam whispered the words with him. "Surely goodness and mercy shall follow me all the days of my life; and I will dwell in the house of the Lord for ever."

When next he woke, he had no idea how much time had passed. He shut his eyes and raised his hand up. This time it didn't take quite as much courage to open his eyes. His hand was there. But so was the pain and the fever. He wanted to beg someone for a drink of water, but his mouth was too dry to form the words. All he could do was grunt.

When she leaned over him, he was sure he was hallucinating. The nurse wore a white Shaker cap and collar. And Charlotte's face. His mind was imagining her face there on the nurse even as he had drawn it in a hundred sketches. Her beautiful green eyes now brimming with tears. The scattering of freckles across her nose.

Her soft and inviting lips. He wanted to reach up and touch her, but he feared that would make the image fade and the nurse would turn back into the same older woman with the bulbous nose who had poured the noxious medicine down his throat the last time he awoke.

"Adam."

Even after she spoke his name, he still thought she was only a vision drawn from his desire. It wasn't until her teardrops fell upon his hot cheeks that he realized she was really there looking down at him, bathing his forehead with a damp cloth.

"Adam, can you hear me?"

He reached up with his uninjured hand and touched the tears on her cheeks and then traced his own lips with his dampened fingers. His tongue tasted their salt. "Charlotte," he managed to whisper. "Not much of a garden here."

"A garden needs sunshine and rain." She smiled through her tears, then she lifted his head and held a cup of water to his lips. "And a loving hand to plant the seeds when spring comes again."

"My hand," he whispered as panic at the thought of losing his hand grabbed him once more. He clutched her arm with his left hand and held up his injured arm. He moistened his lips as best he could with his tongue. "Don't let them cut off my hand. Even if they tell you I'll die, don't let them."

Her eyes widened at the fierceness of his words. "But they might not listen to me."

He tightened his hold on her arm. "You are Charlotte Vance, the senator's daughter, the owner of Grayson. You make things happen."

"But I have no right to speak for you."

The darkness was creeping back, making everything disappear but her beautiful face. He clung to the edge of consciousness long enough to push out the words. "You have every right. You own my heart. Promise me."

He could see her eyes on him as he began to slip down into the tunnel of darkness. Her words followed him. "I promise."

I am Charlotte Mayda Vance, she repeated silently in her head as his fingers relaxed their grip on her arm and he slipped away from her into unconsciousness. *Charlotte Mayda Vance. Daughter of Charles Vance. Granddaughter of Richard Grayson. The owner of Adam Wade's heart.*

But could she keep his heart beating? He was burning with fever. Perhaps the wound was septic. Perhaps the only way to save him was to take his hand. Why had she promised? A binding promise the same as the one she had made young Landon. Dulcie was right. She did think she could fix everything when she couldn't even fix herself.

There was only One who could fix everything. She knelt by Adam's bed and kept her hand over his heart. "Dear Lord, I will do whatever you want if you will help Adam. Whatever I must."

She didn't realize she'd prayed the words aloud until the man in the next bed spoke. "Ain't no use trying to bargain with the good Lord, miss. He done owns it all, you know."

Charlotte turned to look at the man. He had a bandage around his head and his chest. "Are you a preacher?" she asked.

"The men in my company think so, but I never called myself such. But my sainted mother taught me the Scriptures, and believe me, knowing the Word has been a powerful comfort these last few months."

Adam groaned and Charlotte turned her eyes back to his face. She didn't look back at the other man even as she asked, "What should I do?"

"Be not afraid, only believe."

"Is that Scripture?"

"The Lord's very words. Ain't no reason in the world not to trust them. Just say your prayers and get still in your heart and you'll know what to do."

"But what if he dies?" Charlotte whispered the words.

"Been a lot of dying going on and some more in here will be going to meet their Maker afore the day dawns tomorrow. A trip all of us has to make come our time." The man's voice softened.

"But you just do your praying. I'm thinking it may not be his time."

Charlotte glanced over at the man with gratitude. "Is there something I can get you?"

"A new ear would be nice." The man attempted a smile as he touched the bandage around his head. "But failing that, a drink of water would be good, and then maybe later between your prayers for your sweetheart there, if you could find me some paper to write to my sainted mother in Alabama, we'd both be much obliged, I'm sure."

Her prayers were ongoing. Even as she walked among the other men, helping them take a drink, turning their pillows, spooning broth into their mouths, her prayers never left Adam. When the doctor came to stand over Adam, she was there by his bedside. She helped unwrap his bandages without quaking. She stared at the wound and felt a turning sickness in the pit of her stomach, but she didn't look away. She couldn't turn her eyes away.

"We may have to amputate," the doctor muttered more to himself than to any ears listening.

"Nay," Charlotte said. She shook away the Shaker word. She couldn't be Sister Charlotte who bent her head and practiced obedience. She was Charlotte Mayda Vance. The owner of Adam Wade's heart and she had made him a promise. She cleared her throat and pushed strength into her voice. "No. You can't cut off his hand."

36

The doctor looked up at her with some surprise and more than a little irritation. "Miss, I suggest you leave the medical decisions up to me. While it is certainly tragic for a man to lose one of his extremities, it is my duty to keep the men here in my care alive." He wore gray Confederate trousers under a surgeon's wrap that showed the evidence of many wounds treated.

"You can't amputate his arm. He instructed me to tell you that." Charlotte looked down at Adam's face in the dim light. What if he couldn't fight off the fever? Nevertheless, she kept her voice firm and sure. She had promised and she had prayed. "I know him. He's Adam Wade, an artist for *Harper's Weekly*."

That seemed to give the doctor pause. "Hmm," he said as he turned his eyes back to Adam. "Adam Wade. I've seen his illustrations."

"You have to give his arm a chance to heal."

"Or to kill him," the doctor said so grimly that it almost wiped away his Southern drawl.

"There are many ways to die," Charlotte whispered.

"And this way won't be a good one." The doctor's frown grew fiercer as he shifted Adam's arm a bit to better study the wound. He was silent a moment before he gave in. "But I suppose we could wait a few more hours if you're sure he would want to take that chance."

"He would," the man in the bed beside them spoke up. "I heard him telling the girl not to let you get out your saws. Weren't a shred of doubt in his words."

"But did he consider what might happen if we delay proper treatment? You don't think I like amputating arms and legs, do you?" The doctor sounded angry before he let out a long sigh as he wiped his hands on a towel stained with blood. He looked very tired. "Neither do I like pulling sheets up over men's faces."

"You won't." The words were barely audible, but yet it was easy to hear the determination in Adam's voice as his eyes flickered open. He looked first at the doctor and then at Charlotte. He reached for her with his uninjured hand.

Charlotte took his hand and without thought raised it to her lips. With her other hand, she stroked Adam's face as she smiled down at him. The stubble of his unshaven beard was stiff and welcome against her hand.

"So the two of you know each other pretty well," the doctor said as he began to wrap a new bandage around Adam's arm. He didn't wait for her to say anything. "But aren't you one of those Shaker women?"

"Yea," Charlotte said. "In some ways."

"But it appears not in every way." The doctor

glanced up at Charlotte with an amused look. "One of your Shaker sisters was telling me earlier that you all don't hold with a man and woman knowing one another in the biblical sense of the word. Is that true?"

"It's true the Shakers believe all should live as brothers and sisters. That the love of a man for a woman causes much distress," Charlotte said softly with her eyes on Adam's. "But I have not been able to forget the garden."

Adam's lips moved, but he seemed too weak to push out any words. He stared at her a moment before his eyelids drooped and then slowly closed. Charlotte's heart jumped up in her throat as she gripped his hand tighter and bit her lip to keep from crying out. Relief washed through her when she saw his chest continue to rise and fall.

"What garden is that?" the doctor was asking. "The one where Eve met the serpent and sin came into the world?"

"For all have sinned and come short of the glory of the Lord," the man in the next bed spoke up again.

"That's God's own truth. Preach it, Sebastian." The doctor glanced over at the man he called Sebastian before he finished fastening the bandage and straightened up. Then he looked directly at Charlotte. "Keep watch and don't neglect to let me know if his fever worsens.

Better alive with one arm than dead with two. Artist or no artist."

When the sun began to go down, the three other sisters returned to Harmony Hill, but Charlotte refused to go with them. She stayed by Adam's bed, bathing his face and neck through the night to keep the fever at bay. Sometime after midnight his breath became more labored and he felt hotter in spite of the cold rags she was laying on his forehead. Torn between her promise to Adam and the doctor's dire warning, she fell on her knees beside Adam's bed and prayed in desperate silence.

Dear Lord, I spoke a promise I shouldn't have spoken even as I have so many times before in my arrogance. Forgive me, Lord, and help me to know what you would have me to do for this man I love. I know Sister Altha would tell me that my sin of loving him has brought on this trouble, but I can't believe it is a sin for me to love him. Is it? His fever burns so hot. Help me to know what to do. Must I keep my promise to him or should I wake the doctor?

She laid her head down on Adam's chest and listened to the fast beating of his heart. In the bed next to Adam's, Sebastian raised up to ask, "Is he worse, Miss?"

"He's very hot. Do you think I should wake the doctor?" She lifted her head to look across at Sebastian. "I prayed for the Lord to help me know what to do, but I still don't know."

"Be still, and know that I am God."

Charlotte knew that was Scripture and even as she heard those words, she remembered the verse Sebastian had offered her earlier. "Be not afraid, only believe," she whispered. "I'm supposed to trust him, aren't I?"

"We all are, miss. We all are. So just get still in your heart and see what he's telling you. Then you gotta believe it. I ain't never knowed him to lead me wrong."

She shut her eyes and sought the peace of spirit that she knew Sister Martha had. The gift to be simple and depend totally on the Lord. She couldn't be a Shaker like Sister Martha, but she could stop trying to fix everything herself and put her hand in the Lord's hand. Bit by bit into the quiet stillness in her mind came the picture of a garden. Not the garden at Grayson. Not any of the gardens at Harmony Hill. But another garden. And there in its center was Adam with his sketchbook. Adam holding a pencil, capturing the beauty of the garden on his paper.

She stood up and dipped the cloth in the basin once more and gently swabbed Adam's face. Across from her, Sebastian breathed out a satisfied sigh as he lay back on his pillow. "But the mercy of the Lord is from everlasting to everlasting."

As the first light of dawn began pushing through the windows, Adam's fever broke.

Adam rose up out of the darkness that had held him captive and slowly opened his eyes. But this time instead of lifting his arm to see if his hand was still there, he sought sight of Charlotte. It mattered more that she be there than his hand. He tried to speak her name, but his voice came out as little more than a croak.

Even so she leaned over him. Tendrils of her beautiful red hair had escaped her Shaker cap to fall around her face. She smiled at him. "The doctor says you are better, Adam. Thanks be to the Lord." She raised his head and held a glass to his lips. He swallowed the water greedily.

"And my hand?" He still didn't raise his arm up to look at it. He kept his eyes on Charlotte's face. With her there beside him, he could bear whatever she said. "Were you able to keep your promise?"

"It was a promise I should not have made, but one that the Lord honored."

At last he lifted his injured arm off the bed and wiggled his fingers. He welcomed the pain that shot up his arm. His hand was still there. His fingers would hold a pen or a brush again. He moved his fingers again and laughed out loud at the pain.

Charlotte laughed too, understanding his joy without him having to explain. "He must have more pictures for you to draw," she said.

"But not of the war," he said.

"It's not over." All traces of her laughter disappeared.

"Far from it," Adam agreed. "But I have drawn my last scene of death."

"Then what will you draw? As well as I remember, you don't care for doing portraits."

"True." He tried to lift his head up to see her better. She helped him to a sitting position and doubled up the pillow behind his back against the wall. After the effort of moving, he had to rest before he could find his voice again. She waited without speaking until he was able to go on. "But there are many scenes of life I can draw."

She didn't turn away from him, but her eyes seemed suddenly shielded as she asked, "And where will you seek those scenes?"

"Wherever you are." He lifted his left hand to caress her cheek. He didn't have the strength to hold it there over a couple of seconds, but the soft feel of her skin remained on his fingertips.

"Grayson is no more," she said.

"Is Grayson the only place you dare seek life?"

"Nay." She shook her head a little and changed her word. "No. The Shakers have taught me that love can flower in many places."

"And have they taught you so well that you don't want to leave them?" he asked.

"They taught me to believe, but not as they believe. I am not a Shaker." Her eyes burned into his.

"Then will you come away from Harmony Hill and marry me, Charlotte Vance?"

Joy exploded in her eyes, but then the joy seemed tempered by something else as she turned her face away from him.

His heart constricted and he could not stay silent to wait for her answer. "I love you, Charlotte. I hoped you felt the same."

She looked back at him. "I do love you, Adam. With all my heart, but I have made a promise to another."

Now anger burned through him. "To who? Edwin?"

"Nay." She didn't seem to notice the Shaker word this time as she laughed. Then the laughter faded from her face. "It's Landon who asked for my promise and I gave it to him. I promised that I would always be his sister and never desert him."

"Landon?" Adam frowned. At first he didn't know who she was talking about, but then the name dredged up a memory of a small boy hiding under a table. "You mean Selena's son?"

"Selena's son perhaps, but also now my brother. Selena left the night of the fire and hasn't been heard of since. Landon's governess brought him to Harmony Hill and the Shakers took him in, but I made him a promise. A promise as real and binding as the one I made you about your hand." Tears trickled out of the corners of

491

her eyes and down her cheeks. "So even though I have often dreamed of putting my hand in yours and walking away from the Shakers, I can't leave him behind to do so."

"Are you saying my competition is a boy of six who wants to be a whaleboat captain?" The twitch of a smile played at the corners of his mouth.

Charlotte looked surprised for a second before she said, "That's right. I remember now. You wrote that you had met Landon."

"Once." Adam let his smile spread across his face as he reached for Charlotte's hand again. "And to tell the truth, I don't think he's big enough to keep me away from you."

"But . . . ," she started.

He reached up and lightly touched her lips to silence her. "Your promise is my promise. Your brother is my brother." He gently brushed away one of the tears on her cheek before he let his hand drop back to the bed. "I ask again. Will you marry me, Charlotte Vance?"

"Yea," she said, smiling through fresh tears brimming in her eyes. She sniffed and wiped them away impatiently. "Wait. I can't answer you with a Shaker yes." She jerked off her Shaker cap and threw it up in the air. "Yes, Adam Wade, I will marry you. Today. Tomorrow. Whenever you want."

"And what of Grayson?" He had to know for sure where he stood in her heart.

Her face softened as she leaned closer until he could feel the whisper of her breath on his face as she said, "You are my Grayson. Now and forevermore."

Her love gave him strength to reach his hand up behind her head to pull her closer. She willingly surrendered her lips to his, dried and cracked by the fever though they were. And there in the midst of a roomful of groaning men, he found the love he'd been seeking. Nothing could ever separate him from that feeling again, for he would carry it always in his heart even unto death and beyond. Such was a gift of God.

The man in the next bed let out a whoop of laughter before he said, "I am my beloved's, and my beloved is mine."

Charlotte raised her head to look over at the man. "That can't be Scripture, Sebastian."

The man laughed again. "Oh, but it is. King Solomon himself. He went down into a garden and found love."

"And so did we." Adam put his finger under Charlotte's chin and turned her face back to him. He thought he might drown in the beauty of her eyes. "So did we."

ACKNOWLEDGMENTS

Writing a book can be a solitary journey, but few journeys are ever completed without the help of others along the way. That's certainly true for me. I thank all those who have encouraged me over the years by cheering me on and then reading my stories.

I especially thank my editor, Lonnie Hull DuPont, for her enthusiasm for my stories and also her wise comments that help make my stories better. Thanks too to Barb Barnes who makes sure I have all my ducks in a row with her careful editing. I appreciate the great work of the whole team at Revell and Baker Publishing Group who take what I write and turn it into a beautiful book with an enticing cover that invites readers into my story.

I will never be able to thank my husband and family enough for their love and understanding over the years and my kids for learning to sleep over the sound of a clattering typewriter when they were babies.

And of course, I am forever thankful to the Lord for this gift of words and for allowing me the blessing of living my dream to write down stories.

Last but not least, I thank you readers. Without readers, a story is nothing but a bunch of words on paper. You bring the words to life as you let the story play out in your imaginations. Thank you.

Ann H. Gabhart and her husband live on a farm just over the hill from where she grew up in central Kentucky. She's active in her country church, and her husband sings bass in a Southern Gospel quartet. Ann is the author of over a dozen novels for adults and young adults. Her first inspirational novel, *The Scent of Lilacs*, was one of Booklist's top ten inspirational novels of 2006. Her novel, *The Outsider*, was a finalist for the 2009 Christian Book Awards in the fiction category.

Visit Ann's website at www.annhgabhart.com.

Center Point Publishing
600 Brooks Road ● PO Box 1
Thorndike ME 04986-0001 USA

(207) 568-3717

US & Canada:
1 800 929-9108
www.centerpointlargeprint.com